200

BRITISH MOTORCYCLES OF THE 1930s

OSPREY
COLLECTOR'S
LIBRARY

BRITISH
MOTORCYCLES
OF THE 1930s

The A–Z of pre-war marques—
from AER through to Zenith

Roy Bacon

Published in 1986 by Osprey Publishing Limited,
27A Floral Street, London WC2E 9DP
Member company of the George Philip Group

British Library Cataloguing in Publication Data

Bacon, Roy H.
    Motorcycles of the 1930s.
    1. Motorcycles——History
    I. Title
    629.2'275'09   TL440
ISBN 0-85045-657-6

Design Gwyn Lewis

Filmset by Tameside Filmsetting Limited,
Ashton-under-Lyne, Lancashire

Printed by BAS Printers Limited,
Over Wallop, Hampshire

Contents

A pair of Triumph Speed Twins from 1939 or 1940 on official duties and complete with wartime headlamp masks

Foreword by Bob Currie

Many diehards still insist that the Golden Age of Motorcycling skidded to an abrupt halt as the midnight chimes rang out on 30 December 1930, and that anything that came thereafter was but the greyest of grey porridge. Total poppycock, of course, for despite the Great Depression which cast a shadow over the early part of the period covered by Roy Bacon's present survey, there was plenty of inspired stuff yet to come.

Can one dismiss the Ariel Square Four as grey porridge? Or the Series A Vincent-HRD Rapide? The sleek apple-green-tanked BSA Empire Stars? That model which was to set a fashion for the world, Edward Turner's incomparable Triumph Speed Twin? You'll be meeting all these and many more in the pages which follow.

Of course, it is tempting to don rose-tinted goggles and look back with nostalgic affection at the superbikes of the time, passing swiftly over such utter lemons as the enclosed-engine New Hudsons and the dreadful own-engine (actually, made by Levis) Coventry Eagle Silent Superbs of 1932. But the truth was that the British industry was all things to all men, and there was plenty of enduring metal even at the bottom end of the market.

Snooty clubmen turned up their noses at the rock-bottom-cheapie 250 cc Red Panther—an overhead-valve model for under £30, egad!—but the British factories built better than they knew,

and right through the war period there were plenty of Red Panthers, and 150 cc Unit-Minor New Imps, soldiering on in uncomplaining fashion; chrome peeling, cracked mudguards a-flapping, but still running for long after their expected life-span (they had to, anyway, for new bikes were non-existent).

If one had to point to 'The Model Which Won The War', most of you would indicate the Norton 16H, BSA M20 or Matchless G3L. You could well be right, militarily speaking, but on the Home Front it was none of these. No, the model that carried the district nurse on her rounds, took the munitions worker to his blacked-out hush-hush factory, and enabled Captain Mainwaring's Home Guard volunteers to reach their defensive positions around Warmington-on-Sea was the humble single-speed autocycle—just a glorified pushbike, powered (if that's the word) by the lowly but ever-willing 98 cc Villiers Junior De Luxe engine.

Grey porridge? Phooey! All—well, all right, *most*—of the British motorcycles of the 1930s are well worth remembering, and in this book friend Roy has made a fine job of doing just that. Enjoy it!

Bob Currie,
Editor,
The Classic Motor Cycle,
Birmingham,
February 1986

Between wars

From 1919 to 1939 motorcycling underwent great changes. The period began with machines of near veteran style, went through the flat-tank era of the 1920s, turned to saddle tanks and chromium plate for the depressed 1930s and ended with a call-up for machines and men. In that time design changed the appearance and many features, with the greater effects occurring in the 1920s, a decade often termed the Golden Age of Motorcycling.

The start of that decade saw many machines still with belt final drive, although most had a gearbox. Handchange was to start to give way to the foot pedal from late in the decade, but was still to be seen into the fifties. Engines were singles or V-twins in the main with few exceptions and four-strokes outnumbered two-strokes. Valves moved from the side to overhead on many machines in the 1920s, which also saw the advent of ohc in some numbers.

Motorcycle electrics progressed to replace acetylene gas lights, but ignition remained the province of the magneto for most models. Lighting was fitted as standard to many, but was often listed as an extra to hold the quoted price to a low level. Engine lubrication, tyres, brakes and steering all improved as engineers applied the lessons of metallurgy to the motorcycle, so that by the end of the 1920s and the close of the vintage period (1 January 1915 to 31 December 1930) machines were good and reliable.

This was as well, for in October 1929 came the Wall Street crash and this ushered in the Depression of the thirties. Money was short and trade poor so firms kept to a staple diet of low-priced economy models with few frills but plenty of options to entice every possible customer to buy. The exotic did not vanish, but few were to survive more than a season or two and there were far fewer odd but interesting variations on the scene.

Machines became typically four-stroke ohv singles with separate gearbox in a rigid frame with girder forks and saddle. Lubrication was dry sump and the electrics a mag-dyno, with the third brush giving way to the regulator box around 1937. A saddle tank was often the only painted part not in black, but the brightwork had its chrome veneer, which was much less trouble to keep nice than the nickel that preceded it.

There were trends and fancies then as now with twin-port engines popular for many years despite the extra cost of the second pipe and silencer. A fancy that failed was enclosure—which the makers liked as it was cheaper than polishing the parts it hid—but it did not catch on, although it continued to appear sporadically over the years.

So the English motorcycle progressed through the 1930s, reacting to the influences of trade and politics, laws and taxes, and what technical developments the public could afford. Those still in business then went to war and after that many carried on for some years, with the change to telescopic forks the only significant improvement —which went to show how tough and endearing the designs were in the first place.

Most models were built to a very conventional English design, but there were some less so, such as the Ariel Square Four, the OEC, the AJS and Matchless fours and, of course, the Scott. Sadly many of the more interesting and progressive designs were not to survive in those hard commercial years, for, as ever, press and public acclaimed innovations but bought the tried and tested model. Always there was the feeling that it was best for someone else to spring their cash the

Very nice period picture showing a lady rider on a 1932 Royal Enfield Cycar being assisted by the RAC. Little protective riding gear at that time but handy for the shopping

first year while you waited for any problems to surface and be dealt with. 'Maybe next year if work holds out' was so often the word, but for some manufacturers next year was not to come.

So the bulk of the industry built singles up to 500 cc and V-twins to around twice that size. The latter were mainly side-valve plodders made to haul a big sidecar along at 40 mph, but among them were some real gems that could perform well with a chair and were really fast used solo—a true 100 mph on the road at a time when much of the Great North Road was two lanes, narrow and bumpy.

The conventional English machine had an engine with a vertically split crankcase in which a built-up crankshaft with roller big-end ran on ball or roller mains. The timing chest went on the right, the magneto aft of the cylinder and a dynamo was strapped to its back. Lubrication was dry sump with the oil tank under the saddle, and side valves were as common as ohv. Head and barrel were in iron with the valve gear often exposed. Carburation was usually looked after by an Amal and the exhaust pipe went on the right for most by the middle of the decade.

The transmission went on the left, with chain drive back to a separate gearbox with outboard clutch, except on Velocette, of course. The box had the output sprocket concentric with the input and over the decade changed from three speeds and handchange to four speeds and footchange. Final drive was by chain on the left and this dictated that the oil tank went on the right with the battery on the left of it. A toolbox went in the rear quarter of the frame and a saddle and pillion seat carried the riders.

The frame was built up from tubes brazed into forged lugs and was rigid at the rear. At the front went girder forks with friction damping. Braking was by drum brakes front and rear with single leading shoes controlled by hand and foot. In time the brake pedal finished up on the left, once footchange was adopted, but for much of the decade it could be found on either side where hand gearbox control remained.

V-twins were much the same but bigger, longer and heavier, while the bottom end of the market was looked after in the main by machines powered by Villiers two-strokes. These were also constructed on the same lines but to a lighter scale.

The lightweights went through some legislation problems at the start of the decade, with the first change coming during 1929. In the Budget the weight limit for the lightweight taxation class was raised from 200 to 224 lb and a number of firms quickly took advantage of this, especially on their 250s and light 350s. The difference was important at the time, for below the limit the tax dropped from £3 to £1 10s. 0d., which was a significant sum in those days.

Then, in the middle of 1929, there was an election and a change of government and the weight change was cancelled, too late for some firms to back-track. There were protests, but such is government inertia that it was not until April 1930 that the limit was raised to ease the problems of a hard-pressed industry a little. It must also have improved safety, for firms were often listing models with acetylene lighting to drag the weight down below the 200 lb mark and capture customers. The same machines would also be sold with electric lights, and the change meant that the owner was not penalized for selecting the better system.

In August that year a Road Traffic Act was passed which raised the minimum age for a licence from 14 to 16 and compulsory insurance became mandatory, but the old general speed limit went. This meant that it was as fast as you liked, but at the same time the offence of careless driving was introduced, so the speed had to be safe in the eyes of the police. Other changes called for proper pillion seats, so a tied-on cushion was no longer acceptable, and a statement as to physical fitness when applying for a driver licence was not now required.

Near the end of 1931 the industry coaxed a further concession out of the government with a reduction of tax to 15s. for machines below 150 cc. This brought a rash of Villiers-powered models in 1932 along with one or two rather nice ohv singles. In recognition of the Chancellor of the Exchequer concerned, these machines were often called Snowden models.

This move introduced the concept of taxation by capacity, still in use half a century later, and it was fully adopted by the 1932 Budget. With this, from 1 January 1933, up to 150 cc paid 15s., 150 to 250 cc paid 30s. and over 250 cc paid £3. Machines under 224 lb registered by 31 December 1932 qualified and remained at 30s., hence the run-on by such models that season.

The happy days of no speed limit did not last for long, and in March 1935 the 30 mph town limit appeared along with driving tests and moves to improve safety on the roads. The limit was a real problem in some regions as it was applied to lighted roads and in the industrial North large areas ran into each other with little break. In time came by-passes, but these were few in the 1930s and congestion in towns due to through-traffic caused many hold-ups as the volume of vehicles built up.

And build up it did as the economy gradually improved. More people bought cars and motorcycles as the years rolled by and the machines themselves became brighter and were better equipped. Autocycles appeared to draw customers on to the bottom rung of powered transport and the industry provided plenty of rungs from then on up the ladder.

The British motorcycle dominated road racing for most of the decade before having to give best to the blown multis from Europe. Off-road, in the ISDT, the country was equally successful, and in the lonely world of record-breaking British men and machines produced many fine performances on the slenderest of resources. Perhaps the finest were the capture of the very tough one-hour record and the outright world speed title.

So the decade came to a noisy end and the motorcycles put on their khaki paint and went to war. The 1930s came to a close having placed their mark on the motorcycle as surely as the 1920s had. In those years it matured and settled down. Post-war it was to have twins!

A 1930 Radco with 247 cc Villiers engine in a typical street scene of the time when a rider wore a hat rather than a helmet

AER

A. E. Reynolds was first a Scott dealer and then the man behind some very special, de luxe examples of that marque built from 1931 to 1934. When Scott's triple failed to materialize and that firm was unwilling to take up his ideas on a series of engines based on a 125 cc module he moved on to his own notions of what was to be done.

The result showed how far ahead he was thinking and the prototype was first seen in the Island during the 1937 TT period. It was still a twin-cylinder two-stroke, but of 340 cc and air-cooled. The engine was all-alloy with pressed-in cylinder liners and the head and block were each in one piece. The crankcase comprised four castings all well ribbed for strength and cooling, and with air passages to cool the area between the cylinders. The case had two end sections whose joint lay on the cylinder centre and the central part was split horizontally with a split centre bearing.

The crankshaft was built up and carried a flywheel on the right end and two sprockets on the left. One drove the transmission and the other the magneto and a Pilgrim oil pump. A single Amal supplied the mixture into the back of the block and the two exhausts ran back at waist level to silencers. A four-speed Burman gearbox was fitted and the rest of the machine was conventional.

The production model did not appear until 1938, and by then the Amal was on a curved induction pipe, ignition was by flywheel magneto and a dynamo had appeared in front of the crankcase, where it was chain driven and in turn drove the oil pump. On the chassis side there were duplex downtubes in place of the simple loop of the prototype and Webb forks. The finish was silver, blue and chrome plate for the tank and polished aluminium for the primary chaincase.

For 1939 the 350 twin continued and was joined by a second model with a 249 cc Villiers engine. This went into the same cycle parts and again the dynamo was mounted in front of the crankcase. The twin exhaust systems were low level.

The war brought production of the machines to a halt, and long after it the last half-dozen were still sitting on the top floor of the shop, dusty but mainly complete, although not all had an engine.

The 1938 AER with twin cylinder 340 cc engine and dynamo mounted in front where it drove the oil pump

AJS

The old-established firm of A. J. Stevens made the mistake of diversifying in 1930. As producers of a fine and successful range of motorcycles during the 1920s they chose the wrong time to take their existing skills of building sidecar and car bodies to establish themselves not only as car makers but also to offer lorries and single-decker buses as well. A further offshoot was to use the wood-working equipment of the body shops to make radio and radiogram cabinets, then massive pieces of furniture, and AJS found themselves in that business also.

Sadly the Depression finished this and in 1931 the bank foreclosed, the Stevens family settled their debts to the full 20s. in the pound and the AJS name was bought by Matchless. The tools were moved from Wolverhampton to Woolwich and little by little the two marques became closer and closer in parts and design. Late in 1937 the group became AMC, although both marque names were to continue for many years. The Stevens brothers retained some equipment and continued to build machines under their own name.

This commercial hiatus had less effect on the AJS machines than expected, for the models ran on without much alteration in the range or its contents. There were nine models in the 1930 lists, with the smallest a neat 249 cc ohv twin-port single with a vertical cylinder, magneto installed ahead of the engine and a dry sump lubrication system. This last feature was common to the sv and ohv range and all models had a year-code letter R prefix to their type number, with the 250 being the R12. The R5 was a similar machine but with a 348 cc side-valve engine.

The other sv and ohv models all had the then fashionable inclined engine, and to suit its installation in the frame the magneto moved to the rear, where it was chain driven from the timing gear. There were four of these models with the 348 cc R4 and 499 cc R9 being the de luxe side-valve machines, while the similar-size R6 and R8 models had twin-port ohv engines.

The largest model of the range was the R2, which was a 998 cc V-twin with side valves, and like all the other machines it had a three-speed gearbox. Its magneto was hung out in front of the engine and its single carburettor fitted into the vee between the cylinders.

Completing the range were two overhead-camshaft models, the 346 cc R7 and 495 cc R10.

The 1931 transverse twin AJS model S3 with 498 cc engine, outboard camshafts and the distributor driven from the left one

These were much as the factory machines of the previous year and like all AJS ohc singles had the camshaft chain driven on the right and a cast alloy case for it running from crankcase to cambox. The case also extended forward to the front-mounted magneto and carried an oil pump on its outer face. These two models did have dry sump lubrication. The rest of the machine was along standard lines with the oil tank under the saddle, but it was built for racing rather than the road, so came without lights and with long exhaust pipes with a minute muffler on the end.

While most of the range continued into 1931 with a letter S prefix, few if any S7 or S10 machines were built and the camshaft models dropped out of sight for a year or so. For the other machines there were new handlebars with integral levers and the front brake cable was run inside the fork leg. Except on the S5 and S12 an optional instrument panel was available.

The models otherwise continued as they were except for the smallest side-valve. This became the S4 as expected, but its capacity was increased to a round 400 cc by lengthening its stroke. The V-twin was modified to move its magneto out of harm's way to a point behind the rear cylinder.

Early in 1931 four new models were listed, with two of them having the Big Port name. A major change was made to the lubrication system, which became total loss but retained its dry sump appearance. This was because a by-pass was taken from the main delivery so that some oil returned to the tank, but only as an indication that the system was working. These were the 348 cc SB6 and

AJS model S4 from 1931 with inclined 400 cc side-valve engine and nice tank-top instrument panel

498 cc SB8, of which the first had the engine vertically mounted with the magneto ahead of it. The other models were a 348 cc side-valve and 248 cc ohv, both with vertical engines, and these two, along with the SB6, all came under the 224 lb weight limit. With them came a note that the inclined-engine S4 could be had with a 348 cc engine as well as its 400 cc one.

In April 1931 came news of one more machine in the range and this was the Stevens attempt to achieve sales by offering technical advance and novelty. It was always a doubtful method and AJS suffered the same result as most others, but such models certainly enlivened the scene.

The machine was typed the S3 and had a 498 cc V-twin engine set across the frame to drive back to a three-speed gearbox with chain final drive. Construction was advanced for the time, although side valves were used. Unusual was the fitting of light alloy cylinder heads and the location of the valves on the outer sides of the barrels. To match them the camshafts also had to be set well out and the two of them were chain driven from the front of the crankshaft within an alloy cover. On the front of this went an oil pump for the total loss system with a pump by-pass return to the tank.

A single Amal fed the two cylinders unevenly, as was usual with a V-twin, and ignition was by coil with a distributor driven from the rear end of the left camshaft and neatly tucked in behind the crankcase casting. It was matched on the right by the dynamo, but this was simply driven from the crankshaft by a flat belt.

The gearbox was some way aft of the engine and connected to it by a shaft that drove the clutch from its rear end. A pair of universal joints took care of any misalignment and the clutch drove a bevel pair, so the gearbox layout was a conventional AJS three-speeder.

The frame had duplex downtubes, as is common with the transverse vee layout, and the rest of the machine followed the style of the times. Full electrics were fitted with a tank-top instrument panel that looked an afterthought, and in production the front mudguard was so wide that the fork tubes had to pass through it.

It was a pleasant machine, but the clutch action prevented good gear changes. Otherwise it was smooth and quiet, and maybe it was these features that stopped it selling well even though it was launched at a price that cannot have included any profit for AJS. The cash flow crisis and subsequent sale of the firm came too quickly for many to be made and it was dropped from the Woolwich programme.

For 1932 the new owners of the name were sensible enough to realize that moving the production centre was enough trauma for one year so they kept the machines unchanged. They took the prefix letter T. Models dropped were the 400 cc single and 498 cc V-twin side-valve along with the camshaft ones. This left the 348 cc in T5 side-valve and T6 or TB6 ohv form and the similar 498 cc T9, T8 and TB8. It was a restricted range but a good restart.

In July 1932 the V-twin reappeared but in a revised form with square engine dimensions of 85.5 mm and a 982 cc capacity. It now had dry sump lubrication and the mag-dyno was positioned behind the rear cylinder, where it was more out of the way. For all its early appearance it was in effect a 1933 model and the engine was a Matchless unit.

In 1933 the year-code prefix letter was dropped and from then on each model had a prefix number of the last two digits of the year, hence 33, 34, 35 up to 39. The model numbers continued as they were and the 350 and 500 cc single-port ohv machines continued to include the letter B in their typing. This was linked to the continued use of the Big Port nickname of the 1920s and both machines continued to be offered also in their twin-port form as the models 33/6 and 33/8. The year prefix is not generally used in this text to avoid tedium.

The 249 cc model 12 was revised to copy its larger brothers and became the model 33/12 Big Port with inclined engine, rear-mounted magneto and high-level exhaust. The 348 and 498 cc side-valve models 5 and 9 copied it, so for that year all the more touring machines were in the same style with inclined engines.

The two camshaft models were reintroduced for 1933 thanks in part to the appearance of George Rowley at Brooklands and in the ISDT using one of the older machines. George spent most of his working life with AJS and rode them in races, trials and everything in between with great success. The machines retained the chain drive to the camshaft, but in other respects they were all new.

The 998 cc V-twin AJS on the firm's stand at the show of 1931 models. Note footboards and Klaxon horn

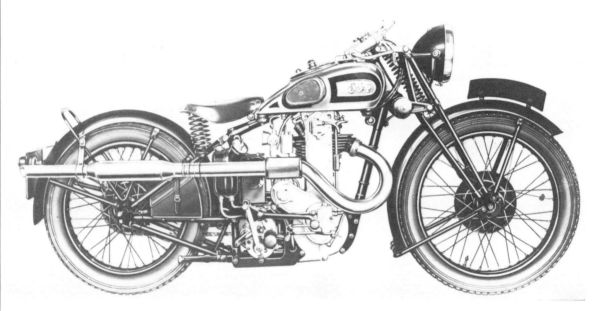

Engine dimensions did stay at 70 × 90 mm and 79 × 101 mm, but the magneto was moved behind the cylinder and driven via a vernier coupling, a feature to be found on many AJS machines. Both capacities were built in racing form, with long, open exhaust pipe and no lights, or in competition form. The latter was called the Trophy model in recognition of Rowley's success in the ISDT and came with a 6.8:1 piston for the 350 and a 6.5:1 for the 500 in place of the racing 7.5:1, lights and a raised exhaust system. For alcohol running 11:1 pistons were available.

Lubrication was dry sump with the main oil pump bolted to the lower part of the camshaft

Above **1934 346 cc ohc AJS model 34/7 Trophy built for road use rather than racing, hence the raised exhaust**
Top **The 1932 Big Port AJS 498 cc model TB8 with inclined engine and typical of the marque in the early thirties**

drive cover and a cambox scavenge pump at the top driven from the camshaft. The engine drove a four-speed gearbox with positive stop change and the mechanics went into a new frame.

In addition to the 1931 and 1933 camshaft models there were a few 350 cc hybrids built up using the older engine with front magneto in a later frame. They included some of the 1933 engine features.

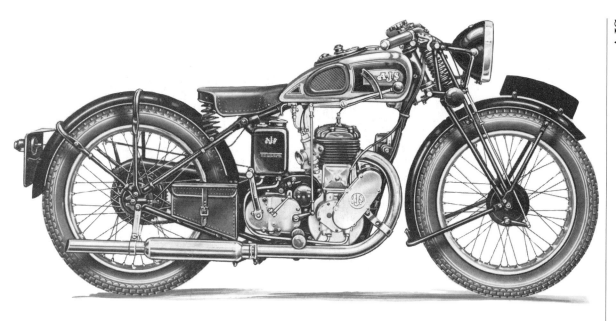

Only the side-valve models 5 and 9 continued to be listed with three-speed gearboxes in 1934. The others had four-speed boxes with the option of hand or footchange, except for the V-twins, which remained with hand, and the camshaft models with foot.

The range stayed as it was through what was a period of consolidation and an export version of the V-twin was offered with swept-back bars, clutch controlled by a left-foot pedal and the gear lever on the left side of the tank.

If 1934 had been near static, 1935 brought a good few changes and the beginnings of a model line that was to run through to the sixties. This was based on the introduction of Matchless-style engines with dry sump lubrication and a vertical cylinder in all but one case.

The general layout was to become familiar to several generations of riders with the timing cover concealing twin gear-driven cams, the oil pump set horizontally in the casting and driven by the crankshaft, twin pushrod covers running up to the cylinder head, dynamo behind the crankcase above the gearbox and the ignition side driven by the exhaust camshaft.

That first year the new models had coil ignition so just had a points housing set in the timing cover. Engine dimensions were revised, so the model 12 became 62.5 × 80 mm and 245 cc while the next size became the model 16 and changed to 348 cc from 63 × 93 mm. The 500 took a new model 18 number but remained with its old dimensions and inclined engine. Models 2, 5, 6, 8

By 1935, and this model 14 AJS of 497 cc, the side-valve engine was upright and the magneto in its front mounting position

and 9 continued and were joined by the 497 cc model 4, which was a side-valve engine with vertical cylinder, coil ignition and the new long 93 mm stroke.

The camshaft models remained in production, but the Trophy version was dropped after 1934 when the machines were built and sold for racing rather than anything else. Improvements included hairpin valve springs and bronze cylinder heads for 1935 and some machines had kickstarters while others were supplied without; these had a blanked-off gearbox end cover. On the chassis side front fork check springs were added.

In March 1935 three more models joined the range, all with vertical engines, dry sump lubrication and ignition by a magneto mounted just in front of the cylinder, where it was chain driven from the exhaust camshaft. The dynamo remained where it was just above the gearbox.

Other than the magneto the main alteration to the two ohv models was a two-port cylinder head. With these changes the 245 cc machine became the model 22 and the 348 cc one the 26. The third machine was the 497 cc side-valve 14, which was similar to the model 4.

1936 brought the 500 into line with the smaller machines, as the models 18 and two-port 8 adopted vertical cylinders, forward magnetos and new engine dimensions to share the 93 mm stroke of the 350. The 12, 22, 16 and 26 all continued and

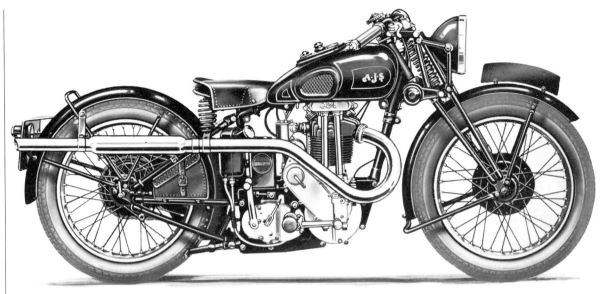

the 350 was fitted with a new head and barrel with more fin area. All models had four-speed gearboxes, but some still retained handchange.

The inclined side-valve engined models 5 and 9 continued for their last year as did the 497 cc model 4, which was still offered as the model 14 when fitted with a front-mounted magneto. The camshaft models 7 and 10 remained in the lists as did the model 2, which was offered in a commercial form as well as in home or export specifications. All gained forked connecting rods.

The AJS sensation for 1936 was a V4 shown at the Olympia show late in 1935. It certainly brought them plenty of publicity and the aim was to race the machine as a factory entry as well as selling it to the public. The engine was air-cooled with 50 × 63 mm dimensions and 495 cc, and the two pairs of cylinders were set at 50 degrees. The valves

Rear magneto on this model 18 AJS of 1936, this being the single-port engine. Footchange Burman and nice raised pipe

were actuated by single overhead camshafts and a chain run up and down between each cylinder pair to drive them. Four exhaust pipes and two carburettors were fitted, while ignition was by twin magnetos, bevel driven, and mounted on the right side of the crankcase. The cycle parts were essentially as any other model and a dynamo could be fitted in front of the engine. Rumour had it that a supercharger could go in its place.

The works raced the four in 1936 and again in 1938, by which time it was still air-cooled but was blown to a minimal extent. Inevitably this caused overheating, so for 1939 it was water cooled. It ran in the 1939 TT and later had its moment of glory at the Ulster, where it led for three laps before a fork

1938 Silver Streak AJS model 26SS of 348 cc. Very extensively chrome-plated which reflects the improved times as the decade progressed

1940 export version of the 982 cc V-twin model 2 AJS had footboards, special saddle, swept-back bars and left-side handchange

link broke, thought to be due to the strains put on it by Walter Rusk keeping it on the road and between the hedges. Post-war it did run again and won a race before blowers were banned.

Of the road models only the prototype is believed to have been built and run and AJS kept to their line of singles and V-twins from then on. Thus there was no mention of the four in the 1937 range, which saw the 12, 22, 16, 26, 8, 18, 7, 10 and 2 all continuing on the lines of the previous year.

Improvements that were made included complete enclosure of the overhead valve gear and isolation of tappet chest for the side valves. There were detail improvements to frames and forks plus a new petrol tank. All models except the export V-twin now had footchange gearboxes and all bar the 12 and 16 used magneto ignition. The inclined engine model 9 and coil ignition model 4 were dropped and the 14, with its front magneto, became the model 9.

Complementing the range were three competition models, types 22T, 26T and 18T. These were for trial or scrambles use and were supplied with single-port heads, raised exhaust system, narrow and plated but close-fitting mudguards, crankcase shield and suitable tyres. As was usual at the time they came with lights and could be used for work and play with minimal changes to suit various events.

There was no mention of the model 10 in the 1937 range and the 7 and 20 were listed as 'details not yet available'. The four never did appear, but by the middle of the year the model 7 was back

245 cc model 12 AJS from 1938 with coil ignition and rather small front brake

in production once more.

For 1938 it was built for road racing only and the engine was fitted with an alloy head and barrel. A megaphone exhaust was used and a Burman gearbox in place of the earlier Sturmey Archer. In keeping with its role it took the designation 38/7R.

There were a good number of detail improvements to the range of three sizes of singles in their one-port, two-port and competition forms. To them was added a super sports model in each size known as the Silver Streak. These were fitted with specially tuned engines and given an eye-catching finish with chrome-plated mudguards, chaincase, chainguard, oil tank, toolbox, wheel rims and headlamp. The petrol tanks were also plated with black panels and blue and silver lining. These models had the letters SS added to their type number. The range was completed by the side-valve models 2 and 9.

All the ohv models were fitted with a new design of cylinder head and rocker box for 1939 and the whole range continued on. There were two additions: the 12M and 16M, which were single-port machines of 245 and 348 cc fitted with magneto ignition rather than coil.

Despite the war a 1940 range was listed late in 1939 and described in February 1940. In the main the models were unaltered, but the range was reduced in various ways. In the 250 class the 12, 22 and 22T were listed, which removed the SS and the magneto-ignited 12M. The 350 range only lost the model 16, but all the model 18s went to leave the 8 in the 500 class with the 8SS as a de luxe version. The model 9 was still there, as was the 7R and the V-twin.

The twin continued to be built in two forms with the first in the conventional English guise. The second was for export and on American lines with footboards and swept-back handlebars. The rear brake pedal was moved to the right as a left-foot clutch was provided along with a handchange gear lever on the left side of the petrol tank. Three speeds and reverse were available in place of the standard four forward gears. An enormous pan saddle was fitted with old-fashioned tension springs to support it.

By 1940 the 22T, 26T and 7R had all gone from the lists as could be expected and the supply of civilian machines gradually dried up as the AMC plant concentrated on their war work.

AJW

AJW were a firm on the edge of the industry who bought in engines, gearboxes and most else to assemble their own package. Very grey porridge one might think, but they were astute enough to keep going right through the 1930s when many others floundered. Production was, however, on a small scale and the best year's production was only 250 machines.

The firm's initials came from Arthur John Wheaton, whose background was publishing, and for his 1930 range he built lightweights to supplement a big V-twin programme. These had special frames based in part on a triangular principle, but not to the same length as Cotton or Francis-Barnett. The AJW included long engine plates that extended back past the gearbox to the rear wheel and each side was a single malleable casting.

Into this went Villiers engines to provide the 172 cc and 196 cc Black Foxes, and 247 cc and 343 cc Silver Foxes. There was also a 196 cc Utility model. The bigger models began with the 500 Double Port, which had a 498 cc JAP engine, conventional cycle parts and a tank with a bulbous nose. It was also listed with a Blackburne engine as an option.

The remaining models were V-twins in the same style and the smallest had a 677 cc ohv JAP engine. Next came one with the 982 cc 8/30 side-valve engine and then one with an 8/55 ohv unit of 995 cc. Top of the list was the four-port special with an ohv engine of 994 cc made by British Anzani. It had inter-connected brakes among its many features and a four-speed Jardine gearbox.

Most of these models continued for 1931 with both pairs of Black and Silver Foxes listed. The 680 and 8/55 were still there as was the 980, now known as the 8 hp and joined by the 8.30 four-cam with the same size of JAP side-valve engine. The Anzani-powered twin was listed for racing only and there were two new models. These were

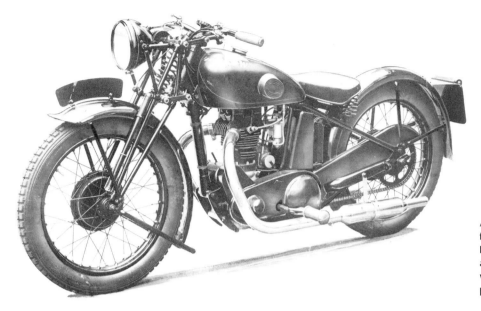

A 1934 AJW Red Fox fitted with a 499 cc Python engine made and supplied by Rudge with four valves in pent-roof form

powered by the 348 cc radial and 499 cc Rudge Python units as used by several firms. The frames of these models had a total of six tubes either bolted or brazed to the headstock, which could thus be said to be well supported.

January 1931 brought a further small model to the range, a new Silver Fox with the long stroke 346 cc Villiers power unit. It and the 247 cc version remained in the range for 1932 as did the two Black Fox machines of 172 and 196 cc. The 348 and 499 cc Python-powered models took the name Flying Fox and the larger one was available with the Ulster engine.

It also had shields and panels to keep the rider clean, although this was in no way enclosure on the scale adopted by other marques. A special feature was a rain deflector fitted to the top of the petrol tank with a pipe near the saddle peak to lead the water away. This gutter was to remain on

many of the larger AJWs for the rest of the decade. In this form it was called the Vixen. Of the V-twins only the 680 remained, with the others available and made to order.

There were only the Python-powered models listed for 1933, with three Flying Foxes with 348 cc, 499 cc and 499 cc Ulster engines. The same trio of motors also propelled the Vixenette, Vixen and Flying Vixen, which were the models with enclosure. A curious feature was that the exhaust pipes were a constant diameter with the silencer baffles built in the end. Neat, but not something to endear the marque to police or public.

They were still there for the upswept pipes in 1934, but the low-level ones had tubular silencers. There were just three models of 499 cc that year, still with the Python engine. The base was the Red Fox, which had the distinction of being the lowest priced 500 on the market at £42. The Flying Fox

Nice 1935 AJW Red Fox now fitted with a 488 cc JAP engine

was essentially the same machine with upswept pipes and valanced rear mudguard, while the Flying Vixen was as this but with the Ulster engine with bronze head.

For 1935 the same three models were listed but with a change to JAP engines. The Red Fox was still the base model but did have a magneto, and it and the Flying Fox had two-port engines and the Flying Vixen a TT replica one. 1936 saw just two models left, with the Red Fox having a three-speed handchange gearbox and the Flying Fox one with four and footchange. Both engines were of the dry sump type and the marque continued to offer 500 cc performances without frills at a low price.

In January they were joined by the Silver Vixen, which was a new model powered by a 495 cc Stevens engine, a product of the firm started up by the AJS family left when that firm moved to London. The engine had a vertical cylinder, hairpin valve springs and total loss lubrication, a feature well dated by the mid-1930s. Ignition was by rear-mounted magneto, which was chain driven from a camshaft, and the dynamo went on the front of the crankcase and was belt driven. A four-speed box and conventional cycle parts completed the model, which had a chrome and blue petrol tank.

The Silver Vixen was short-lived as it was back to the two Foxes for 1937, and the high-level pipes of the Flying model now had a small megaphone attached to their ends. As with others, the sole concessionaires were Pride and Clarke of London. For 1938 only the Flying Fox was listed, but this now had a single-port JAP engine with fully enclosed valve gear. This went into a revised frame that began as a normal tubular diamond type, but had a box structure of plate and angle round the gearbox and bolted on chainstays. The lower of these had lugs at each end and the rear ones were slotted for the wheel to push out forwards, as on a racing bicycle.

This one ohv model was joined by a pair of two-strokes for 1939. Both used 249 cc Villiers engines with the exhausts running straight back on each side. The standard Lynx had a flywheel magneto and three speeds, but the de luxe version had coil ignition, a dynamo and four speeds. The frames of both were duplex type, part bolted-up construction with tubular seat stays with the other members of angle section.

All three models were listed for 1940 and post-war the firm continued in one way or another into the sixties.

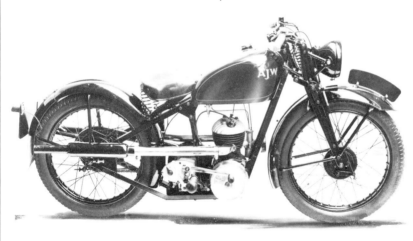

Left **AJW two-stroke from 1939 fitted with 249 cc Villiers engine and sold as the Lynx**

Right **One of the AKD models from 1930, possible of 248 cc capacity and rather basic. Note the stand under the engine pointing forward and ready to cause an accident if the spring fails**

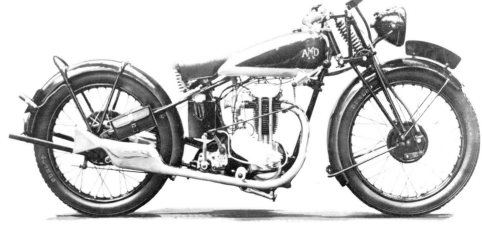

AKD

Ariel

As the Abingdon this make dated back to Edwardian days, but they were better known in engineering circles for their range of tools in general and King Dick spanners in particular. From 1925 the motorcycles took the initials of the two parts to become AKD.

They used their own range of ohv engines and for 1930 listed eight models. All had engines set vertically in a straightforward frame with girder forks and a saddle tank. The magneto went to the rear and the lines were rather vintage and quite conventional. All had three-speed gearboxes.

Three machines had 172 cc engines and were the single-port model 10, two-port 80 and sports 70. Next came the 196 cc 20 with two ports and the same size model 60, followed by the 248 cc sports model 90 and de luxe 100. Finally came the one side-valve of 296 cc which had an outside flywheel between the crankcase and the primary chain and was typed the model 40.

For 1931 the machines were given names in place of numbers and a smaller model was introduced for the 150 cc class. This was the Comet and it had a 148 cc ohv engine inclined in its frame. The three 172 cc ohv models continued as one- or two-port versions of the Orion and the sports Mercury.

There was only one 196 cc ohv model left as the two-port Jupiter and just one of 248 cc, which also had twin ports and was labelled Neptune. The final model was new and called the Polar. It had a 349 cc side-valve engine inclined in its frame and it took over the job of the model 40.

The whole range went forward as it was for 1932, but during that year the firm stopped building motorcycles and concentrated on hand tools.

The range of Ariel singles had their basic design laid down by Val Page late in 1925, when he first joined the firm. For the 1927 models he moved the magneto behind the engine with chain drive from the camshaft and so set the pattern for 30 years. Cylinders may have been inclined for some years, but the essence was untouched.

In the redesign for 1926 most of the cycle side had remained unchanged and veteran, but Page did deal with the poor stopping power of the old models by fitting seven-inch brakes to both wheels. For 1927 there was a new frame, which gave problems, plus a new gearbox and saddle tank. The frame was redesigned for 1928, when the Ariel house trademark first appeared, and dry sump lubrication adopted in 1929 with the twin-plunger pump bolted to the inner timing case and driven by the camshaft. Thus by the end of the vintage period the design was well established and in little need of radical alteration.

So the 1930 range was much as the one for the previous year and comprised three each of 250 and 500 cc plus two of 557 cc. These last were the model A, with side-valve engine with a vertical cylinder driving a three-speed gearbox, and the model B, which was the de luxe version.

In the 500 cc class the E was the standard model with two-port head and dimensions of 81.8 × 95 mm to give 499 cc. The F was the de luxe version, while the G was the special with polished engine internals. It also had a backrest pad bolted to the rear mudguard to emphasize its sporting nature.

The smallest models were all based on 65 × 75 mm dimensions and of 249 cc, but the LB was a side-valve engine and the others ohv. Both had twin-port heads and the LF was the de luxe model and the LG the tuned sporting one. All were known as Colts by the riders, although the name really belonged to the ohv models only. All had three-speed gearboxes and similar cycle parts.

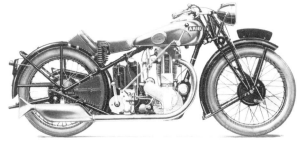

There was a considerable change for 1931, for the trend was to inclined engines, and Ariel backed their horse both ways by following the new style and keeping some of the old. They also notched up a sensation at the show where the Square Four made its debut.

The 250 cc models were still the side-valve LB and ohv LF, but their cylinders were inclined forward by 30 degrees. Two versions of the ohv model were offered with one- or two-port heads and listed as the L1F31 and L2F31. Ariel had for that year, and the next, adopted a year dating suffix for their models, and thus the 250 side-valve was the LB31.

Next in size but not launched until the spring was the MF31, which was a 30-degree inclined ohv engine with 72 × 85 mm dimensions and 346 cc capacity. In other respects it was as the 250s.

The big singles came in two sizes and two sets of three, with two 500 cc ohv models plus one of 557 cc with side valve in each, the first with vertical cylinders and the second with them inclined forward by 60 degrees. In the first set were the

Above **The twin-port model G Ariel of 1930 with 499 cc ohv engine**
Above left **Sloping side-valve 557 cc engine of 1932 Ariel SB32. Silencers and splayed frame suited the four as well**
Top Inclined 346 cc 1932 engine of the MH32 Red Hunter

VB31 and VF31, very much as the year before, and with them went the VG31. This differed from the 1930 version in that it had a four-valve head to improve engine breathing.

The slopers formed a similar trio, with the SB31 the side-valve model and the SF31 and SG31 the ohv ones. All had four-speed gearboxes and frames with duplex downtubes to straddle the engine. The first two also had a transverse silencer box mounted close up to the engine and just ahead of the frame tubes. From this pipes ran back to twin conventional silencers. The SG model had a four-valve head similar to the VG.

The most impressive new model was of course the Squariel as it was nicknamed. The design was Edward Turner's and the engine layout unique. The prototype was exceptionally compact with all four cranks overhung and gears in the centre coupling the shafts and taking the power back to the three-speed gearbox built in unit with the engine.

This was a little too special for economic production at that time, so the left rear crank gained an outer web and this drove back to the four-speed gearbox. The engine was based on dimensions of 51 × 61 mm and a capacity of 498 cc. A single camshaft ran across the top of the cylinder head to open the valves and was chain driven on the right. An ignition distributor went on the left end of the camshaft and a magneto behind the block with its chain drive also on the right. Alloy cases enclosed both chains. Lubrication was by connecting rod dippers which picked up oil from sump troughs to feed the big-ends, plus a pump to feed the cambox. The oil was carried at the rear of the crankcase.

The four engine was still a compact unit and able to slot between the duplex downtubes of the sloper single frame and drive the same gearbox. The cycle parts were much as the rest of the range and included a tank-top instrument panel.

It continued for the next year as the 4F/5.32 and was joined by a 601 cc version achieved by boring out to 56 mm. This was the 4F/6.32. The rest of the range continued much as before, minus the VF and SF models. Only the twin-port 250 ohv remained, as the LF32, but the 350 was available with one or two ports as the M1F32 or M2F32.

New was the MB32, which was a 346 cc side-valve lightweight that slipped under the 224 lb tax barrier. It had an inclined engine so was much as the smaller LB32. In the 500 cc class the VG and SG remained in the lists and the VG changed its bore and stroke to that of the SG. They were joined by a new name, the Red Hunter, which was given to the VH32. This was a tuned version of the four-valve, vertical-cylinder VG and was set-off by red tank panels and rim centres. It also had a well-worked-on engine, racing carburettor and magneto plus other sporting goodies.

Early in the New Year it was joined by the 346 cc MH32, a tuned version of the MF model with inclined engine and twin-port but only two-valve head, but it had the same red finish. Completing the range were the two 557 cc side-valve models, the VB32 with a vertical cylinder and the SB32 with a sloping one.

In January 1932 the company learnt that it had won the Maudes Trophy for the previous year in recognition of the Ariel Sevens test which ran seven models in tests that featured the same number.

Despite this success the group had problems and during 1932 ran into financial trouble, but Jack Sangster, whose family had been involved with it from Victorian days, was determined to save it. He managed this and re-established Ariel with a slimmed-down workforce, factory and range. One who moved on was Val Page who went to Triumph, and at Ariel Edward Turner was put in charge of design and quickly slimmed the range to use many common parts both for the single-cylinder engines and on the cycle side.

The diversification of vertical and sloping engines was discontinued and all the singles settled into the mould they were to stay in for many years. The four continued in 601 cc form only with the 498 cc version available to order for a short while. The frame changed to a single downtube and was common to the range, as were Burman gearboxes.

All the ohv singles had twin-port heads and the tourers were the 346 cc NF and 498 cc VF, both of which could be had with three- or four-speed gearboxes. The 557 cc VA side-valve models had the same option, while the de luxe VB came with four as standard. The Red Hunter range was extended down to the 248 cc LH in February by reducing the bore of the 350 to 61 mm, while the VH changed to a two-valve head. The 346 cc version of the Red Hunter became the NH and the lists were completed by the VG, which was the de luxe 500 with four speeds but handchange. Unlike its forebears it had a two-valve head.

The year 1934 brought enclosed valve gear, rubber-mounted handlebars and new forks, along with the continual swing from hand to foot-change. The model range continued as it was with the addition of the LF, a standard version of the 248 cc model. The others followed the lines set by their type letters with the capacities represented by L, N and V and the build state by F for standard, G for de luxe and H for Red Hunter. For the side-valve models the letters A and B were used for the same purpose.

The one significant change for 1935 was to the engine dimensions of the VH, which reverted to the long stroke 81.8 × 95 mm. For the rest there were single- and twin-port heads, high or low exhaust systems and three- or four-speed gearboxes with hand or footchange.

The F build went at the end of the year, so the 1936 range brought in the de luxe LG and NG to accompany the VG and the trio of Red Hunters. The VA also went, while the VB increased its stroke

to 102 mm and its capacity to 598 cc. The 4F/6 continued and all models had four-speed gearboxes with footchange.

Also listed were competition versions of the Hunters, which had single-port heads, no lights, sump guard, nail catchers, special mudguards and competition tyres.

At the end of 1936 the company name became Ariel Motors and stayed at that for the rest of its life. The 1937 range of singles was exactly as for the year before with the three ohv sizes built in de luxe and Red Hunter forms and the one side-valve model. All the de luxe machines were fitted with twin-port heads, while the Hunters had the option of one or two. The competition versions remained in the lists.

If the singles were little changed the four underwent a major revamp. This had been carried out by Edward Turner for the 1936 season, but development problems delayed it, together with Turner's move to Triumph. Thus the new four, known as the 4G, was not shown until the 1937 season and went into production in September 1936.

The engine was completely redesigned. It was enlarged to 995 cc using 65 × 75 mm dimensions and altered to ohv operation using a single central camshaft. This was driven from the rear crankshaft by a chain on the right, which also drove the mag-dyno. A nut on the end of the camshaft drove the duplex plunger oil pump and lubrication was dry sump with an oil tank under the saddle.

The crankshafts were conventional forgings, each with a central flywheel bolted in place. The connecting rods were light alloy forgings with plain

Above left **Typical Ariel side-valve engine built for many years and in this case of 557 cc and fitted in the model VA of 1933. Note Bowden carburettor**
Above **Edward Turner making a point about his Ariel Square Four 601 cc 4F at a show of 1934 models**

big-ends and the two crankshafts were coupled by gears on the left. Both head and block were cast-iron, so it was a heavy unit but compact enough to fit in the normal Ariel frame. The performance was smooth and quick with 10 to 100 mph in top being the claim even if 9 to 95 might have been more realistic.

At the same time a 599 cc version of the 4 was proposed as the model 4F. This came by reducing the bores to 50.4 mm, but, in the main, these machines seem to have been exported. About 400 are believed to have been made.

It was detail improvements and the range remained as it was for 1938 and nearly the same for 1939 with no major changes for the 346, 499 or 598 cc singles. The 250s became the de luxe OG with single-port head and the OH Red Hunter. They adopted a lighter frame and cycle parts along with a lightweight Burman gearbox. The side-valve VB was joined by a new version of the VA, but with an 81.8 × 95 mm, 499 cc engine to give the firm a machine to offer against the opposition's 500 cc sv models.

The 4G continued and was joined by the 4H, which was a cheaper standard model, the original now being typed the de luxe one. With them came a smaller edition, the 4F, with the bore reduced to 50.4 mm and the capacity to 599 cc, but in other respects it was as the 4G.

Also new for all models except the 250s was a spring frame designed by Frank Anstey. This used a linkage to connect the wheel spindle to the frame and to a plunger box on each side. The link lengths were designed so that the spindle moved in an arc about the gearbox sprocket for constant chain tension, but introduced too many pivots and rather overlooked the movement of the gearbox to set the primary chain tension. The movement was rather limited and was undamped, but it was an interesting option that continued to be used on the Square Four at least up to 1959.

The whole range continued as it was for 1940, but the firm then concentrated on a service version of the NG for the duration plus a number of the OG and a small batch of the VA from spares stocks. The services found the Ariel single just as tough and reliable as it had been in civilian life.

1938 competition version of the Ariel 499 cc model VH

Ascot Pullin

The Ascot Pullin only reached the 1930 market as a job-lot sold off by the liquidator to Rennos, the London dealers, and some stayed there for two decades unsold. It was a machine with an unprecedented amount of new features and as such could have expected a rocky ride from the motorcycle public at the best of times. Following its announcement late in 1928 and some major development problems that arose in 1929 it could not have chosen a worse time to attempt to be 'The New Wonder Motor Cycle'. Before the year was out the receiver was in.

The machine was stated to be a fast tourer and the sales brochure listed 52 new or exclusive features and they really were advanced in the main. The engine set the style, for although only a single with pushrod operation of its two overhead valves it was laid flat, so the head faced forward and had its three-speed gearbox built in unit in a section of the casting above the crankcase area.

Engine dimensions were 82 × 94 mm and capacity 496 cc. A downdraught carburettor supplied the mixture and the twin-port head connected to a low-mounted pipe and silencer on each side. Ignition was by a magneto mounted on top of the engine and gear driven, while lubrication was dry sump with a separate oil tank. The cylinder was well spigoted into the crankcase.

Primary drive was by double helical gears on the left and the gearbox was of crossover design, so its output sprocket appeared high up on the right. The chain to the rear wheel ran mainly outside the frame and was thus easy to enclose.

The frame was part of the special nature of the machine, for it was built up from steel pressings into which the mechanics were fitted. Various covers then hid the works from view and provided access. The pressings did not stop there, for the fork blades were made in the same way, as was a tank-top toolbox and a handlebar-mounted instrument panel.

This carried speedometer, ammeter, oil pressure gauge, light switch and a clock, while all the controls were built in and the cables hidden from sight. Contents gauges were fitted to both petrol and oil tanks. The braking system was equally advanced, with hydraulic and interconnected brakes—the original Ascot Pullin design was inclined to total failures so they quickly changed to Lockheed components. Both standard and de luxe models were listed and the latter was fitted out with legshields, a mirror, a screen and, best of all, a windscreen wiper. Finish was in deep blue with the frame panels in cream and the fittings chrome-plated.

It was an impressive and innovative machine and was launched at a price that could hardly have included either profit or much to pay for all the press tools. The word then went round that it did not steer and it was soon found that at speed it could throw its rider. There were other problems and the sedate performance did nothing to entice customers to it so few were sold.

Other financial problems dragged the firm down and once again it was shown that new ideas were not the route to salvation.

Baker

F. E. Baker was involved with American machines in Edwardian times, the Precision make of engine and machine either side of World War 1 and the Beardmore-Precision in the early twenties. This last was too innovative to succeed and he then turned to Villiers-powered models to retrieve the situation. He used a bolted-up frame much as the Francis-Barnett, but with a top tube brazed to the headstock to skirt round the patents.

For 1930 there were six models, all with Villiers engines, with the 172 cc model 55 and 65 the smallest. The latter had the Brooklands engine. There were also two models of 196 cc with the 50 the standard one and the 58 with the Super Sports engine. Finally there were the 60 with 247 cc and the 62 with 343 cc.

In March 1930 a four-stroke was added with a 249 cc James side-valve engine and this was a sign of an impending merger. Late in the year Frank Baker sold out to the James company and they went on to use his frame for some of their models.

Below **A two-stroke Baker with auto-lube from 1929, possible with 247 cc engine**

Top left **The Ascot Pullin with its full enclosure and very advanced cycle features**
Left **Ascot Pullin on show at Beaulieu about 1959. 496 cc ohv engine but a model with problems and a short life**
Right **The 1930 Baker fitted with 249 cc side-valve James engine**

Baughan

H. P. Baughan was a trials man first and last, involved for many years with the ACU Western Centre and ISDT selection tests. He and his staff at the works in Stroud, Gloucestershire, were more often, it seemed, organizing something for the ACU, preparing reports or producing results sheets than running a business. For all that the firm prospered by moving into a new field at the right time.

The firm began in 1920 with the production of cyclecars, but their day-to-day business remained service and repair work for quite a while. The motorcycles began to come in 1928 and from the first were nearly all built for competition. This was most unusual for then such machines were standard road models to Colonial specification.

The other item that focused attention on Baughan was that the first machines were sidecars and they had the sidecar wheel driven. They were immediately very successful and this brought protests, and while the ACU refused to ban them they left the way open for trials organizers to do so. Baughan dealt with this by fitting the works

machine with an alternative chair minus the drive as called for.

Production began around 1930 and was always limited, so each machine was really hand built to a customer's order. Due to this a range of engines was listed from 300 cc sv to 500 cc ohv and could come from Blackburne, JAP or Sturmey-Archer. The rest of the machine was equally open to option, with the basic frame, forks, tanks and wheels laid out with trials work in mind.

Not all machines were built as sidecars, but when they were the drive to the wheel was incorporated. This was done by changing the rear wheel to a live spindle running in ball races in housings in the frame fork ends. From the left the spindle drove a simple dog clutch and this in turn a cross-shaft, with two fabric alignment joints, to the sidecar wheel.

It worked very well and could be used to reach farm or cottage off the beaten track in addition to its trials competitions. On a hard surface the dog clutch was easily disengaged, which was as well. If this was not done the outfit would try hard to go straight on at the first corner it came to.

From then on a range of models was listed each year with 250, 350 and 500 cc engines from one or more of the three firms and in either side-valve or ohv form. Only a dozen or so were built in a year, but they continued in this way until 1936, when motorcycle production ceased and the firm moved to other fields.

A solo Baughan from 1935 fitted with a 348 cc Blackburne engine and full competition equipment

Berwick

This was an experimental model built to appear at Olympia and unusual in that it was a lightweight with shaft drive. The prototype was made by the Berwick Motor Company of Tweedmouth on the east coast of Northumbria, but a move was then made to Banbury, where preparation for production was put in hand.

The engine was a modified Villiers and it was intended to offer both 247 and 343 cc sizes. To suit the shaft drive it was turned so the crankshaft lay along the machine, and this was extended to drive the three-speed gearbox bolted to it. The clutch went in a flywheel between the two and the flywheel magneto at the front. The cylinder was mounted vertically with the carburettor at the rear and the exhaust on the left.

The gearbox had handchange and its output shaft went on the right. A universal joint attended to the alignment and the shaft itself was enclosed.

It drove an underslung worm at the rear wheel.

The effect was one of unit construction and it went into a duplex frame as most such did. This had a fabricated headstock with the two tank rails and two downtubes both emerging from the base of the gusseted area. The first ran nearly straight back to the rear wheel and the second went down and under the power unit to the same point. A massive section of the rear mudguard went between the two pairs to brace them and act as a seat stay.

At the front went Brampton girders and each wheel had a 7 in. drum brake. The finish was in black with gold lining for the tank, which held nearly two gallons.

Sadly no more was heard of this interesting design.

The strange Berwick with its turned Villiers engine and shaft drive. Note how rear mudguard section acts as a frame member

British Anzani

This company was a builder of engines rather than complete machines, but did produce a prototype in June 1939 that was interesting because it foresaw a post-war trend. This was the clip-on, which attached to a standard bicycle and thus took the work out of travel. It had a short boom period post-war along with the autocycle, although both were swept away in time by the moped.

The British Anzani unit was of 44.5 × 39 mm dimensions and 61 cc. It was a simple two-stroke and, like many later, drove the rear wheel with a friction drum in contact with the tyre. Unlike post-war designs the engine was located on the left side of the rear wheel with the cylinder parallel to the frame tube running from saddle to wheel spindle. Its roller ran on bearings mounted above it and was connected by chain to the crankshaft, where there was a ten-tooth sprocket. The roller was 3 in. in diameter and its sprocket had 17 teeth.

A lever enabled the roller to be held clear of the tyre or in contact and the latter condition was assisted by a spring. The tank for the petroil went above the engine and a flywheel magneto on the left provided the ignition.

At the time British Anzani were themselves too busy to contemplate production and then came the war. Thus no more was heard of the unit, but it was an interesting foretaste of what was to come to satisfy the demand for transport at the lowest cost.

Brough Superior

The Brough Superior was the machine of legends, an early superbike before the term was coined and 'The Rolls-Royce of Motorcycles'. George Brough was also a master of the art of publicity, grabbing the best parts for his machines and truly making the whole greater than the sum of its parts. Much of the legend came from performance by specific men and machines and from the show-stoppers George produced year after year for Olympia and Earls Court.

Another view is that George Brough made the machines he most liked to ride, which might account for the gradual move from out-and-out performance, in totally sporting style, to the high-speed sports tourer. And for the show bikes.

There is hardly such a thing as a standard Brough Superior as, for the price charged, there was very individual attention. There was a standard range, but this was really just the starting point from which the customer could refine his basic choice of SS80 or 100 to the machine *he* wanted with the exact specification *he* desired. No wonder it was expensive, but run by a showman like George, rather like a large club, it worked well enough. Part of the expense came from the firm's practice of assembling each machine completely and getting every aspect right before anything was plated or painted. When correct it was stripped, finished and reassembled for final testing.

With this background it is hardly surprising that the Brough story is peppered with show specials, works specials, customers' specials and modified models each with a name and a story. Best known owner outside the world of motorcycling was T. E. Lawrence, who had a string of Broughs known as George I to VII. Then there was Spit and Polish, Old Bill, used by George himself in competition in the early 1920s, Ike's Bike, Leaping Lena, Moby Dick, the works scrapper, and the Karbro Express, a road machine stretched out to near 1500 cc and pulling an incredibly high gear.

George Brough was a perfectionist and as a hard rider one of the most stringent and critical inspectors of all the machines that carried his name. Many customers were personal friends and all would have their needs and wishes discussed before their machine was put in hand. Service and back-up was to the same style and standard for George knew only too well that if you charge high and exclusive prices then you must also keep the client happy. He won't carp at the bill but he will object if his spares are not sent off at once.

The client took his starting point for his order from one of three models which in 1930 were the 680, the SS80 and SS100. All used V-twin JAP engines prepared to the highest standards and the first was a relatively small one of 677 cc with 70 × 88 mm dimensions. It had ohv and a fair degree of go but to George was too small to be of much interest. In its basic form it had a rigid frame and three-speed gearbox, but as the Black Alpine was normally supplied as a springer and with four speeds. In this form the finish was in black and known as all-weather, with the petrol tank in eggshell black with a silver line in place of the usual plating. Hence the name, although the finish with its minimal use of plated parts could be specified at no extra cost on any model when ordered, as could the spring frame, although there was a price for that.

The other two machines were bigger, as they had always been, with the SS80 being fitted with a 981 cc side-valve engine and the SS100 with a 995 cc ohv unit. Both pulled high gears.

All three machines were topped off by the famous Brough fuel tank, which gave them their

Above left **The V-four Brough Superior on show at Olympia for 1927 with 994 cc side-valve engine**
Above **Top view of the Austin-engined Brough Superior with its twin rear wheels and the prop-shaft running between them**

distinctive air. It was made from many hand-beaten pieces all soldered together and was a Brough trademark. Possibly it was the most important feature that George himself contributed aside from his demand for perfection from everyone.

A smaller model joined the range for 1931, a baby to George Brough, but a fast 500 twin to anyone else. It used a 491 cc ohv JAP V-twin engine and was priced a little nearer to what the average was for such a size, but was still expensive by the standards of the times. It maintained the cachet of the marque admirably, but was not kept in the range for 1932. The market for small but de luxe machines was minute and only nine 500s were made. It made more sense for Brough to build bigger machines for more money.

Aside from this it was time for another stunning special to grab the headlines and excite the customers. While just about all the machines that left the Brough works were special in some way or another the works specials, one-offs and prototypes were even more so. For many the most interesting were the various fours.

The first appeared in 1927 and was a transverse V–4 with side valves and 994 cc capacity. The vee angle was 60 degrees, with the single camshaft in its centre, and the engine drove straight back to the clutch and gearbox built in unit with it. Bevels turned the drive for the chain to the rear wheel.

The machine was a sensation at the show but less so on the road.

George came back in 1928 with an in-line four fitted with a 900 cc Swiss-made MAG engine and similar transmission arrangements. This machine had a Bentley and Draper spring frame with the suspension spring horizontal under the saddle, the usual Castle forks and twin headlamps. It was smooth to ride and covered many miles on the Continent, but had some engine problems, so no more were built.

There was an interlude involving a prototype fitted with a twin-cylinder two-stroke Villiers engine and a one-off racing machine with a single-cylinder JAP, but George always came back to the need for a 4 if the result was to be smooth, quiet and in the Gran Turismo style he was beginning to seek. Water-cooling was thought necessary as a means of keeping the noise level low and dealing with any cooling problems and from there it was only a short step to using an existing car engine. The obvious choice was the Austin 7, as it was small and light, so George set to work on Sir Herbert Austin.

This is thought to have been the most difficult part of the project, but in the end Sir Herbert agreed to supply engines bored to the maximum oversize to raise the capacity from 750 to 800 cc and fitted with an alloy cylinder head and a water pump. Attached to it was the usual clutch, gearbox and a propeller shaft, which was of course on the centreline of the machine.

To get round the problem that most solved by shifting either drive or engine, George in his inimitable way left the mechanics where they were and moved the wheel to one side. Then to balance it he fitted another, so there was just room for the shaft to pass between them, and declared it a sidecar-only model.

With a reverse gear in the box it was a de luxe machine for hauling a chair, but it was also sold as a solo. That opened up all sorts of possibilities and Brough legends. Only ten were built as they fell foul of the taxation authorities, who claimed that as it had four wheels it was a car and ignored the regulation that allowed the twin rears to count as one. All of the Austin 4s were made in 1932, but the last was not sold until two years later. Nearly all survive.

The standard 680, SS80 and SS100 all continued in the lists with their options and extras, but in essentials were little altered except for detail improvements. Thus the side-valve engine gained

alloy heads and quieter cam gear, the 680 had the mag-dyno shifted to make room for a footchange and the SS100 Alpine Grand Sports had its gear lever on the side of the tank and a special close-ratio gearbox.

For 1933 the SS80 was redesigned to a shorter wheelbase, lower saddle and increased ground clearance and to go with this there was a revised and improved JAP engine with detachable heads. All models had the option of being fitted with interchangeable wheels held to the brake drum by a hub nut with two knock-off ears. The system was as used by Norton in 1932 and was mainly used on export machines.

Even Brough Superior were feeling the pinch of the Depression years, so early in the year they announced that their V-twins could be bought without electrics, speedo or number plates at a reduced price. At the same time they added two more side-valve models to the range.

The first was the 11.50, which used the massive JAP side-valve V-twin of 1096 cc to pull either a very highly geared solo or a massive sidecar outfit. At just under £100 it was not cheap by 1933 standards, but was by Brough's. The second model was less expensive still for it used a 680 cc JAP side-valve engine in a set of cycle parts that were spartan for the firm but fairly de luxe for any other.

The side-valve 680 failed to find much favour and few were built, so it was not in the lists for 1934. Neither was the SS80 or the straight-four, although the last of these was sold that year. This left the 11.50, 680 ohv and the SS100, which was

Above left **The working area of the Brough banking sidecar chassis showing the scroll formed in the back of the wheel which raised the chair body after a left bend**
Above **Brough Superior 680 Black Alpine from 1935 with ohv engine and sprung frame**
Right **The small 491 cc V-twin Brough of 1931 of which only nine were made**

much modified, plus a very special sidecar chassis.

The SS100 was fitted with the 8/75 JAP V-twin engine, known as the 'two of everything' motor. It had two carburettors, two magnetos, two double oil pumps and an abundance of power. There was a new frame, Castle forks and all the carefully executed details expected of the pride of the Brough range. It was guaranteed to do 110 mph solo and 90 with a chair, but sadly the engine proved troublesome and not more than ten were built.

Unlike the standard Brough sidecar, which was very conventional, the new chassis was a one-off and unusual in that it allowed the machine to bank to the left under the control of the driver. A pedal released the mechanism so that the chassis dropped under its own weight and the control of a hydraulic damper. To get it up again a scroll was formed in the back of the sidecar wheel and a chassis peg engaged into this. The rotation of the wheel and the outfit's momentum thus raised the chassis, which was then locked by a second peg.

The three models were still listed in the same way for 1935 with the spring frame option that had existed from 1928 and the 680 built as the Black Alpine with this feature as standard. The big side-valve was made as the 11.50 Special and had a twin-choke carburettor thanks to the 60-degree vee angle of the JAP engine. This differed from all the others and the extra room just allowed the manifold to be installed with the carburettor body with its two throttle slides mounted side by side on it. The two mixing chambers faced left and were supplied by a single float chamber.

In July 1935 the SS80 returned to the lists but in a new form, for it now had a Matchless 982 cc V-twin engine fitted. The tappet covers were marked 'Brough Superior' and 'SS80 Model' and the magneto chain cover also carried the Brough name, but in reality it was built in Plumstead. For the rest it had a four-speed gearbox, duplex frame, full equipment and the enviable Brough finish.

The SS100 went the same way for 1936 when it too was fitted with a Matchless engine, this time one with ohv and hairpin valve springs. It came as standard with Castle forks, which were an option for the others. The three machines continued with detail changes for 1937, when they were joined by the SS80 de luxe Special, which had Castle forks as standard and, according to reports, a new twin carburettor arrangement with rod linkage and single cable on the lines used by a modern four. This design also went on the SS100, but is unknown to marque experts, so was unlikely to have reached production.

By 1938 it was time for the next show special and with it came plunger rear suspension, which went on all models except the standard SS80. The SS80 was also the only one not fitted with a new easy-action roll-on centre stand.

The special was seen at the Earls Court Show held late in 1937 and was less spectacular than the fours which preceded it. It was based on the SS80 engine with this set transversely across the frame. This put the ports and timing gear at the front while the drive side was extended back to the single plate Austin 7 clutch. A sprocket just ahead of this drove the mag-dyno mounted above the clutch housing on the machine centreline.

A three-speed and reverse Austin 7 gearbox was bolted to the back of the housing and was unusual in that the second and top gears had synchromesh—common enough in cars but not motorcycles. The two upper ratios were engaged by a foot pedal, but first was selected by hand. At the rear of the gearbox went a spiral bevel pair which drove the rear wheel by chain and allowed the kickstart to operate in its normal plane. The clutch had hand or foot operation.

The engine and gearbox were housed in a frame based on the standard design, to which plunger rear suspension had been added. It was also modified with a shortened downtube which split to run either side of the engine as usual with the type of layout. This was needed to clear the oil tank as well, for this was bolted to the front of the crankcase to form a bulbous nose. From it enclosure panels ran back to encompass the mechanics and the electrics, although the battery was left to stand unashamed above the gearbox.

The public were still wary of the much dreaded

torque reaction inherent with the transverse engine and showed limited interest in the new concept, so limited that only the show model was sold; but this was ridden extensively enough to wear the machine out. The public distrust hardly mattered to George for the twin was interim. He had his eyes on his dream—the Golden Dream for 1939, and it went on view at the show late in 1938.

Two were built, one in the usual black and chrome for road testing and the other in gold for the show. Hence the Golden Dream name it gained before the week was a day old.

As usual it was the engine that set the Dream apart and for it George chose a flat-four layout of unique type. The aims were to gain smooth power impulses, complete engine balance, no vibration and even cooling for all four cylinders.

This last meant either water-cooling or a fan and cowling for most people. Not so for George and his team of Ike Webb and Freddie Dixon. They arranged the four cylinders as two flat twins, one above the other, so all four exhausts had the same cooling draught available to them. The crankshafts lay along the machine and were geared together to rotate in opposite directions.

This first model had 68 × 68 mm dimensions and a 988 cc capacity. The top crankshaft was meshed with larger gears on the two camshafts which lay on the horizontal centreline between the cylinders and carried two cams at each end.

The second engine had 71 × 63 mm dimensions and a 998 cc capacity. In both cases the pistons all moved from side to side in unison, for there was only one crankpin for each flat twin pair

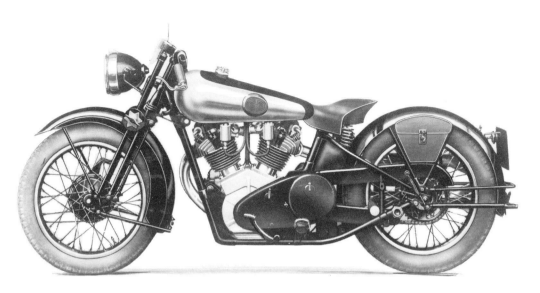

Above left **The twin carburettor installation on the 1935 Brough Superior 11.50 engine**
Above **Top of the line was always the SS100 Brough and this is the 1936 version**
Right **The side-valve Brough Superior mainstay for many years was the SS80 and this is the 1937 one**
Below **The show special seen late in 1937 and based on the SS80 but turned to create a transverse V-twin housed in a frame with plunger rear suspension but with chain final drive**

of cylinders. They were in line because one rod was forked to straddle the other and thus when the two right pistons were at tdc the two left ones were at bdc.

For the design at the show the camshafts were chain driven in two stages. The first was from the top crankshaft down to the oil pump set below the engine in the wet sump. The second ran from that shaft up to embrace the two camshaft sprockets. The cams moved tappets and short steel pushrods that lifted the overhead valves.

Engine construction was on car lines with the light alloy crankcase casting being split on its vertical centreline and extended out to form the cylinders. Iron liners provided the running surface for the pistons, and while iron, one-piece, heads were fitted at the show, alloy ones were proposed for production.

The rods were short and in alloy, twin Amals provided the mixture and an exhaust system went on each side. Ignition was by a special mag-dyno driven from the rear of the top crankshaft and incorporating a distributor to feed the sparking plugs. It was based on that used by the Ariel Square Four.

A three-speed gearbox was bolted to the rear of the engine with a kickstarter on the black

prototype and a hand start lever on the gold show model. There was also a four-speed box made but not finished off. From the box a shaft ran back within a tube to the rear wheel, and an underslung worm and wheel turned the drive round the corner.

The frame and cycle parts were positively prosaic in comparison but well up to the usual Brough standard. Plunger rear suspension and specially widened Castle front forks looked after the ride and the details and finish incorporated all of George's ideas and ideals for his Dream machine.

Sadly it proved harder than anticipated to develop fully, and then the war came and with it the end of Brough Superior motorcycles. Right to the last days the three basic models continued to be listed, but from October 1939 the firm was committed to high-precision work.

It was perhaps only right that the company who used the slogan 'The Rolls-Royce of Motorcycles' should do much work for Rolls-Royce during the war and were one of the very few entrusted to machine Merlin crankshafts.

The 1938 Brough Superior Golden Dream pictured in the Beaulieu gallery in 1959. Very special flat-four engine with shaft drive

BSA

At one time during the 1930s the BSA slogan that 'One in Four is a BSA' was simply a fact. They dominated the market and were always well ahead of their rivals, one year building twice the machines of their closest rival.

They were successful in surviving the Depression because they concentrated their efforts on building machines the public would and could buy. There were very few excursions into the interesting, the innovative or the exciting, and this avoided the costs, the lack of sales or the commercial heartache so many others suffered.

BSA concentrated on a range of plain and straightforward models built in traditional sizes and without any signs of oddity in their specification or construction. What the customer got was a very well-made machine, reliable, sturdy, priced to a level he could afford and backed by a first-class chain of dealers for spares and service. In the 1930s this was what most buyers wanted because it was all they could afford.

Dreams might have been a Brough or even a car, then a real luxury item with heavy running costs, but reality was getting to work on time. For many a motorcycle became the way to do this in preference to the tram, bus or bicycle and at weekends it offered the countryside.

BSA appreciated all this, so built their range of models to suit, and in 1930 it was an extensive one running to some 18 basic machines. In addition there were variations and options and accessories, so customers could easily turn their standard machine into something a little special and unique to them, a welcome fillip in those hard times.

On the smaller machines the specification could be important, for it naturally affected the weight and this could determine the taxation class. When the limit went from 200 to 224 lb it helped, but could still be marginal. The effect in those Depression years was dramatic as the tax rose from 30s. to £3 in an era when you could buy a second-hand machine for less.

One area of variation was the electrics, with magneto, mag-dyno or Maglita being available and machines offered without lights, with acetylene lamps and bulb horn or with a lighting set. The Maglita was a device that in theory acted as both dynamo and magneto in one unit, but as so often happens with compromises it failed to do either job all that well.

The smallest machine in the range was a 174 cc two-stroke built in unit with a two-speed gearbox as the A30-1 or a three-speeder as the A30-2. It had been the firm's first two-stroke and its construction was unusual with overhung crankshaft, flywheel on the left and magneto mounted on top of the gearbox. Between crankshaft mains and flywheel went the ratchet gear for the left kickstart and two or three gearbox pinions. These drove mating gears on a shaft in the box and the clutch went on the right of this shaft outboard of the final drive sprocket. Thus the machine had a crossover box just as the Bantam, their next two-stroke, was to have.

The cycle parts were conventional and the machine not successful as its power output was minimal, so it went from the range at the end of 1930.

In the 250 cc class there were two models and in the BSA style as used up to 1935 they were typed B30-3 and B30-4. The system was a letter to indicate engine size, two digits for the year and a number for the model. As this last depended on the range size there was no continuance from year to year, but it usually began at the smallest and ran up. The effect was that the largest model number varied from 10 to 15 over the years 1930–35.

The B30-3 was a typical BSA with vertical cylinder and the magneto mounted ahead of the engine and gear driven. The oil was carried in a sump cast into the front of the crankcase and was only pumped to the crankshaft bearings. The engine drove a three-speed, handchange gearbox with right-side kickstart, and the two were housed in a simple tube frame with duplex downtubes and girder forks. An Amal supplied the mixture and the exhaust system went on the right. Finish was black with a green tank.

The B30-4 was the ohv version, with its pushrods neatly enclosed in twin tubes and fitted with a chrome-plated tank with green top panel. Similar in style were four other machines, two being of 350 cc with side valves and the other pair with 500 cc ohv engines.

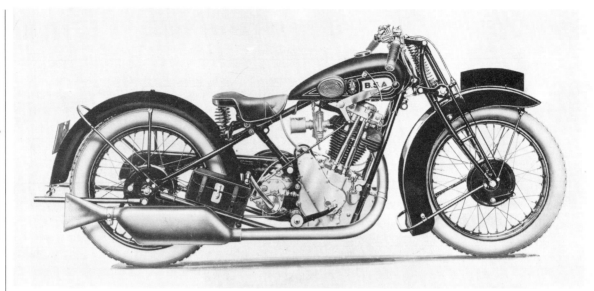

The L30-5 was a 348 cc sv model built for solo use, while the L30-6 had a stronger frame and was only sold to go with a sidecar. Both were much as the 250, but the 500 pair were on older lines. They were built as the S30-19 and S30-18, with the latter a lighter version of the first and meant for solo use only. With reduced weight it had a sprightlier performance from a common engine.

This had a vertical cylinder with ohv and the magneto was mounted in front of the crankcase ahead of the frame. In this position it was chain driven from the exhaust camshaft in real vintage style. The gearbox contained three speeds and had handchange and the cycle parts ran on normal lines.

The remainder of the single-cylinder models had inclined engines in the style set by the Sloper model in 1927. With its low seating position and saddle tank it was a trendsetter, and more so when it gained a two-port head. For 1930 it and its companions went into a new frame with a forged steel backbone running from steering head to saddle nose. BSA were to make much of this feature up to 1936.

Above **BSA model G30-15, a 985 cc V-twin from 1930**
Above left **1931 249 cc side-valve single BSA model B31-1. Basic get-to-work transport, good and cheap to buy and run**
Top **The BSA Sloper model in its 1928 form, here without lights which would have been an extra**

The Sloper itself was the S30-13 and its lightweight version the S30-12. The 493 cc ohv engines had twin-port heads and were inclined forward to give the name. The design was much as for the vertical engines, with the oil carried in a sump cast into the crankcase, but the magneto went aft of the cylinder and was gear driven. An Amal supplied the mixture and the remainder of the machine was conventional.

The Sloper was listed with many options and one was a tuned engine. To distinguish it from the standard ones it had a red star stencilled on the timing cover and from this came the star theme that was to run through to gold when times improved.

Along with the two ohv models there were four with side valves, all built on the same lines, but in two sizes and two weights. The stock 500 was the

Above J34-11 BSA or the 499 cc ohv V-twin for 1934
which had first been designed for the War Office

Below The BSA 499 cc model with fluid flywheel
in the crankcase and elaborate timing chest

S30-9 and its lighter version the S30-7. By boring the engines out 5 mm to 556 cc the H30-10 and lighter H30-8 were created. There was also the smaller L30-11, a 348 cc ohv machine with sloping cylinder built to a lighter scale but otherwise as on the 500.

A feature of the Sloper was its braking system, which had two brake pedals, the right one working the rear brake and the left one the front. The latter could be supplemented by an optional hand lever.

Completing the range was a pair of side-valve V-twins with chain-driven front-mounted magnetos and constant loss lubrication with mechanical and hand pumps. Capacities were 771 and 985 cc with a single Amal in the vee, exhausts on the right and heavy-duty construction. The type numbers were E30-14 and G30-15 respectively. There was also a G30-16, which was a heavy-duty, sidecar-hauling-only model with an extended wheelbase.

For 1931 the range was cut back to 12 models, but the variations, options and extras continued so that all customers could be satisfied. The 250s were little changed and continued as the B31-1 with side valves and B31-2 with ohv. A de luxe version of the latter was offered as the B31-3, and this came with an oil gauge in the tank, a stronger frame and added fittings.

In the 350 class there were two side-valve models, the L31-4 and de luxe L31-5, and they were joined by the new L31-6. This had an ohv engine with vertical cylinder on the lines of the 250 and replaced the L30-11 Sloper of the previous year.

The 500s also numbered three, all with sloping engines, with the S31-7 side-valve, S31-9 ohv and S31-10 de luxe ohv, all much as in 1930, as was the H31-8 side-valve 556 cc machine in the same style. This last came with footboards as standard so had a heel-operated rear brake, while the two ohv Slopers continued with their dual brake pedals. The two V-twins also ran on as the E31-11 and G31-12 in the same two sizes.

1932 saw the side-valve 250 disappear, but the ohv one continued as the B32-1. The sv 350s stayed as the L32-2 and L32-4, while there were three of that size with ohv. The basic model was the L32-3 and the de luxe version with bigger brakes was the L32-5. There was a second L32-5 available and that was called the Blue Star and had a tuned engine with raised compression ratio, better cams and stronger valve springs. On the chassis side it had footchange and upswept exhaust pipes for its twin-port cylinder head, but was still offered with acetylene lighting or a mag-dyno.

In the 500 cc class the only model to continue was the Sloper as the S32-8 but with a four-speed gearbox. The other three models all had new vertical engines with 85 × 88 mm dimensions and front-mounted magneto. The sv model was the W32-6 and the others were both typed W32-7, one being the Blue Star version. The sv 556 cc model with inclined engine ran on as the H32-9 and the big 985 cc V–twin as the G32-10, the other twins being dropped.

Among the new fitments that came that year

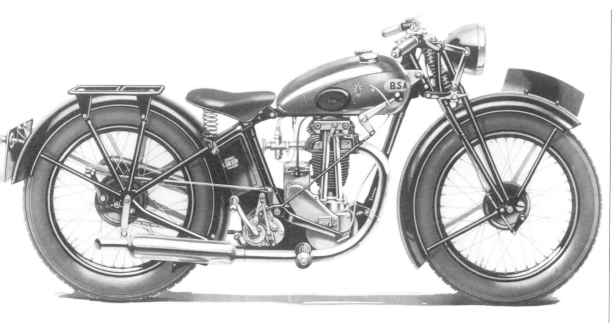

Above **1935 149 cc X35-0 model which looked after the bottom end of the BSA ohv market**
Above left **1934 499 cc BSA Blue Star W34-9 with front mag-dyno and sump cast in with the crankcase**

was a pawl for locking the front brake lever on for parking; it disengaged when the lever was squeezed further. Also new was a trough formed in the base of the primary chainguard which was topped up with oil from the crankcase to keep the chain happy. The handlebar-mounted instrument panel gave way to one set in the tank top, while an internal improvement was forged steel flywheels for all models.

For the 250 cc market in 1933 the side-valve B33-1 and ohv B33-2 were joined by a Blue Star version, the B33-3. The last of these followed the lines of its predecessors, but the other two were really cut to the bone to suit the times. Engines were vertical and lubrication total loss. A Maglita was chain driven from the crankshaft to provide sparks and current, the chain cover was simply a guard and a handchange three-speed gearbox was fitted. It was pretty basic to meet the needs of the Depression. The side-valve 350 was dropped and the ohv changed to the 71 × 88 mm dimensions, which were to remain a BSA favourite for very many years. Two models were offered, the standard R33-4 and the Blue Star R33-5.

The sv 500 continued as the W33-6, but its larger brother had its stroke extended to 105 mm, which raised the capacity to 596 cc. It was listed as the M33-11. For 500 cc ohv riders there were three machines, the W33-7, the Blue Star W33-8 and the

Special W33-9. This last had a more highly tuned engine for sports riding or even a little road racing. The range was completed by two 985 cc V-twins, the basic G33-13 and the G33-12, which was modified to make it more suitable for solo riders.

1934 brought a new model at the lower end of the capacity scale. This was the X34-0 with 52 × 70 mm, 149 cc ohv engine much on the lines of the 250s. These ran on as the sv B34-1, ohv B34-2 and Blue Star B34-3. The ohv 350s also continued as the R34-4 and Blue Star R34-5, but were joined by a special version, the R34-6, on the lines of the 500 of the previous year.

This remained in the lists as the W34-10 along with the W34-8 and Blue Star W34-9. The sv machines remained as the W34-7 and M34-12 and the bigger ohv as the M34-13.

Improvements to existing models were mainly detail, but a sign of the slightly improving times was that all models were supplied as standard with full electrical equipment. The days of scraping the barrel and acetylene lights were firmly put in the past, while models with the mag-dyno mounted in front of the engine were provided with a shield to protect it.

Very new in the 500 class was the model FF, so named because its transmission comprised a fluid flywheel and pre-selector gearbox. The flywheel was formed in the left half of the crankshaft, which still carried a sprocket on its outer end. This drove the gearbox, which had three speeds pre-selected by a handlebar lever and engaged by moving a foot pedal. No clutch was needed as the fluid did this job and the kickstarter turned the engine via gears in an extended timing cover. For the rest the model was much as the others of that capacity, but the new transmission dampened the normally good performance down to a humdrum level. The prototype was displayed at the 1933 Olympia Show, but the model never entered production.

Of more interest was a small ohv twin which joined the 985 cc one, which continued as the G34-14. The smaller had originally been designed for the War Office and then modified for civilian use. Dimensions were 63 × 80 mm to give 499 cc and the valves were exposed for the first year. A single carburettor fed into the vee and the exhaust pipes made their own ways back to twin silencers. The mag-dyno went in front of the engine, which had a dry sump, and the model typing was J34-11.

In February 1934 a third 249 cc ohv model appeared as the B34-17. In effect it was a lower-priced Blue Star and this reduction came from minor specification changes. Downswept exhaust pipes were fitted, only one toolbox, no oil gauge and the petrol tank was painted without any plating.

It was short-lived, for both it and the Blue Star were replaced in 1935 by a new model typed the B35-3. This was of 249 cc and retained the usual engine dimensions, but was of revised design with vertical cylinder, pushrods contained within a single tube, rear mag-dyno and dry sump lubrication with the oil tank under the saddle. A four-speed footchange gearbox was fitted and the cycle parts followed the usual BSA lines.

A larger version of the new machine was built as the 348 cc R35-4 and replaced both the existing standard 350 and the Special to leave the R35-5 Blue Star from the year before. Most of the rest of the range continued with minor changes and improvements and type numbers similar to those used in 1934.

1936 brought changes to the machines and their names, with the Empire Star models being introduced to mark the Royal Silver Jubilee of the previous year. Down at the bottom end the 149 cc became the X0 model, but otherwise remained the same lightweight machine. The sv 250 became the B1 and the standard ohv the B2, while the de luxe with four-speed gearbox was the B3 with footchange, and the B18 light with hand operation.

In the 350 ohv class there were no fewer than five models with two distinct engine styles. The base model was the R4 de luxe with its pushrods enclosed in a single tube, dry sump lubrication and

a four-speed, footchange gearbox. The same basic engine also went into the R19 Competition model, which had trials tyres, chrome-plated mudguards, raised exhaust system and a sump plate.

The other three models had engines with the oil tank cast into the front of the crankcase, from where oil was pumped into the big-end. After draining to the sump it was picked up by the flywheels and returned to the tank. The engines had the mag-dyno mounted ahead of them and the standard model was the R17. More sporting was the New Blue Star R20 with two-port cylinder head and waist-level exhaust systems. Unlike the standard machine, footchange was fitted for the four-speed gearbox and this was also a feature on the top-of-the-line R5 Empire Star.

In the 500 cc class this style and type of machine was repeated with the standard Q7, New Blue Star Q21 and Empire Star Q8. All three had revised 82 × 94 mm engine dimensions, which reduced the capacity a little to 496 cc. The side-valve models took the same form but retained their old dimensions as the 499 cc W6 and 596 cc M10.

For riders who preferred a V-twin the 499 cc ohv continued as the J12 and the 985 cc sv as the G14. Between them a new version of the ohv appeared with 71 × 94.5 mm dimensions and 748 cc capacity. Otherwise it was much as the 500; but one variation was the front brake, which went on the left for the 750 while staying on the right on the smaller twin.

In addition to the major changes to the range there were a good number of detail improvements. One of the most noticeable was the adoption of an aluminium primary chaincase on the Empire Star models. A quick-action, quarter-turn filler cap appeared on the petrol tanks and external aluminium surfaces were coated with a special finish.

While the previous years had been ones of consolidation, 1937 brought a major revamp to the singles, which were fully redesigned. The man responsible for the engineering was Val Page from Triumph, who had been at Ariel earlier and was to return there in due course. The design was to continue post-war to the end of the pre-unit days.

The 150 ohv model was dropped, so the smallest machines were the B20 side-valve and B21 ohv 250s, together with the B22 Empire Star. All used 63 × 80 mm dimensions and a common, light crankcase with timing gears on the right to drive the rear-mounted mag-dyno. Dry sump

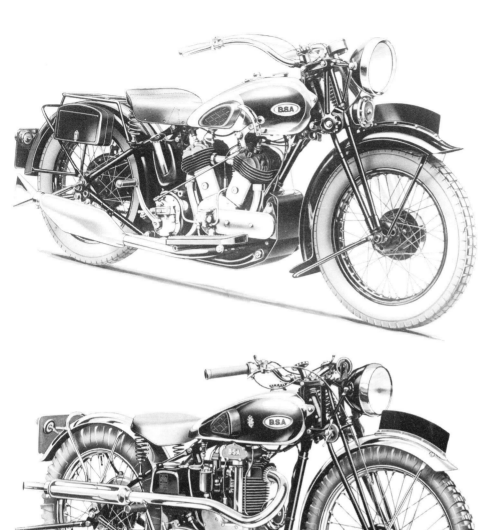

The big V-twin for
1936, the 985 cc
model G14 still with
handchange and
external oil pump

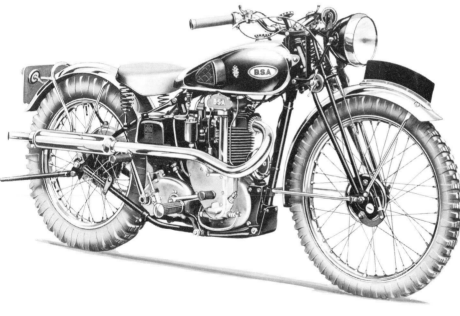

Competition R19
from the 1936 BSA
range and of 348 cc
with tyres,
mudguards and
crankcase shield to
suit its purpose

For those who still
wanted a magneto
BSA listed this
249 cc B20 in 1938
as well as the C10

lubrication supplied oil from a tank under the saddle. Construction was simple and robust, reliable and easy to service, so it was to continue with little change for all models.

Separate four-speed gearboxes were fitted with footchange on the Empire Star and hand on the others. The frame was a simple tubular one with light girder forks and the cycle parts were conventional.

Next in size was the 348 cc B23 with side valves and a trio of ohv models of the same capacity, all of which used the traditional 71 × 88 mm dimensions.

These were built to the same light design as the 250s and comprised the B24 Empire Star, the B26 Sports with handchange gearbox and the B25 Competition. This last had competition tyres and mudguards and waist-level exhaust and was built for trials use. A fourth 350 was the M19, which was built on a heavier scale for engine, gearbox and frame. The engine was distinguished from the lighter models by the tappet access cover, which moved from the crankcase to the pushrod tunnel. Internally the construction was heavier and the crankshaft supported more robustly. Its dimensions differed from the others at 68.8 × 94 mm.

The M series extended to four more models of larger size with side-valve ones represented by the 496 cc M20 and the 596 cc M21. These repeated the heavier construction of the M19, and the first was to do sterling service during the war and the second to remain in use until 1963, much used by the AA in their distinctive yellow livery.

Two ohv 500s were produced using the same basic design, these being the M22 Sports and M23 Empire Star, both of which had footchange rather than the hand system retained by the side-valve models. All the 500s used the 82 × 94 mm dimensions and the M21 those of the M10.

To complete the range there were two of the V-twins, the Y13 with the 748 cc ohv engine and the 985 cc G14 side-valve model. Neither of these received any significant changes and none of the Blue Star models were built after 1936.

The new range was consolidated for 1938 with little alteration, except for 82 × 112 mm dimensions and 591 cc capacity for the M21, but was joined by two new and significant models. The first was triggered off when Wal Handley came out of retirement to ride a specially prepared Empire Star at Brooklands in June 1937. He duly won his first race at over 100 mph, so was awarded the usual Brooklands gold star, and from this exercise came the famous model of the same name.

For the catalogue it was prosaically typed the M24, but was a full sports machine with an all-alloy bench-tested engine and TT carburettor. The gearbox shell was cast in magnesium alloy and the frame was built in a better, lighter-gauge tubing without sidecar lugs. An unusual feature was a toolbox set in the top of the petrol tank and a crankcase shield was fitted as standard.

Two additional versions were listed, one for competition and the other for track racing, for which it was prepared in Brooklands style. It is doubtful if any of the track models were ever built, but the competition one proved popular for the trials events of the times.

Left **The much-maligned BSA grey porridge C10 of 249 cc and side valves in its original 1938 guise**

Right **The M23 Silver Star of 1939, 496 cc and with the option of a close-ratio gearbox**

The second new model came at the opposite end of the range and was the C10 side-valve 250. It had an engine built on similar lines to the others but with a single gear-driven camshaft to lift the valves via bellcrank levers, skew gear-driven contact points housed in an angled housing on the timing cover for the coil ignition and a chain-driven dynamo mounted behind the cylinder.

A separate three-speed, handchange gearbox was fitted in the simple cycle parts, but dry sump lubrication was retained, with the oil stored in a compartment in the petrol tank. The silencer had a cheeky uptilt to its tail and the machine was an adequate if basic performer.

Early in 1938 BSA began an attempt for the Maudes Trophy using M21 and M23 models. The side-valve was fitted with a chair and the two machines were then subjected to a long journey, severe hillclimbs in Wales, magazine-style road tests at Brooklands, more Welsh hills and finally two cross-London rides in heavy traffic using top gear only. For all this they won the trophy.

For the last year of the decade the basic C10 was joined by a de luxe model with footchange gearbox and the C11 ohv. This used the same bottom half, box and cycle parts as the de luxe C10 and a simple all-iron design with crossed pushrods and alloy rocker box lid to fully enclose the valve gear.

With the arrival of the C range the B20 was dropped, but the B21 continued in standard hand and de luxe footchange versions for those who insisted on a magneto supplying their sparks. The B23 was also listed in standard and de luxe forms.

The ohv 350s continued as the B24 Silver Star in single- or twin-port styles, with the latter fitted with waist-level exhaust pipes and tubular silencers. Complementing these machines, which replaced the Empire Star, were similar one- or two-port versions of the standard model B26. To complete the set the B25 Competition model continued to be listed and was also available with a twin-port head.

In the larger sizes the M20 was offered in standard form or de luxe with tank-top instrument panel and qd rear wheel. Both models were also built as the larger-capacity M21 and all used the footchange gearbox.

The ohv M22 continued and was joined by a twin-port version, while the M23 became the Silver Star with the option of a close-ratio gearbox. It was also available with the twin-port head. Top of the single range remained the M24 Gold Star, which had gained two extra bolts for its pushrod tunnel early in 1938. For 1939 it had the instrument panel set in the tank common to the larger machines and the close gears as standard. The wide gears were an option.

The range was completed as always by the massive G14 V-twin, which was still much as it had been in 1930. It still retained the oil pump bolted to the outside of the timing chest and this still had its sight glass. The auxiliary hand pump had, however, gone. The machine itself continued to fulfil its role of a sturdy plodder to pull a sidecar along and it did this as well as always.

BSA laid on another long ride for two of their machines in 1939 in an attempt to retain the

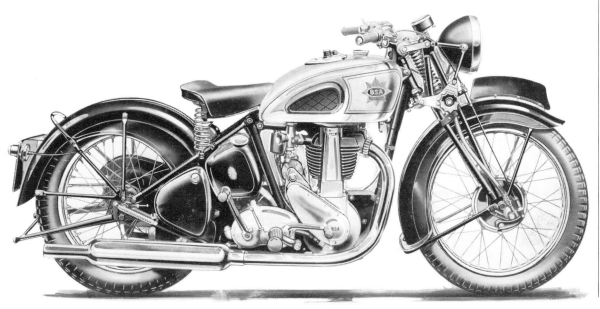

Maudes Trophy. This time they went all round the coast of England and Wales and added in Welsh hills and Brooklands, all of which was to be done without the engines stopping except for the final track tests. This proved over-ambitious, for they had problems with the fuel feed and the electrics, although these were rather minor. They completed the full test in fine order, but were not to keep hold of the trophy, which went to Triumph.

Despite the stringencies of wartime, BSA had not one but two new models in their 1940 range. This was all the more surprising as many older ones were dropped. Out went the B21, B23, B24, B25, B26, M22 and M24. The side-valve C10, M20, M21 and G14 all remained and with the ohv C11 and M23 received minor changes.

The two new models were both of 348 cc capacity and the more mundane was the C12, which had side valves and was modelled strongly on the C10. It thus kept to the coil ignition, skew-driven points and rear dynamo, while its transmission was by a three-speed, footchange gearbox.

The second model was the B29 and the forerunner of the post-war big singles. It retained the usual BSA 71 × 88 mm dimensions but was based on the M-series heavy-duty crankcase with its total of four main bearings. The valve gear was fully enclosed and the valves were controlled by hairpin springs within the one-piece head and rocker box. It was a basically simple and sturdy engine that was tough and successful.

However, before BSA could really reap their reward with it they had to build thousands of prosaic M20s for the Services.

1939 BSA 348 cc B23 in standard form, superseded by the C12 the next year

Calthorpe

This marque name was first seen before World War 1, and by the end of the 1920s was best known by one machine, the Ivory Calthorpe. This had a distinctive finish to petrol tank and mudguards, which made it stand out from the many sombre black machines of the times and had been introduced for 1929.

By 1930 it had become Ivory the Second, with a new inclined 348 cc ohv engine. This had dry sump lubrication, the magneto mounted to the rear of the engine and the dynamo at the front. The oil was carried in the front section of the crankcase and the pushrods went within a single tube up to the rocker box.

A three-speed gearbox provided the transmission, with its hand lever working neatly in a gate built into the right knee-grip. The cycle side was conventional, with the frame having duplex downtubes to span the crankcase oil tank and girder forks going at the front.

Contemporary and later reports indicate that it was a well-made motorcycle that was very nice to ride and performed better in the all-round sense than many. At the time its finish told against it, for traditional enthusiasts would go for black with gold or silver lining and viewed anything with

Above **348 cc Ivory Calthorpe III from 1931. Its bright colour made it stand out from its contemporaries**
Below **Ivory Minor Calthorpe of 1932 fitted with a 247 cc two-stroke engine and finished in the same style as the larger models**

coloured mudguards as effete, which was their loss, although a black and gold finish was available as an option.

For 1931 it became the Ivory III, with a four-speed gearbox, the option of coil or magneto ignition and a tank-top instrument panel. It was joined by the Ivory IV in 1932, and this was of 494 cc but in other respects the same and also offered with the choice of ignition systems. Competition versions of the III and IV were also listed.

At the show a third Calthorpe appeared as the 247 cc Ivory Minor and this differed from the others in having a two-stroke engine, although it retained the finish. The engine was based on a

Villiers and had auto-lube, but the oil tank was cast into the front of the crankcase in the same style as the four-strokes. Otherwise it was a simple lightweight with tubular frame, duplex downtubes and blade girder forks.

In September 1932 the range for the next year was given out as the three existing models plus a Sports version of the 494 cc Ivory Major. Two months later it had shrunk back to just the 500, but still with the option of coil or magneto. A few 348 and 247 cc models were available until the stocks were sold off.

For 1934 the Major continued unchanged and was joined by an Ivory Minor. Unlike that of 1932 it was a 247 cc edition of the Major, so had the same inclined engine with twin-port head and dry sump lubrication with the oil tank cast into the front of the crankcase. Ignition was by mag-dyno, which was gear driven and sited behind the cylinder. The rest of the machine was as for the larger model but on a reduced scale in the matter of tyre sections and tank sizes. Magneto-only and coil ignition versions continued to be available at a lower cost.

A third model was listed for 1935 and this brought the return of the original 348 cc machine as the Ivory Junior. It was much as before, and the other two models had few changes. The 247 cc had a larger tank and the 494 cc a revised lubrication system which removed the section of the oil tank to the rear of the crankcase proper. Ignition of all three models became coil with magneto as an option.

In 1936 the 348 and 494 cc engines were fitted with new heads and barrels with total enclosure of the valve springs and gear. The competition versions of these two machines also reappeared while the 247 cc one was left as it was.

For 1937 Calthorpe became one of the ranges sold exclusively by London dealers Pride & Clarke. For this purpose they lost their old colour and became the Red Calthorpe, which somehow lacked the same ring. The range itself stayed as it was with three road and two competition models, but the 350 changed its dimensions to 72 × 86 mm in order to share the 500 bottom half. This took the calculated capacity to just over 350 cc.

It was the same red finish for the same range for 1938 plus a green finish option, but sales were not enough and the firm went into liquidation. It was

sold by the receiver to Bruce Douglas, a member of the motorcycling family of Bristol and in May 1939 a new range was announced. There were three models with 245, 348 and 497 cc ohv Matchless engines with vertical cylinders and re-marked timing covers. Although one report mentions four machines it is unlikely that any other than a prototype or two were ever built before war preparations led to the new company being given notice to quit their premises at Bristol Airport.

Post-war the Calthorpe name revived briefly, but was for a machine built by the firm that became DMW. This was a 122 cc Villiers lightweight shown in prototype form as the Calthorpe-DMW in October 1947 but as a DMW when production began late in 1950.

Carlton

Chater-Lea

This make first appeared in the early 1920s and sold in small numbers as it was not widely advertised. Models built used bought-in engines and other components in a similar manner to many others and in 1930 were typified by the 500 cc DP with Sturmey-Archer engine, hand-change and chrome-plated tank.

The make then dropped from sight but reappeared in 1937 when it was one of a number of firms that used the 122 cc Villiers unit-construction engine to build a lightweight machine. In this one the engine had its cylinder inclined forward a little and the usual three speeds with a direct hand lever on the box. Lubrication was by petroil and ignition by flywheel magneto, which also looked after the direct lighting.

The engine unit was housed in a simple loop frame with blade girder forks. The twin exhaust pipes ran into a front expansion box which had a pipe on the left running back to the rear of the machine. Full equipment was provided, with legshields, rear carrier and electric lighting fitted as standard.

The model was just what the commuter needed and thus proceeded into 1938 without change, while for 1939 all that appeared was a choice of tyre sections. It was the same for 1940, but production then ceased and did not start up again post-war, when Carlton returned to the bicycle business they had always been in.

Chater-Lea began by making bicycle parts for other firms in Victorian times and in due course went on to do the same thing for motorcycles. In the Edwardian era they started to put some complete machines together and for them used all manner of English and European engines.

During the 1920s they were campaigned at Brooklands by Dougal Marchant and he broke world records using them, including setting the absolute 350 cc record over 100 mph for the first time. The marque was also a leader in style, for as early as 1924 they began to fit saddle tanks in place of the older flat type and this transformed the machine's appearance.

In the mid-1920s the firm decided to produce their own camshaft engine and the result was a 348 cc face cam design that was still in use in 1936. The bottom half was of conventional built-up type, but with a bevel gear on the right end of the crankshaft. This drove a vertical shaft with splined couplings at each end and at the top went two face cams, the inlet above the exhaust.

Two part rockers followed the cams and lifted the valves. At first the valve gaps were set by using valve stem caps of various thicknesses, but later a screw was used in the rocker. A cap went in the top of the shaft housing and its removal gave access to the cams, while the shaft itself was extended below the bevel gear to an oil pump set in the base of the crankcase. This supplied oil up the vertical shaft to the cams and rockers, while a second pump, fed separately from the oil tank, looked after the crankshaft and its bearings.

The magneto was bolted to the front of the crankcase and was driven by gears from the left side of the crankshaft from between the two roller mains, while if a dynamo was supplied, this went in front of the magneto where it was chain driven from the crankshaft. The engine went into an open diamond frame with girder forks and rather vintage lines. A single exhaust system went on the

Above left **The 1930 Carlton in this case fitted with a Sturmey-Archer engine**
Left **Later 122 cc Carlton with Villiers engine and built from 1937–40, this being from its first year**

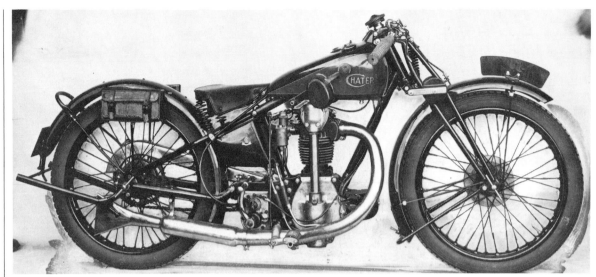

right and the fittings were of the period. For 1930 a magneto cut-out was built into the main oil tap as a safety precaution.

In 1928 the firm moved from London to Letchworth Garden City, then a development town, and for the following year offered two other machines as well as the 348 cc Camshaft Super Sports one. One had a 545 cc side-valve engine much on the lines of the ohc with front magneto and this dated from the early 1920s and was sold as the Sports model. The third machine was a two-stroke and had a 247 cc Villiers engine in a bolted-up frame. It was listed as the Super Sportlette and was a run-on from the 1929 programme so was soon dropped.

For 1931 the ohc model became the Super Sports, but there was no other real alteration. Gearboxes continued to be handchanged and were three-speed Sturmey-Archer units. In 1932 the model names became Camshaft and Side-valve, but otherwise the two machines continued in their rather vintage style from year to year.

The last camshaft model left the works in March 1935 and, along with the rest of the final batch, had a four-speed gearbox with footchange. The final Side-valve went to the AA in July 1936 as one of some 1200 combinations supplied over the years.

The company remained in existence and at Letchworth under the control of the Chater-Lea family, but turned to sub-contract work for the motor trade and other firms. Half a century later they were still there in business.

Chell

This Wolverhampton company announced two models for the 1939 season. Both were powered by Villiers engines, one of 98 cc with a two-speed gearbox and the other the 122 cc unit-construction motor with three speeds.

These units went into a loop frame fitted with pressed-steel forks and wheels with 4 in. drum brakes. A two-gallon saddle tank carried the petroil and direct lighting came from the engine's flywheel magneto.

The machines were available with rigid frames or with rear suspension and came complete with speedometer, rear carrier and horn. Production only lasted a few months, after which the make vanished from the lists with few machines built.

Top **1930 Chater-Lea Camshaft model with 348 cc engine**
Centre **545 cc Chater-Lea called the Sports model in 1930**
Bottom left **1930 Super Sports Chater-Lea two-stroke with 247 cc Villiers engine**
Below **1939 Chell with 122 cc Villiers engine**

Cotton

The Cotton hailed from Gloucester, and from their start in 1920 was hallmarked by its frame. This dated back a further seven years to when Francis Willoughby Cotton first laid down his triangulated design that was still little changed in 1939. He was also a trained lawyer so well able to fend off any attempts to poach the design, and during the 1920s the temptation was certainly there.

Stanley Woods had his first TT ride on a Cotton in 1922 and went on to win the Junior on one the following year. There were two seconds in 1924, two in 1925 and complete success in the 1926 Lightweight, when they took the first three places. This was to be the peak of their Island fortunes, but it served to establish the small firm in the public's eye.

This worked well up to the Depression, but by 1930 the effect was wearing off and they ran into harder times. To cope they offered an extensive range of models using proprietary engines, but always in their very stiff, rigid and light frame.

Engines were Blackburne or the slightly cheaper JAP plus one Sturmey-Archer and one Villiers two-stroke. The models were numerous, but all had a Burman gearbox, and in 1930 the ohv machines had saddle tanks while the others retained the older style with it between the top frame rails.

The two-stroke was of 247 cc, while the side-valve machines came in 295, 348 and 495 cc sizes, all with Blackburne engines. The 495 cc had the engine inclined, but the other three were installed vertically. All the ohv machines had their engines at the slope and were listed with one- or two-port Blackburne engines in 348 and 495 cc sizes, the latter in a choice of engine dimensions. Both could also be held with JAP engines and there was a further model with a two-port 242 cc JAP engine.

For 1931 the side-valve Blackburnes were out and only ohv models were listed in the three classes, with JAP or Blackburne engines plus the one Sturmey-Archer. Also available were 348 and 499 cc Rudge Python motors, so there was plenty of choice for the motive power for a Cotton.

In 1932 all models had saddle tanks and the side-valve ones back with JAP engines. There were also two models for the 150 cc class, one with a sv JAP engine and the other with a Villiers two-stroke. At the other end of the scale there was a 596 ohv machine with Blackburne engine along with the trio of ohv engine makes as before.

For 1933 the range extended a little more to include 250s with two-stroke Villiers, side-valve and ohv JAP, and ohv Python. With 17 models, one of each per week would have amounted to good sales in those times.

The range was up to 19 models for 1934 with the addition of 150 and 250 cc ohv Blackburne-powered models and 245 and 596 cc ohv JAP ones.

Above **1932 Cotton model 1J with 148 cc side-valve JAP engine in the triangulated frame**

Right **JAP-powered Cotton from 1937 and typical of the marque throughout the decade**

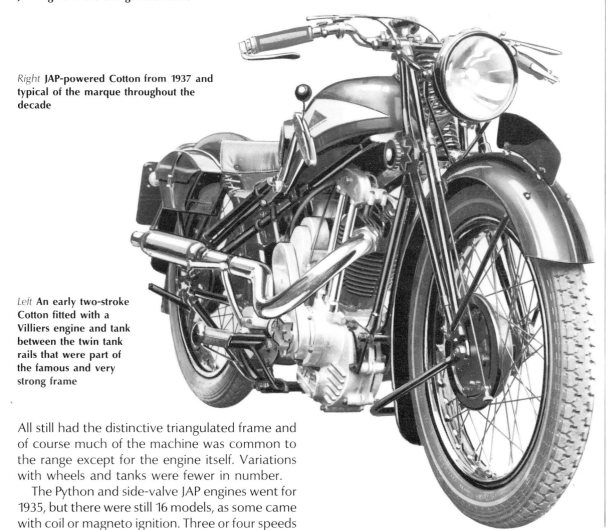

Left **An early two-stroke Cotton fitted with a Villiers engine and tank between the twin tank rails that were part of the famous and very strong frame**

All still had the distinctive triangulated frame and of course much of the machine was common to the range except for the engine itself. Variations with wheels and tanks were fewer in number.

The Python and side-valve JAP engines went for 1935, but there were still 16 models, as some came with coil or magneto ignition. Three or four speeds and hand or footchange were transmission options and the JAP and Blackburne engine options continued. A change was to the 150 cc JAP engine, which became an ohv unit.

For 1936 there was little change other than the addition of a super sports 500 with a JAP engine. One of the Blackburne-powered models, the 25B, took the same super sports designation. 1937 saw a different story, for all except one of the Blackburne engines went, and that left was as a 250 ohv option. There were three new models in the range with new 250, 350 and 500 cc JAP engines, each with chain-driven high camshaft and short pushrods enclosed in a single tube to give an air of ohc. These were mounted vertically in the familiar frame with four-speed, footchange gearboxes. Most of the other models remained, but in revised form and with a new type number system.

1938 was as 1937 except that the 150 ohv model had a Blackburne engine rather than a JAP, but this was to clear stock as the Blackburne factory had ceased production in 1937. Neither was in the 1939 list. For that year there was a new JAP engine in 500 and 600 cc sizes in the Cotton, and although still with ohv its appearance was in complete contrast to the high-camshaft engine. In place of a pushrod tube were horizontal fins that stretched from crankcase to cylinder head top without pause. It looked like a tall two-stroke and as well as its looks also had odd valve springs. They were wound like hairpins, but left with the ends pointing fore and aft. The centre coils went on a fixed pin and the ends reached out, one to the inlet valve and the other to the exhaust valve.

These engines were installed vertically in the familiar frame and built in standard or de luxe forms. The 500 cc high-camshaft model ran on with the others with 250 or 350 cc sloping engines, and at the bottom of the list still came models with 150 cc Villiers or 250 cc sv JAP engines to compete for the ride-to-work market.

Right at the end, during 1939, an even smaller two-stroke model made its appearance with the Villiers 9D engine of 122 cc. Low-priced it may have been, but it still retained the triangulated frame with twin downtubes which swept under the engine and gearbox unit. Forks were Webb pressed steel and the whole machine was smaller than the usual Cotton.

While never a large company Cotton certainly stood out from the crowd of runners using similar engines due to their frames and their TT successes.

Coventry Eagle

This company was located in Coventry and had its roots in Victorian times—bicycles and early powered tricycles. They always used proprietary parts, but in a neat assembly with a good finish, so they survived longer than some of their competitors.

During the 1920s they introduced their Flying 8 series with big V-twin JAP engines and very stylish tanks, somewhat like the Brough, and at the other end of the scale came utility models. The latter went into pressed-steel frames from 1928, which was novel in England even if more common for Europe.

The beginning of the 1930s saw Coventry Eagle offering a good range of models to cover most people's aspirations. All were in their traditional finish of black with cream tank panels and a carmine tank nose, which gave them a distinctive air. All had a letter F prefix to signify a 1930 model.

At the lower end of the range were four machines with Villiers engines in the duplex, pressed-steel, channel frame. This had the fuel tank perched on top and pressed-steel forks as well. The smallest-capacity model was the F21 with a 147 cc two-speed unit, but the others had three speeds. These were the F23 of 172 cc and two of 196 cc, the F24, and the F25 with super sports engine.

The rest of the range had tubular frames and four of these had vertically-mounted JAP engines with a rear-mounted magneto. The smallest was the 300 cc sv F35, then the 346 cc sv F45 and ohv F46, and largest was the 490 cc ohv F55. Both ohv models had two-port heads. There was one further

Top **1931 Coventry Eagle Flying Eight with side-valve V-twin engine**
Centre **The pressed-steel frame of the Coventry Eagle was a feature for many years and is here seen on a 1931 example with a 196 cc engine**
Right **Very basic 1932 98 cc H16 Coventry Eagle Marvel**

249 cc Coventry Eagle Pullman model N11 of 1937 with semi-elliptic rear springs and massive cast-alloy silencer

model with a JAP engine, the F50 with an inclined 482 cc side-valve unit.

The other three singles had Sturmey-Archer engines, either sloping as in the case of the 495 cc sv F52 or just inclined a little. The latter were the F44 with 348 cc and F54 with 495 cc engines, both ohv, with twin-port heads and dry sump lubrication.

At the head of the range came a trio of V-twins, all using JAP engines. They were all Flying 8 models and the F130 was the sports one with a side-valve engine. The F150 was the equivalent police model, but had a four-cam engine still with side valves, while the F160 was the super sports version with ohv.

The range thinned down a little for 1931, but did have an extra 196 cc Villiers model listed in standard and de luxe forms. This was the G22, also called the Wonder, and all models used the letter G prefix. Unchanged were the G24, G25, G44, G46, G52, G54, G55, G130 and G150. The others were dropped, but new was the G45, which had an inclined 346 cc Sturmey-Archer engine with side valves and dry sump lubrication. The 172 cc two-stroke model became the D25, with vertical engine in the pressed-steel frame.

The letter H was used for 1932, when the range slimmed down some more and the Flying 8 models were no longer listed. The four-strokes were down to just four models, with the 346 cc ohv JAP model becoming the H40 and the H44, H45 and H55 continuing much as before.

The real interest was in the two-strokes, and back in July 1931 a 147 cc version of the 196 cc

Wonder had been announced as the Wonder Junior. When the full range was listed in November it was, however, no longer there.

Most interest centred on the Silent Superb H19 model, which had a 147 cc Coventry Eagle engine and was built with a full luxury specification. The engine was actually made for Coventry Eagle by the Levis factory. To ensure it was quiet its twin exhaust ports were connected to a large cast-aluminium expansion box, which was curved to fit between the frame members and round the crankcase. At its rear were attached twin chrome-plated silencers.

The engine had coil ignition, with the points on the end of the dynamo which went above the gearbox and was chain driven from the left end of the crankshaft. A large flywheel went on the right under a cover and a three-speed gearbox was fitted.

The frame was an improved version of the pressed-steel type, fitted with blade girder forks and a neat toolbox between the right chainstays. The machine came fitted with massive legshields that curled under the rider's feet to give ample protection.

The Silent Superb was excellent value for money at £23 10s., but for those who could not stretch to this there was the H18 Eclipse, which was the same thing with a single-port engine and two-speed gearbox. This pulled the price down to 19 guineas.

Even cheaper was the H16 Marvel that used a 98 cc Villiers engine with two-speed gearbox in a tubular frame. For all that it still had legshields. Finally came the H22, which at first was simply the 196 cc Wonder model of the year before. Before the year was out the makers had a change of mind and the model became another Silent Superb but fitted with a 196 cc single-port Villiers engine. It still retained the coil ignition and separate dynamo of the smaller model rather than the more usual flywheel magneto.

There were only three models for 1933, for trading was very hard in those times. Sensibly the firm dropped the four-strokes, which were much as many others, and concentrated on their speciality of a two-stroke that was different. Dropped also were the Levis-Coventry Eagle engines, which had proved unsatisfactory, these being replaced by Villiers. The J19 Silent Superb was modified and joined by a 247 cc version, the J20. Both now had the gearbox casing housed in the main crankcase casting so that rotation of it adjusted the primary chain. This was enclosed in a cast-alloy case along with the dynamo chain, but the coil ignition had given way to a flywheel magneto on the right crankshaft end.

The frame was also altered, with the wheelbase

1938 P50 Coventry Eagle with 497 cc Matchless engine and natty megaphone silencer

being extended and a second toolbox appearing on the right. The capacity of the three silencers was increased and controls and wiring tidied up.

The third machine was the J18, which revived the Wonder name and had a 148 cc Villiers engine in the pressed-steel frame. For this model the three-speed gearbox remained separate and it was much as the machines of the previous year.

In May 1933 the Silent Superb range was extended by adding two models to it, one with a 148 cc Villiers engine and the other with a 247 cc Villiers. Both had three-speed gearboxes and retained the separate dynamo, although ignition was by flywheel magneto. The use of three silencers continued and a pressed-steel cover enclosed the primary and dynamo drives.

It was these two models that continued for 1934 as the K1 and K2, but the 250 was also listed in two other forms. One was the K4, when it came complete with a sidecar, and the other the K2A, where it was in competition form with high-level exhaust system, no legshields, an undershield and more suitable mudguards.

The third model for that year was the K3, which had a 245 cc ohv JAP engine and a pressed-steel frame similar to the others, but extended and stiffened to suit the four-stroke motor. In April 1934 it became the K6, with enough revisions to warrant the new type number. The engine was still inclined in the pressed-steel frame but had a cast-

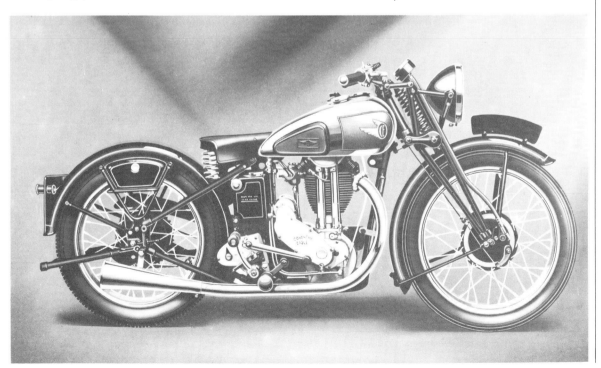

alloy chaincase and the three-speed gearbox mounted close to the crankcase. Lubrication was dry sump with the oil tank in the space between the chainstays on the right. Ignition was by mag-dyno, which went behind the engine and was driven from the timing gear. The cycle side remained much as before and continued to include legshields as standard.

In effect it was the range as before plus Utility models for 1935. Thus the 148 cc Silent Superb became the L2 and the 247 cc the L5 de luxe alongside an L4 standard model. The Utility machines were the L1 and L3, which had direct lighting and no dynamo or battery. The version with the high-level exhaust was the L6 and the one with the JAP ohv engine the L7. As nothing kept its original number there was some confusion.

The initial announcement of the 1936 range showed little or no change other than an M year letter. Missing was the model with the JAP engine, and all six machines were now called Silent Superb as the utility tag had been dropped. The more basic models continued with pressed-steel chain-case and the choice of direct or dynamo lights, while the M5 and M6 had the cast-alloy oil-bath case.

If the first part of the 1936 range failed to cause much of a stir, the second did, and was a sensation at the Olympia show. There, the firm launched a trio of models they called Pullman Two-seaters, with the option of the established 247 cc Villiers engine, the newer 249 cc one with a flat top piston or a 246 cc ohv Blackburne modified to suit the installation. The first of these had three speeds, but the other had four and all had footchange.

It was the chassis that was so special and it was an extension of the pressed-steel design. For the Pullman the frame began with two deep channel-section members that ran from the front of the engine to the tail of the rear mudguard. Three cross-members braced the sides and the structure rigidity was further improved by the fixings for the engine and gearbox. A further panel went beneath the mechanics to enclose them and this was formed to prevent drumming and aid stiffness.

The top part of the frame was also unusual and the head lug was supported from two directions. Two sets of three steel strips ran from the head down to the front of the side channels while to the rear ran two pieces of angle section. These bolted to two pressings which supported the saddle and provided a platform for the petrol tank, which was held down by a single wide strap. At the front of the chassis went legshields formed in one piece, and these with their cross-bars further stiffened the assembly. In fact the top bar was extended out and fitted with rubber buffers so the machine could be leant against a wall.

There were access panels where needed in the sides of the main frame members and at the rear went a massive rear mudguard-cum-valance. This completely enclosed the wheel down to the frame, but the whole was simply secured with six hand nuts so was easily removed when needed.

The frame extended so far to the rear because the machine had rear suspension and was unusual in fitting semi-elliptic springs. These lay outside the side members with their link at the rear end and the rear brake had a torque stay to the frame to avoid spring wind-up. Front suspension was in comparison prosaic with pressed blade girders.

Even the centre stand was unusual, for it was operated by a long hand lever on the left which was held by a clip when not needed. The usual front stand was provided by using the mudguard stay.

The silencing arrangements were in the style expected of the firm. For the M11 model, which was fitted with the long-stroke Villiers engine, they began with a finned cast-aluminium expansion chamber placed in front of the cylinder. It connected to an exhaust port on each side of this and passed the gases on to a second finned chamber carried ahead of the crankcase. From there they went into a pipe within the chassis to a vertical tubular chamber just ahead of the rear wheel and from this an outlet pipe carried them to just below the bumper bar fixed to the rear end of the frame.

The M10 with the older Villiers engine dispensed with the first chamber, so its two front ports were connected directly to the second box. The same type of arrangement was used for the M12 with the Blackburne engine. For all models a battery went beneath the seat on top of the chassis, and on the two-strokes a panel enclosed the area from it to the back of the cylinder. The four-stroke had the oil tank in its place.

The Blackburne engine had a skew gear-driven camshaft and dry sump lubrication. The valves sat side by side in the head and were lifted by straight rockers moved by the pushrods on the right of the engine. Ignition was by magneto and the car-burettor was not enclosed by the panelling.

One further model joined the range, and this was the M9, which was as the M5 but fitted with the long-stroke 249 cc Villiers engine from the M11. It did not survive to 1937 and neither did the M10 or M12. For that year there was only one Pullman model, listed as the N11, but with modifications. The most obvious change was that the rear springs moved inside the side frame members, but in addition the front down struts became a channel section and were augmented by further pressings.

The 148 cc and 247 cc Silent Superbs continued much as they were in their pressed-steel frames and with a letter N year prefix. Four versions of the larger model were still listed with direct lighting, dynamo, de luxe or with high-level exhausts.

New for 1937 were three four-strokes with ohv Matchless engines of 245, 348 or 497 cc. These models were called the N25 Flying 250, N35 Flying

The model Q9 Coventry Eagle of 1939 with 98 cc Villiers engine and plunger rear suspension

Coventry Eagle R14 98 cc autocycle of 1940 with neat side shields to enclose the engine and protect the rider

350 and N50 Flying 500. The engines were all mounted vertically in the frame, had a rear-mounted magneto, enclosed valve gear but exposed springs, and dry sump lubrication. Frames were tubular and fitted with Webb forks to match, while the gearbox had four speeds and foot-change.

1938 brought two new models while the rest of the range continued with minor improvements and a letter P as the year prefix. The new machines were both called Cadets and came in 122 cc and, for export, 98 cc versions. Both used Villiers engines in a simple tubular frame with blade girders and could be fitted with legshields. The larger model was the P8 and the other the P7, while both offered basic utilitarian motorcycling.

The six Silent Superbs continued with few changes for 1939 as did the two Cadets and three Flying models. All had a letter Q prefix, but the Pullman was no longer listed. New were the 98 cc Q9 and 122 cc Q10, which were simply Cadets with plunger rear suspension. This was elementary in nature with a compression spring, a rubber buffer for rebound and no damping other than friction. Heavier-gauge springs were fitted if a pillion seat was specified at the time of ordering the machine.

At the show Coventry Eagle had one further model to offer, the Q12 Auto-ette. This was an autocycle propelled by a 98 cc Villiers Junior engine and much as others of its ilk. The frame was thus a simple tubular one with the engine hung from it in front of the pedalling gear. The fuel tank fitted within the frame members and the front forks were heavy-duty cycle ones and thus rigid. It gave basic transport at very low costs.

A reduced range was announced for 1940 with two Silent Superbs continuing as the 148 cc R1 and 247 cc R4. They were joined by a 98 cc version using the smallest Villiers engine to make the R0. Two Flying models were listed as the R35 and R50, and the list was completed by the R12 Auto-ette.

In March this was joined by the R14 version, which had neat side shields added to enclose the engine unit. At the front end they flared out to protect the rider's feet without impeding his pedalling action. The shields were made in one piece with the chainguards on each side of the machine.

Like the rest of the range it was well thought out but like many others, the marque failed to survive the war.

Coventry-Victor

This make of machine was first seen in 1919, with the flat-twin engine type they always used and had built for others from 1911.

By 1930 they had two engines, one a 499 cc ohv and the other a 688 cc sv. They were installed with the cylinders fore and aft to drive a three-speed Sturmey-Archer gearbox and the mechanics went into a duplex frame. The engine was mounted higher than the gearbox and had a large external flywheel on the left and its magneto on top of the crankcase. Each cylinder had its own exhaust system and both went on the left on the side-valve model with the rear cylinder silencer above the front. The machines were named the Royal Sports for the ohv and Super Six for the sv.

In addition to the two road models there was also a speedway machine powered by the 499 cc ohv engine and suitably modified for this sport. The frame had a reduced wheelbase to aid cornering, and this was adopted for the road models for 1931. Late that year the firm began to produce three-wheelers, still using the flat-twin engine layout, and in time these took over from the motorcycles.

For 1932 the 499 ohv model took the name Royal Grand Sports and the speedway machine became Dirt Track No. 1. There was also a No. 2 and this had a 600 cc ohv engine. For 1933 this was taken to its logical conclusion and went into a second version of the Super Six, while the 499 cc ohv and two Dirt Track models all continued.

None of this lasted long, for the days of the flat twin in speedway had passed and the road models were looking very vintage and had few changes. For 1934 the range was down to two models, the 499 cc Royal Grand Sport and the 688 cc sv Super Six. The following year there was only the side-valve model and by the end of 1935 that too was no longer listed.

From then on the company stuck to its three-wheelers, until they too lapsed in 1938.

Cyc-Auto

This machine was a pioneer of the pre-war autocycle and post-war clip-on and moped, all of which sought to provide basic powered transport by adding a small engine to strengthened cycle parts.

The Cyc-Auto was announced in March 1934 and was possibly unique in having its crankshaft axis along the frame and used a worm and wheel in the cycle bottom bracket to turn the drive and give the required reduction ratio. The engine sat in front of the bracket with a vertical cylinder and a

Wico magneto bolted to the front of the forward flywheel casing.

Behind the engine went a silencer formed as a streamlined casing to the engine and through which the engine shaft passed on its way to the worm. The carburettor was an ETC and the whole unit was held in place by two bolts. Petroil was stored in a cylindrical tank under the rear of the saddle and the rest of the machine was bicycle with a coaster rear and stirrup front brake. It was possible to disconnect a dog clutch between the worm wheel and the bicycle sprocket so that the machine could be pedalled home if this became necessary.

This was the model A, and for 1935 it was joined by the B, which had an open frame. In 1936 the frame size was changed from 23 in. to 21 in. for the A model and 19 in. for the ladies' open-framed B model. At the same time the frame was strengthened by adding a horizontal tube a few inches above the bottom bracket to brace the seat and downtubes. There were other detail changes and lubrication of the worm gear was changed from grease to oil, so a dipstick appeared to check its level.

For 1937 the standard machines became models C and D, and were joined by the CV and

Coventry-Victor 688 cc Super Six showing the old-fashioned lines and the flat-twin engine they used in side- and overhead-valve forms

Above **The 1935 Cyc-Auto in its early A model form with its own make of engine and unusual worm gear in the frame bottom bracket**
Below **1939 edition of the Cyc-Auto Ladies model with the Scott engine**

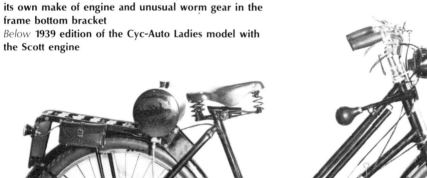

DV, which had a Villiers engine with flywheel magneto. This continued for 1938, during which year the original firm ran into money problems and sold out to the Scott company. They moved premises and revised the Cyc-Auto engine unit to add a clutch immediately behind the engine while continuing to offer the Villiers at a lower price.

For 1939 the machines were simply offered in Ladies' or Gents' form and still carried the Cyc-Auto name, although the engines were made at Shipley in the Scott works. Both models were also available in de luxe form with a sprung front fork and hub front brake. A tradesman carrier version was also listed.

In these forms the Cyc-Auto ran up to the war and on for a little while before production ceased until the end of hostilities. Post-war it was to continue in production up to 1958.

Dayton

Diamond

Dayton were a bicycle firm who occasionally produced autocycles over the years. Their first came in 1913, but lapsed in the early twenties. They reappeared in 1939 with a new autocycle fitted with a 98 cc Villiers engine with petroil lubrication and flywheel magneto ignition.

The frame was of the open type, but of heavier construction than that of the bicycles and it had a rigid front fork and light rear stand. Both wheels had drum brakes with cable operation and the machine was sold complete with lights, horn and tyre pump.

It was only built for that one short season. Postwar, Dayton opted for Villiers-engined scooters.

This company dated from before World War 1 and ran as one of the minor makes up to 1928. It then turned to other work, including building SGS machines for a couple of years, but reappeared in April 1930 with a single model. This had a 247 cc Villiers engine in a diamond frame, a three-speed Burman gearbox and conventional appearance.

For 1931 it was joined by two four-strokes of 245 and 346 cc, both with ohv JAP engines, three speeds and similar cycle parts. In January a further model appeared with a 346 cc Villiers engine and this was called the Blue Diamond. This machine had auto-lube and a flywheel magneto to power the direct lighting or was available with a dynamo.

The two-strokes continued for 1932 as did the 346 cc ohv model, but not the 245 cc one, whose place was taken by one with a 490 cc sv JAP engine. The gearboxes continued to be three-speed Burmans and all had the option of hand or footchange.

Dayton autocycle with 98 cc Villiers engine as built for 1939, its only year in production

There was no range given for 1933, but the firm did continue, and to suit the new taxation limit produced a model with a 148 cc Villiers engine. This went into a simple frame with blade girders and was much as many others.

From then on the company turned to trailers and milk floats, although late in 1935 there was a note in the press that they would make motorcycles to use Villiers engines to special order. It seems unlikely that any appeared.

Below **148 cc Diamond from 1933, the final year the firm was listed**
Bottom **A 1931 Dot V31 with 247 cc Villiers engine with auto-lube**

Dot

Devoid of Trouble it was said and the make was five years established when Harry Reed, the founder, won the 1908 twin-cylinder TT. He was

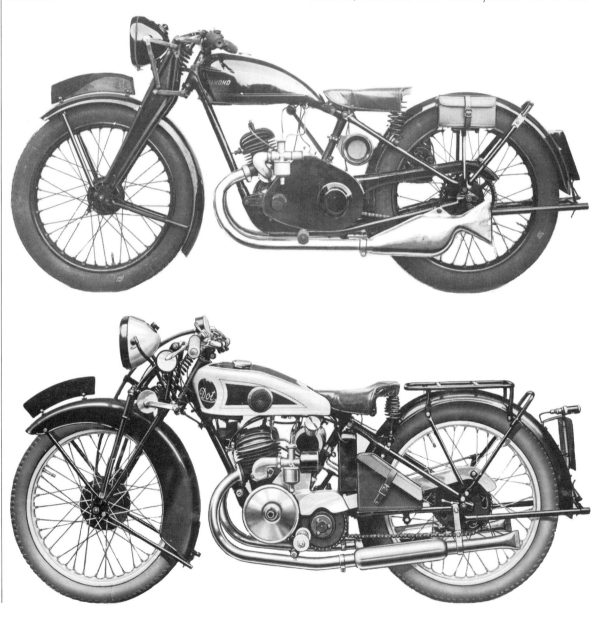

also second in the 1924 sidecar TT, while the Twemlow brothers were placed in 1928 and 1929, but this was something of a swansong.

They had built some interesting models in the 1920s, but by 1930 the range was down to a pair with Villiers engines and a four-stroke. The two-strokes were both of 196 cc with one machine having the sports and the other the super sports engine. They were the V5 and V6 and built on conventional lines. The V7 had a 346 cc ohv JAP engine.

In May 1930 a model with a 247 cc Villiers sports engine was added to the range and this unit was inclined forward in the standard frame. This was the only one of the range to go forward into the 1931 list, as the V31, and it was joined by the VL31, which had the short-stroke 343 cc Villiers engine. The third model was again a four-stroke, but in this case the engine was a 349 cc ohv Bradshaw unit and the model the B31.

May 1931 brought an addition at the lower end of the scale. The new model had an inclined 98 cc Villiers engine, two-speed Albion gearbox and simple frame with blade girder forks, centre stand and Dunlop rubber saddle. The flywheel magneto provided the direct lighting as well as the ignition, and lubrication was by petroil. The usual Dot colour scheme of red with light tank panels was used.

A month later the company added one more model by fitting the 346 cc long-stroke Villiers engine into the V31 cycle parts. The next to arrive came in September 1931 and was a 147 cc Villiers engine set vertically in the 98 cc machine and still with a two-speed gearbox. Unlike the smaller model the 147 did have a kickstart lever and a full-length exhaust system.

When the 1932 range was announced it was down to three models, all now with names. The smallest was the 98 cc machine, which now had the kickstart as standard and no longer an extra. It was listed as the Midget, while the 147 cc model was the Minor and had moved up to a three-speed gearbox. The third machine, the Major, had a 148 cc Villiers engine with twin exhaust systems and was fully equipped. It too had three speeds and a similar frame and forks to the other models.

This small range was not enough to sustain the works and during 1932 they turned to other products. This led to the building of three-wheeled delivery trucks, powered by Villiers engines, and eventually, in 1949, back to motorcycles.

Douglas

The Douglas firm was well established before World War 1 and even by then was famous for its flat-twin engines. Nearly all their models were built with power units of this type and in the 1930s they continued, with one exception, to be installed along the frame. This always meant that the front plug suffered from mud and water, while the rear's problems were overheating and access. The company also went through many financial hard times despite, or because of, excursions into other realms.

By 1930 the firm was in a sound position with good sales, new models designed by Freddie Dixon and some very successful dirt-track machines. However, despite the adoption of saddle tanks, the machine's appearance was rather vintage due to the length inherent in the engine type and layout. Also the dirt-track models were soon to be challenged and then vanquished by others with vertically mounted single-cylinder engines. The speedway JAP was about to begin its long reign of the tight ovals.

The range for 1930 was based entirely on flat twins, which came in three capacities and with side or overhead valves. Smallest were the L3, with a 348 cc side-valve engine based on 60.8×60 mm dimensions, and the H3, which was an overseas version with heavier tyres.

The engines followed the construction lines used by Douglas for many years with the valves and exhaust system on the right, a single carburettor feeding into a manifold and the magneto mounted on top of the crankcase. Lubrication was claimed to be dry sump, but was really wet sump with a submerged pump. The oil was carried in a finned chamber bolted to the underside of the crankcase and after circulation drained back into it. A dynamo could be fitted along with electric lighting, but the acetylene system was also available.

The frame design was straightforward with

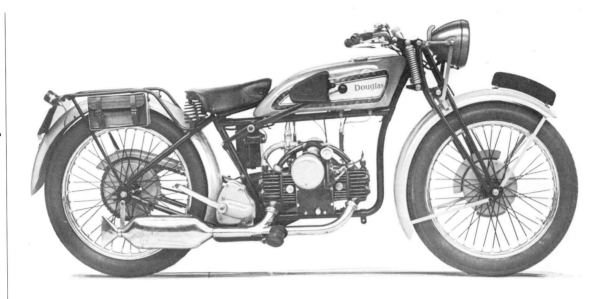

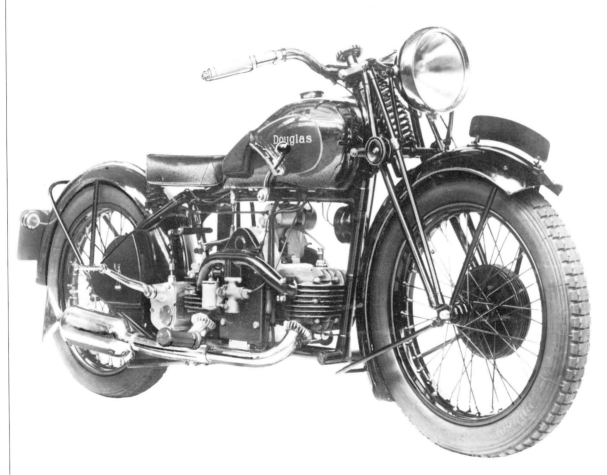

Above **The 1934 Douglas model Z of 596 cc with the usual flat-twin engine associated with the marque**
Top Douglas Terrier model A32 from 1932 with a 348 cc engine and a tartan border to its tank panels

Right **The engine room under the panels of the Douglas model X of 1934 which was first sold as the Bantam the year before. A rare single for the make** girder front forks and rigid rear. The wheels had hubs with separate 8 in. diameter drums and inside these went Douglas patent semi-servo brakes. The design was an internal band that was expanded by a link lever, pulled off by three tension springs and held in approximately the right place by four adjuster bolts. It was a design that dated from 1925 and was to remain with the firm up to 1939.

The larger side-valve models were the S5, with 62.25 × 82 mm dimensions and 499 cc capacity, and two bored out to 68 mm and 596 cc, these being the S6 and T6. All these machines, including the 350, had a three-speed gearbox fitted behind the engine and handchange. A kickstart or a hand lever were available and the gearbox was fixed in the frame. Chain adjustment was by moving the engine forward and rear wheel back, a variation of the normal method.

Along with the side-valve models were the ohv ones in 500 and 600 cc sizes, and speed and dirt-track forms. The engines were of an older design, with the camshaft above the crankshaft, more primitive lubrication, twin carburettors and exposed valve gear. To keep the wheelbase down the gearbox was mounted above the rear cylinder, which was no trouble with a rigid frame. The clutch, as usual with a Douglas, was built into the outside engine flywheel but not fitted to the dirt-track models, for that sport used a rolling start in those days.

The dirt-track DT5 and DT6 models came minus brakes, left footrest, silencer or full mudguards, but all these were supplied for the SW5 and SW6, which could thus be ridden on the road to competition events.

For 1931 Douglas adopted tartan borders to their petrol tank panels and kept their range much the same but with two added models and a revised numbering system. The competition models retained the SW and DT code, but the others became A31, B31, etc.

These first two were the 348 cc side-valve models with the A31 reduced in weight below the 224 lb bar. Its oil tank was built into the fuel tank and its gear lever worked within the right knee-grip. The B31 retained the finned sump and other features of the previous year.

The larger side-valve models were the 499 cc C31 and, with 596 cc engine, the standard E31 and touring sports D31. These were much as before, but new were the F31 and G31 of 500 and 600 cc with ohv and gearboxes mounted above the rear cylinder. A four-speed gearbox and a light 500 that would qualify for the reduced road tax were also talked of.

1932 saw a new suffix number, so the range became A32, B32 and so on up to G32, except for the speedway machines, which continued as the DT5 and DT6 and the SW5 and SW6 competition ones. There were three new models and the largest was the 750 cc side-valve H32 based on the 596 cc engine. The other two had short-stroke engines and ohv with the pushrods fully enclosed

and positioned on the right side of the cylinders. The models were the 350 cc K32 and 500 cc M32, and both had three-speed gearboxes mounted above the rear cylinder. The light 500 became the C32 and actually did scrape under the weight limit.

Near the end of 1931 the company was sold off by the family and became a public firm. For a brief while they were involved with the Dynasphere, which used a Douglas engine to drive the one enormous wheel in which the rider sat along with the mechanics.

This was only a passing phase and by June the new company had announced its range, which was some of the existing models with detail changes, reduced prices and the name of a breed of dog for each one. Thus the A32 became the 348 cc Terrier, the C32 the 499 cc Bulldog, and the 596 cc sv machines the D32 Greyhound and E32 Airedale. The big 750 cc H32 took the name Mastiff and there were no ohv models.

This did nothing to remove the financial problems that had already afflicted the new company, but despite these a 1933 programme was prepared and in it were two interesting new models. Even the September 1932 announcement had to admit that two models were not due until the New Year and only one machine was actually in production.

This one model broke Douglas traditions by only having one cylinder which came as a 148 cc Villiers engine set horizontally in the frame. It drove a three-speed Albion gearbox, and this plus engine and dynamo were all mounted on a baseplate

which in turn was rubber-mounted to the frame. The exhaust expansion box bolted to the underside of the baseplate and was connected to a fishtail silencer on each side.

This assembly went into a bolted-up tubular frame with blade girder forks and was enclosed by side panels that hid it entirely. Legshields were attached to the front of the panels and the petroil tank completed the job of keeping the mechanics out of sight. It was called the Bantam.

The second new model which did not make it into production was called the Golden Star and pioneered a new layout for the firm. The engine was a 245 cc side-valve flat twin, but set across the frame with the clutch and four-speed gearbox bolted to it. From this an enclosed shaft on the right drove the rear wheel via spiral bevel gears.

The engine had alloy heads and rear exhaust ports feeding into a silencer box beneath the gearbox. This had a gate change with the hand control on the right. The frame was tubular with some bolted joints and duplex downtubes, while the front forks were in effect of the leading link design with external spring units. The wheels were interchangeable and had Douglas-type 8 in. brakes with finned drums. Legshields were fitted along with a large saddle tank and full electric equipment.

The remainder of the range comprised the Standard 350, Bulldog 500, Greyhound 600 and Mastiff 750 flat twins, all with side valves, plus a 1000 cc side-valve Powerflow model and a 500 cc ohv TT one.

Speed Special Douglas model 5OW1 from 1935. 596 cc with ohv and the gearbox above the rear cylinder

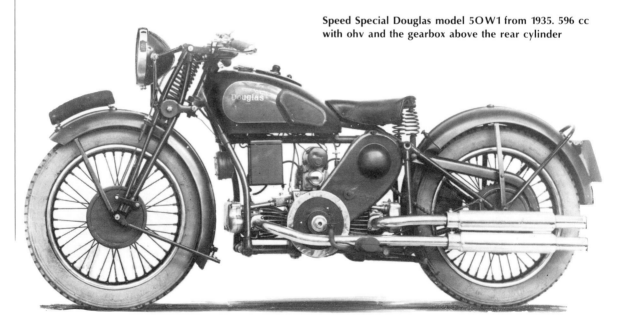

1933 was a bad year for the firm as their financial troubles worsened and an official receiver was appointed. In September the company was re-formed, but for that season there seems to have been little or no motorcycle production. The few machines built were from spares or drawn from left-over 1932 stock.

For 1934 the two-stroke was fitted with a new engine built by Douglas. It retained the 53 × 67 mm dimensions of the Villiers unit but had various internal and external differences. The cycle parts remained as before with the enclosure and twin exhaust systems, while the Bantam name was retained. The two versions were designated the model X and X1 with battery lighting.

Next came a run of five side-valve twins on the lines of earlier models. Smallest was the Y with a 51 × 60 mm, 245 cc engine and next up was the Y1 with 60.8 × 60 mm, 348 cc engine. Then came the Y2, still with the 60 mm stroke but bored out to 72 mm and 489 cc. Finally there were the Z with 596 cc, 68 × 82 mm engine and the Z1 with a 744 cc, 76 × 82 mm version of the same design. Both were fitted with four-speed gearboxes but retained their handchange as standard, although selection by foot was offered as an option.

Along with these models there were two with ohv and engine dimensions of 62.25 × 82 mm and 68 × 82 mm to give 499 and 596 cc. These also had the four-speed gearbox with foot or handchange and this sat above the rear cylinder. They were typed OW and OW1.

In 1935 Douglas played safe on most models, but sprang a surprise with the Endeavour, their first real transverse twin. This used a new 500 cc engine which was also fitted to a more conventional model with fore and aft cylinders. The range were given names as well as numbers and there were detail improvements.

The two-strokes became models 5X and 5X1 and retained the Bantam name, while the 245 cc sv became the Comet model 5Y and the 348 cc sv the Cotswold model 5Y1. The 596 cc was the Wessex model 5Z and the 744 cc the Powerflow 5Z1, while the two ohv machines became Speed Specials and models 50W and 50W1.

The 500 sv became the Blue Chief model 5Y2 and its engine changed to 68 × 68 mm dimensions, 494 cc capacity, and had light alloy heads and barrels, the latter with iron liners. This same unit was turned round for the Endeavour model, in which it drove back to a four-speed handchange gearbox and then by shaft to the rear wheel bevel box. The remainder of the machine followed Douglas practice with some good detail points, but its price when launched was rather high as so often happens with such designs.

By the middle of the year the firm was in financial trouble once more and was rescued by British Aircraft Company, who re-formed them as Aero Engines. The idea was to use the facilities to make aircraft engines, and so Pride & Clarke

1935 Douglas Endeavour with transverse flat-twin engine, a style they were to adopt post-war

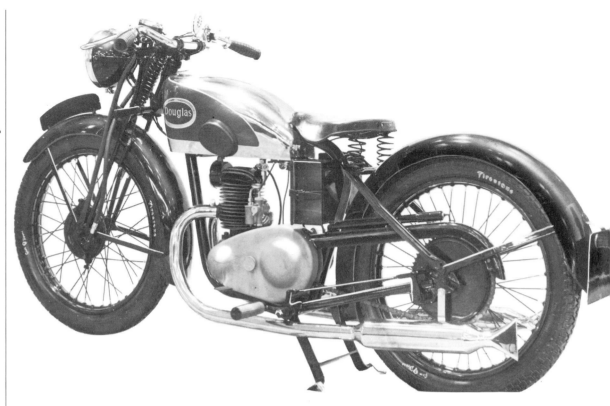

in London became sole agents for Douglas machines, which were assembled from stock to clear out the stores.

In this way the 1936 range comprised the 245, 348, 494 and 596 cc side-valve models from the previous year, all with the name Aero, plus the Endeavour at a reduced price. There was no 750, no two-stroke and no ohv models. There were also no changes until some parts dried up and others were substituted, resulting in hybrids reaching the market.

This situation continued into 1937 with just 348, 494 and 596 cc Aero models being built to sell at very keen prices. For 1938 these were replaced by a two-model range with one a lightweight and the other a revised 600. The Aero prefix was dropped from the name.

The lightweight was the CL38 with a 148 cc two-stroke engine and vertical, twin-exhaust port, cylinder. It drove a three-speed gearbox and the cycle parts were conventional and without enclosure. A 5 in. drum front brake was fitted along with the usual semi-servo one at the rear.

The other model was the DC38, which was much as before but had revised engine dimensions of 74 × 68 mm, which made the capacity 585 cc. The gearbox had four speeds and

Douglas CL38, a 148 cc two-stroke built for 1938 and not in their normal mould

handchange without the option, while the electrics were BTH magneto and pancake generator.

Only the 600 was built in 1939 and then only in small numbers until war broke out and the works turned to defence contracts. This built the company up once more so that post-war they were able to return to the motorcycle field and the flat-twin engine, but from then on transversely mounted.

Right 1930 Dunelt model T with 249 cc ohc Sturmey-Archer engine with face cams at the top of the vertical shaft. Their working face was at an angle to the shaft to match the rockers and valves

Dunelt

Dunelt won the Maudes Trophy in 1929 and 1930 but before then were best known for a 500 cc single-cylinder two-stroke with a double diameter piston. They were built in Birmingham, although the firm, Dunford and Elliott, were steel makers in Sheffield who had come into the motorcycle industry in 1919.

They kept to their two-strokes for a decade, but in the late 1920s began to fit Sturmey-Archer engines, inclined, to their models. It was these that won the Maudes, and they used a 350 in 1929 and a 500 the following year.

Their 1930 range comprised these two machines, listed as the 348 cc Montlhéry and 495 cc Majestic or model S, plus the 495 cc model SD with dry sump lubrication and two others. One was a 249 cc two-stroke with Dunelt double diameter piston typed the model K.

The second was the model T and this had a special 249 cc ohc engine using the face cam principle patented by Lieut. Slater of the Royal Navy. In this, bottom bevels drove a vertical shaft on the right side of the engine and the cams went on the top of this. They were formed as bevelled discs and the rockers followed their form and were laid over to lie across the head to reach the valve tops.

The lower end of the vertical shaft drove the oil

pump for the dry sump lubrication and a magneto was chain driven from the left end of the crankshaft. The engine had a twin-port cylinder head and was inclined in the frame, which had twin downtubes. The gearbox was a handchange Sturmey-Archer and the remainder of the machine typical of the period.

It was not a success, for the valve gear was noisy, and by the time the model reached the shops customers had tired of waiting and bought other marques. So the model T, along with the two-stroke K, was dropped and four models with Sturmey-Archer engines were listed for 1931. All were given the names of birds, and while Cygnet for the 297 cc side-valve machine and Drake for

the 495 cc ohv one were nice, the choice of Vulture for the 348 cc ohv seems to have been a marketing error. The fourth model was the 598 cc side-valve Heron and all had inclined engines.

In February 1931 Dunelt returned to the two-stroke field but with a 346 cc Villiers engine. This

Below **The 1931 Dunelt Vulture with 348 cc Sturmey-Archer engine. Few model names can have been as unfortunate**
Bottom **Dunelt V1 from 1933 with 148 cc Villiers engine**

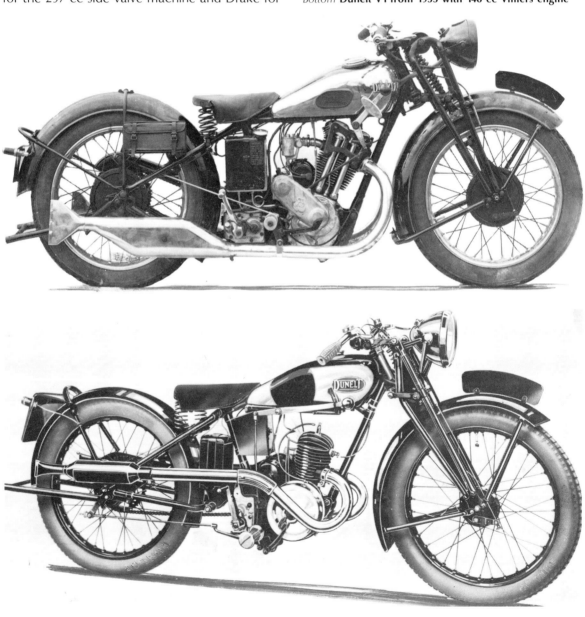

was installed with the cylinder inclined and had a small external flywheel on each side with a sprocket outboard of that. The right one drove a Miller dynamo and the left the gearbox. Ignition was by coil with the points in the end of the dynamo and lubrication by the Villiers automatic pressure system with the oil tank a compartment within the petrol one. The machine was given the name Monarch.

Late in the year manufacture was transferred to the main works and for a time the machines were called Sheffield-Dunelt to highlight this point. For 1932 they were given numbers and the smallest was a new model with a 148 cc Villiers engine set vertically in the frame and listed as the V1. The 346 cc Villiers-powered machine became the V2 and the 348 cc S-A the V3 and these were joined by the V3 Special, which had a tuned engine, upswept exhaust and footchange. It was sold without lights for competition use and its high-level exhaust also went on the 495 cc ohv V4. The final model was the 598 cc sv, which became the V5.

Most of the range remained for 1933, but the V2 changed its engine to one of 249 cc, and there was the T Special. This differed from the other models in having a Python engine which was of 248 cc and of course had the four-valve radial cylinder head. There were also Special versions of the V1, V3 and V4.

The range was smaller for 1934 and only used Villiers or Python engines. The V1, V1 Special, V2 and T Special all continued and were joined by two further models. One was the V2 Special with the 249 cc Villiers engine, but the other had a 499 cc four-valve Python engine and was called the V4 Special.

The Villiers machines ran on for 1935 as they were and continued to be offered with a flywheel magneto and direct lighting or with a separate dynamo. On the four-stroke front the engines were changed to 245 cc and 490 cc ohv JAP units, which were installed inclined forwards.

The smaller had a frame with duplex downtubes directly bolted to the lower members and the twin exhaust pipes ran between the frame tubes. On the larger model the exhausts passed outside the twin tubes and these terminated at a one-piece assembly of engine plates, distance pieces and crankcase shield. Both models had four-speed, footchange, Albion gearboxes.

1935 proved to be the last season for Dunelt and from then on they kept to their main job of making steel for others to use.

Excelsior

This company dates from 1874 in its original form, when it made penny-farthings, and it became involved with motorcycles in 1896. From the turn of the century they appeared in track races and later ran at Brooklands and in the TT. Their machines were mainly utility ones, but, like many in the early days, they would build just about anything if there was a chance of selling it.

In 1929, they had their first Lightweight TT victory and so entered the new decade on a high note. To help them cover the options they listed 14 models and at the bottom end were a trio fitted with 147 cc Villiers engines. These were the models 0, 1 and 2 with two- or three-speed gearboxes, a loop frame and blade girders. Next came models 3 and 4 with 196 cc Villiers engines with petroil lubrication or, in super sports form, with pressure auto-lube.

In the next class came the models 5 and 7 with 247 cc Villiers engines and the latter was for overseas use and had a duplex frame. A little larger at 300 cc were models 6 and 8, with a side-valve JAP engine, and for the more sporting rider the models 9, 10 and 13, with 245 cc ohv JAP engines. These three were built in standard, sports and TT replica forms, the last to celebrate the racing victory. Finally came a pair at 490 cc, the 11 with side valves and the 12 with ohv, both units being JAP engines.

These were additions and subtractions for 1931 with the only 147 cc listed as the A2, but with the 196 cc as the A3, A4 and AE4, which had the benefit of electric lighting. The 247 cc machines followed the same lines as the A5 and AE5, while the model with duplex frame became the A7. There was only one 300 cc side-valve, the A6, but there were three of 346 cc, the A8 with side valves, the A10 with ohv and the A11 with ohv and a duplex frame. In the smaller 245 cc class the ohv A9 was the standard model and the A14 the TT replica. Finally there was the A12 with 490 cc ohv

Above 1930 Excelsior model 3 with 196 cc Villiers engine
Below 1933 water-cooled C6 Excelsior with 249 cc Villiers

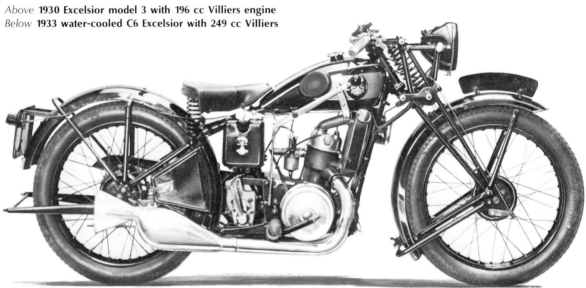

Below 1933 four-stroke Excelsior C4 with 149 cc ohv

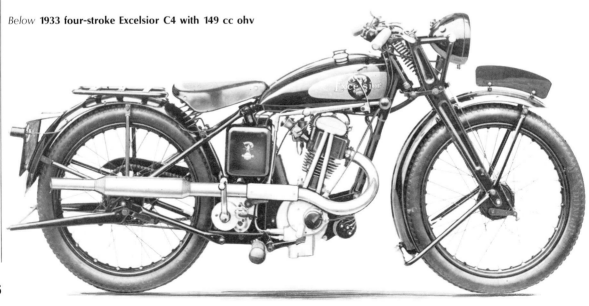

engine and the A13 with a 600 cc side-valve one. All the two-strokes continued to be Villiers and all the four-strokes were JAP.

In March two more models were added to the list, both within the 224 lb weight limit and both fitted with ohv JAP engines. One was of 245 cc and the other 346 cc and both had dry sump lubrication and drove a three-speed Burman gearbox. They were well equipped and came with a lighting set.

One month later, in April, Excelsior created some kind of record by introducing their 98 cc Universal at a mere 14 guineas, the lowest price anyone was to reach. For that money the rider got a Villiers engine, two-speed gearbox with rocking pedal foot control, simple tubular frame and blade girders. A direct lighting set was an extra 25s. or the rider could have an acetylene set for 15s. It really was scraping the barrel, of course. In July 1931 it was joined by a 147 cc version with stiffer frame and similar specification, but this was really an advance on the next year's range.

1932 brought further variations with the two Universal models, the 98 cc B0 and 147 cc B2 and BE2 with electric lighting. There was only one 196 cc, the B3, while the 247 cc models were the B5 and BE5. Also labelled as sports models were the B4 and BE4 with lights which used the long-stroke 148 cc Villiers engine.

JAP engines went into the B8 with 346 cc sv, the B9 with the same size ohv twin-port, while the B10 was again of 346 cc but with a single-port head. The B11 had this style head and 490 cc, while the B12 was the two-port model and the B13 the 600 cc side-valve one. Top of the range was the 498 cc B14, which was a TT replica and used a frame identical with the 1931 works one. It was listed as a 500, but could be supplied with a racing JAP of 250 or 350 cc as an alternative and was also available with a sports 350 cc engine.

February 1932 brought another Excelsior model, this time with the 148 cc Villiers engine with a dynamo clamped to the front of the crankcase. This carried the points for its coil ignition, but the model was also available with flywheel magneto and standard dynamo. It was another low-priced utility machine, but came with full equipment and legshields.

The 1933 range began with the 98 cc Universal C0. It went on to the 148 cc Empire range with the C1, the coil ignition machine, the CV1, with flywheel magneto, and the CE1 with this plus a dynamo lighting set in place of the direct system.

In the 196 cc class the C3, CV3 and CE3 carried the name Service and were to similar specifications.

The basic 249 cc model was the C5 with long-stroke Villiers engine, but more special was the C6, which had a water-cooled unit. The system was simple thermo-syphon and unusual in that it had no hoses. Instead, the bottom tank was bolted directly to the water port between the two exhausts and the other connection was a cast pipe between the cylinder head and top radiator tank. In other respects the model was much as the others with tubular frame, girder forks and full equipment. The engine had auto-lube, flywheel magneto and separate dynamo.

The four-stroke range was much restricted for the home market with the sv 346 cc C8, ohv 346 cc C10, ohv 490 cc C11 and C12, and sv 600 cc C13 all being listed as for overseas but available on the home market. This left the C14 TT replica little changed from the year before and the C4, which was new.

This had an ohv Excelsior 149 cc engine with very long stroke, inclined engine and dry sump lubrication. Ignition was by coil with a dynamo mounted in front of the crankcase and the machine had blade girders and electric lights.

Early in the New Year one further model appeared as the 246 cc ohv C7. This was a bored version of the 149, but with variations. Ignition was still by coil and the engine inclined, but the dynamo went behind it and the lubrication was wet sump. For this a large, well-finned sump was bolted to the underside of the crankcase. The valve gear was enclosed and in place of the pushrod tubes of the smaller model were tunnels cast in head and barrel. The rear of the sump formed one support for the three-speed gearbox, and for overseas a model with magneto ignition was available. A de luxe version with four speeds and more chrome and polish was also listed.

In June 1933 the racing world was introduced to the works 250, which became known as the Mechanical Marvel. The engine, which was the special feature of the machine, was in fact made by Blackburne and had a single vertical cylinder with four radial valves. The method of opening them was to provide two camshafts set high up across the crankcase, one fore and one aft of the cylinder. Each moved one pushrod, in a tube angled out from the cylinder, and this in turn moved a small piston set in the rocker box. Two rockers lay on the top of this and they in turn opened the valves. It was ingenious, and other

Excelsior

77

features were twin carburettors, a skew drive to the magneto and sophisticated dry sump oiling. The cycle parts were much more prosaic and were of the times. The overall result won the TT that year, but proved troublesome to keep in tune and was much less successful in 1934.

Despite this the Mechanical Marvel was listed in the 1934 range as the D14. Most of the others were there also with the 98 cc, three of 148 cc, only one 196 cc and both 249 cc, including the water-cooled version. For the four-strokes there was the 149 cc ohv and the 249 cc ohv, which became the DE7. There was also a dry sump version of this machine which lacked the ribbed sump but had a separate oil tank and was listed as the D7. Larger models were of 346 cc with sv and ohv and the D11 of 490 cc with ohv.

They all now had names: the Universal D0, Empire D1, Service D3, Bantam D4, Scout D5, Water-cooled D6, Pathfinder D7, Chieftain DE7, Marathon D8, Warrior D10 and Powerplus D11, plus the Mechanical Marvel, of course.

Following on the general announcement came one that the water-cooled model was also to be available with total enclosure. It was listed as the Viking D9 and was fully panelled from its legshields to the rear number plate. The panels were detachable for servicing and those on either side of the engine had long, vertical louvres formed in them to allow the cooling air out after it had passed through the radiator.

April 1934 brought another version of the 149 cc ohv model which was listed as the Wasp. Both a four-speed gearbox and a magneto were available for this machine at extra cost.

The 1935 range brought the first mention of the famous Manxman models that did much to lift the firm's name above those who built similar small models with Villiers engines. Not that there was any shortage of these, for most were still listed. The 98 cc one became the E0 and the 148 cc class had the E2 Empire plus the Pioneer E1 and ED1 with dynamo lighting. The latter had a single-port engine specially made for Excelsior, while the E2 stuck to the standard two-port design.

In the 250 cc class there were new 247 cc models in the form of the Meritor E4 and ED4 with two-port engines, the latter also with dynamo lighting. The Scout E5 continued much as before but with a tank-top instrument panel while the Viking continued with water-cooling and full enclosure as the E9. There was no model without the panels so no 1935 version of the D6.

Only the Bantam E3 ran on with the 149 cc ohv engine, but there were three of 246 cc. The Dictator E6 had the Excelsior engine with the pushrod tunnel cast into the cylinder, while the Pathfinder E7 had a similar unit with revised cams and considerably more power. It thus also had bigger brakes and as the Chieftain E8 was fitted with a four-speed gearbox. The final ohv model was the Powerplus E10, which continued with its two-port engine much as before.

The two Manxman models were launched at the show in 246 and 349 cc sizes. They shared a common stroke and were of straightforward but

massive design with a single overhead camshaft driven by shaft and bevels on the right. The valve gear was fully enclosed with just two valves and the top bevel box cover carried the Three Legs of Man insignia. The mag-dyno went behind the cylinder, where it was driven by a train of gears, and these also turned the two gear-type oil pumps and a rev-counter. Lubrication was dry sump and very thorough, with two short pipes connecting the oil tank to the top of the timing chest.

The cycle parts were also obviously intended for racing as well as sports use with a cradle frame, four-speed gearbox, footchange and large brakes and petrol tank. The models were to be listed in sports or racing form and for the latter there were rearsets, bigger tanks, narrower mudguards, different engine internals and an oil drain from the cambox.

The bewildering list of two-strokes was pruned down for 1936 and the smallest became a trio of 148 cc. These were the Pioneer models and came with single-port, with separate dynamo or with this and a two-port engine as the F1, FD1 or FX1. Next were the 247 cc Meritor F4 and FD4 with dynamo plus the 249 cc Scout F5 with its stronger frame and tubular girder forks.

All the four-strokes had overhead valves and the 246 cc Pathfinder F7 was much as before with the inclined engine but now had footchange for its three speeds. New were the 246 cc Norseman F8, 344 cc Warrior F9 and similar-size Clubman F10, which had vertical engines, enclosed valve gear and dry sump lubrication. All three had magneto

ignition, four speeds, footchange and a sturdy frame, so offered a sporting performance without the complexities of the camshaft engine.

The Manxman range was extended to include a larger 496 cc version, the F14, and this closely followed the lines of the two smaller models. All continued to fit a combined toolbox and battery carrier shaped to match the oil tank and this gave the illusion that the latter was of the wrap-round type. The racing models really did have a tank of this form and greater capacity and for 1936 they were separately listed as the FR11 and FR12. The road machines aped the racers with megaphone silencers, but had spiral baffles inside them.

Early in the New Year a new Universal Model was announced with a 122 cc Villiers engine. It was a basic machine with simple loop frame and a wedge-shaped tank fitted under the top tube. Blade girders were fitted and useful legshields were standard along with direct lighting and a rear carrier. It continued the Excelsior tradition of utilitarian models and when released had its twin exhausts running forward, down and to the rear. The lower part of the legshield centre section was formed to accommodate them, but on the model tested in April the legshield was flat, the exhausts ran straight back at waist level and a saddle tank was fitted.

1937 saw the range stabilized with a few deletions, but the 122 cc stayed as the G0. So did two of the 148 cc models as the G1 and GD1, two of 247 cc as the G4 and GD4, plus the 249 cc G5. This last went over to footchange, but for the rest

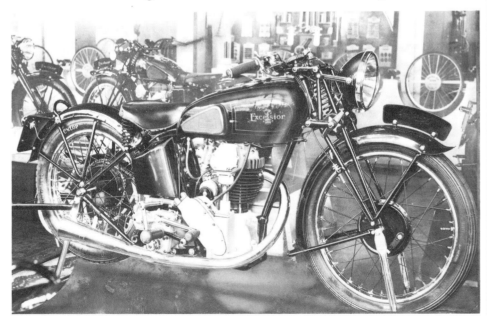

Left **The 1935 Powerplus E10 Excelsior with 490 cc twin-port JAP engine** *Right* **The famous Excelsior Manxman on show in 1935 when it was listed in sports and racing forms. This was its first year**

Excelsior

79

it was the usual story of detail improvements.

The Norsemen and Warrior both ran on as the G8 and G9 with clutch changes and a brighter finish for the wheels. The Manxman received rather more and the 249 cc models G11 and GR11 both changed to a shorter-stroke engine as had been used by the works engines in 1936. That engine, and the works 350, had been fitted with a radial four-valve head modelled on the Rudge system, made under licence, but still using the vertical drive shaft and bevels to turn the overhead camshaft. The Manxman kept to its normal two-valve design but had improvements to its lubrication system and a raised mag-dyno to improve access.

The two 349 cc models, the G12 and GR12, received similar attention, as did the 496 cc G14, which was joined by the Manxman Special G15 of the same size. This was a super sporting model fitted with a bronze head, raised compression ratio, racing-type mag-dyno, close-ratio gears and quickly detachable lights.

For 1938 the 496 cc ohc models were fitted with a decompressor, the 249 cc G5 Scout was dropped and all models changed to a letter H prefix. They were joined by the Autobyk, which was an autocycle fitted with a 98 cc Villiers Junior engine and the usual pedalling gear but without enclosure or legshields.

It continued in the 1939 list along with the Universal J0, which had a longer frame, larger fuel tank and was now listed with either 98 or 122 cc engine. The Pioneer J1 and JD1 continued with the 148 cc engine, which was mounted vertically in a new frame. The dynamo of the JD1 moved to the rear of the engine and both models had covers to completely hide the driving chains, an undershield and legshields. The 247 cc Meritor J4 and JD4 altered on the same lines, with vertical engines and a degree of enclosure.

The two ohv models ran on, with the Norseman J8 changing to a shorter-stroke engine and both having separate magneto and dynamo. The Manxman range adopted hairpin valve springs and Girling cable brakes with wedge operation and were listed as the J11, J12, J14 and J15. The racing versions were improved, with the gearbox bolted directly to the crankcase and a duplex primary chain. They were available as the JR11 and JR12 or as the JRS11 and JRS12 when fitted out with plunger rear suspension.

The 249 and 349 cc Manxman range was then further extended by special versions of the road models fitted with many of the racing parts in the engine. This provided a super sports machine or race replica for the clubman racer and they took a /S suffix in the lists.

The three basic road Manxman models were listed in the 1940 range as the K11, K12 and K14 with no changes but with the option of a bronze head. The pairs of 148 and 247 cc two-stroke models continued, as did the K0 as a 122 cc only. The Autobyk completed the range and was joined by a de luxe version with a new Villiers engine with alloy head. The machine was better equipped than the standard one and had front suspension in the form of fork blades that could move as telescopics against a single central spring.

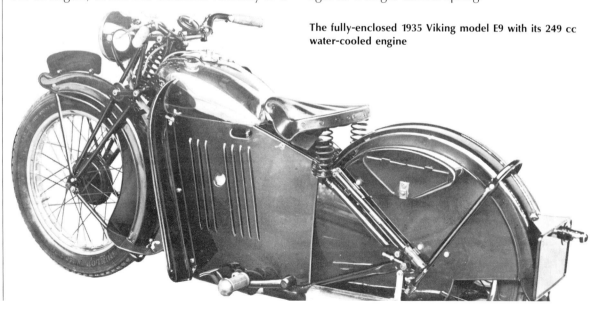

The fully-enclosed 1935 Viking model E9 with its 249 cc water-cooled engine

Above **Excelsior model J0 of 1939 with 122 cc Villiers
engine and simple cycle parts**
Top **1938 Excelsior Autobyk with the 98 cc Villiers Junior
engine and typical of its type**

As late as June 1940 the de luxe Autobyk was
fitted with side shields to cover the engine in the
style that was to become common for all
autocycles. On that note they concentrated on
their wartime production and, post-war, built a
range of lightweights.

Fagan

Federation

This obscure make hailed from Dublin, Ireland, and was assembled using British components in order to avoid the tariff that existed on imported machines in the 1930s. It was only around for 1935 and 1936.

There was just one model which had a 148 cc twin-port Villiers engine which was inclined forward a little in the frame, which was made by Diamond Motors. Ignition was by flywheel magneto, which also supplied the direct lighting, and the gearbox was an Albion with three speeds and handchange.

Other parts were Webb blade girder forks, Harwil hubs and a Lycett Aero saddle. Legshields were included in the price along with toolbags and a rear stand was provided.

The price was £27, but few seem to have been sold and the machine was not listed any more.

The Irish-built Fagan, produced in Dublin using British components including a 148 cc Villiers engine, this being a 1936 model

Millions of people shopped at the Co-op and collected dividend stamps, tin plate 'coins' in the 1930s, and for a while the Co-operative Wholesale Society, or CWS, put up the money for a range of motorcycles. These were built at the Federal Works in Tyseley, Birmingham, and were also sold under that name.

The machines were much as others of the time with JAP engines, Burman three-speed gearboxes and conventional lines. There were just four models listed for 1930 and only one with ohv. This was the 346 cc model 4 and its partner was the 3, with the same size of engine but side valves. Slightly smaller was the 300 cc model 2 and larger was the 498 cc model 5.

For 1931 the 3 and 4 continued, but a revised 490 cc engine went into the 5. It was joined by an ohv version of the same capacity which became the 6. To complete the range a model with a V-twin engine for sidecar work was introduced. This was the 7 with a 677 cc side-valve JAP engine.

In 1932 this range was extended by one more

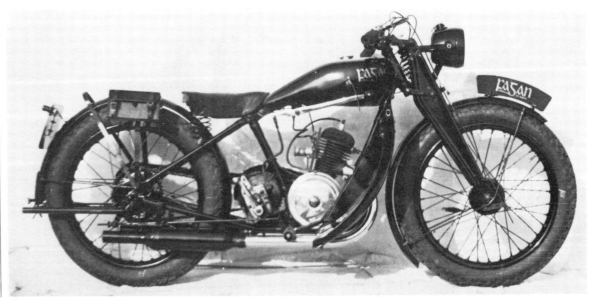

model, the 2, which introduced another make of engine to the Co-op. It was a Villiers 147 cc which drove a two-speed Albion gearbox, had a flywheel magneto and ran on petroil. It went into a simple frame with blade girders and continued for 1933 with the model 2A. This differed in that it had a long-stroke 148 cc Villiers engine and three-speed gearbox.

Only one of the JAP-powered models continued and this was the 490 cc ohv one which became the model 4. It was joined by a 245 cc ohv machine which took the number 3, and both continued with Burman three-speed gearboxes, while all models had handchange.

This range was offered for 1934 and again in 1935 less the 147. The model numbers changed to indicate size, so those left were the 148, 250 and 500, a Villiers and two ohv JAPs. The same three were listed for 1936, but for 1937 the 500 had gone.

This left the 148 and 250, which were listed at prices exclusive of the cost of the horn. The ohv model retained a rather vintage air and had twin exhausts which ran back at waist level. Low-level pipes were listed as an option. After 1937 the Co-op dropped two-wheelers and concentrated on its groceries.

A 1933 Federation of 148 cc, listed as the model 2A

Francis-Barnett

The first machine carrying this company name was built in 1920, but both founders had been involved from pre-World War 1 days. In 1923 they produced their triangulated frame and from then on were known mainly for lightweight machines.

The frame was the essence of simplicity and comprised six pairs of straight tubes and one pair with a small kink. Each was identified with a stamped-on letter and, given the listing, assembly was a matter of minutes. The system was still going strong in 1930 and the firm claimed not to have had a breakage except in accidents.

Into the frame went a run of Villiers engines of 147 cc with two speeds, 172 and 196 cc super sports with three speeds, 196 cc with auto-lube and three speeds and 247 cc. The last was listed as the Empire and was joined early in the year by the Dominion of 343 cc.

Above **1934 Francis-Barnett Falcon 38 with 196 cc engine**
Below **1934 249 cc Cruiser 39 model Francis-Barnett**

For 1931 there were just the two 196s with the names of Black Hawk and Falcon, the first with coil ignition and the second the more sporting engine. In June the 147 reappeared to take advantage of the capacity limit that was to come and was listed as the 19 without lights and 20 when fully equipped.

These two models became the 23 Merlin and 24 Kestrel for 1932, for it became the firm's policy to give most of their models a number and the name of a bird, a practice they were to continue to the end. Thus the Black Hawk and Falcon remained with model numbers 21 and 22, and were joined by a long-stroke 148 cc model called the 25 Lapwing and a 172 cc super sports 26 Condor.

The hard days of 1933 saw the Lapwing

continue as the model 27, with a second version, the Lapwing 28, which had a dynamo, coil ignition and an electric horn. The Black Hawk followed the same pattern as the models 29 and 30. The Falcon 31 was still listed but now, as the most expensive model, had auto-lube, coil ignition, the dynamo and the horn.

Completely new, and launched in the first week of the year, was the 32 Cruiser, a 249 cc machine with full enclosure and a different form of frame construction. This commenced with an I-section forging which formed the head lug and downtube. From the lug two channel section members ran back under the tank to the rear wheel. There they were attached by flitch plates to two more members which ran forward to the base of the downtube. They were braced by an undershield and the seat area was stayed down to the lower members.

At the front went blade girders with each blade made from two pressings, one flat and the other curved, welded together. A long-stroke Villiers engine was fitted in this frame with coil ignition and points on the end of the dynamo. This was tucked in behind the engine, where it was chain driven, and aft of it went the four-speed gearbox. To the rear of that was the battery.

All the mechanism other than the top half of the cylinder was enclosed by a curved panel on each side. These were easily removed for servicing and the one apparent obstacle, the kickstart lever, was made for quick detachment without the need for tools. At the rear, fixed panels filled in the area between the chainstays and matched to the sides. At the front what appeared to be a bulbous panel was in fact a cast-alloy expansion box which fed a second silencer on the right at the rear.

Both mudguards were large and valanced, with the rear easily removed for servicing. Legshields were built in and the whole machine designed to keep the rider clean and free from road dirt.

For 1934 the silencing of the range was improved by following the lead of the Cruiser, with a transverse cylindrical silencer near the cylinder connected to a single rear unit. The Cruiser was altered to auto-lube, with its oil tank under the front of its right side panel and this gave it the benefit of very short oil pipes. There was one extra Lapwing with a four-speed gearbox, but otherwise it was the range as before but with new numbers.

There were major changes for 1935 and a new four-stroke. This was the model 44 and it had a 247 cc engine made for it by Blackburne. Bore and

stroke were equal and the valve gear layout unusual, as the pushrods crossed over and the rockers lay across the head. Ignition was by magneto, which was chain driven and fitted behind the cylinder, while lubrication was wet sump. The oil was carried in a casting bolted to the base of the crankcase and the oil pump was submerged in this.

The frame had a one-piece forging to act as head lug and down member, and into this was fixed a tube which ran back to support the tank and then down behind the gearbox. Angle sections connected this to the down member and supported the sump via rubber linings. The rear frame was tubular, as were the girder forks.

The Cruiser and a single Black Hawk were little altered, but the two 148 cc and two 249 cc models all had a new form of bolted-up frame. The head lug was a malleable casting, the down member twin pressings, the top rail a single channel with a single seat tube and under-engine angles. It made for a more normal appearance and the smaller models were the 40 with flywheel magneto and direct lights, and the 41 with a dynamo. The larger models were the 42 and 43 on the same lines.

1936 brought a second version of the Cruiser as the F/45 and this was fitted with a Villiers engine with flat-top piston, petroil lubrication and twin exhaust ports. As these were on the sides of the cylinder, cast-alloy pipes were used to run the gases round to the normal expansion chamber in front of the crankcase. The standard Cruiser became the F/39 with detail changes which included the provision of a prop-stand.

The 148 cc models continued as the Plover F/40 and F/41, with the latter having dynamo lighting, but only one 249 cc was left in the list as the Seagull F/43. The ohv model took the name Stag and was unchanged as the F/44.

The whole range went forward for 1937 with detail changes only, but a second ohv model was introduced as the Red Stag. This had different tyre sizes, a fishtail on its silencer and red tank panels for which the customer paid an extra £2.

In April 1937 a second Seagull was added as the G/47 and differed by having a four-speed gearbox with footchange and thus the footbrake moved to the left side.

There were no Stags in the 1938 list, Blackburne having ceased engine production, but the two-strokes all continued with a letter H prefix. All except the H40 had a new petrol tank and the four-speed Seagull adopted the Villiers engine

Top **Francis-Barnett 1935 Plover 41 with 148 cc engine in frame with built-up downtube**
Centre **The Stag F/44 model with 247 cc ohv Blackburne engine in 1936. A rare four-stroke Francis-Barnett**
Left **The simple Francis-Barnett 122 cc Snipe J48 of 1939 which gave basic transport. Note the built-up frame**

with the flat-top piston. The H43 one stayed as it was.

February 1938 brought a new model name, Snipe, and two machines with either 98 cc or 122 cc Villiers engines. They were aimed at export markets in Norway and Holland, where capacity or weight limits gave tax concessions. Once again it was the frame that was unusual with channel section down member, angle tank rails and tubular engine unit loop and rear frame, all bolted together. Construction had to be light, but the machines were not skimped.

The Snipe engine was fitted with a more powerful generator and hence better lights for 1939. Otherwise it was the range, now eight in number, as before with improvements to keep the marque at the forefront of the utility market. At the show one new model was added in the form of the Powerbike. This was a 98 cc autocycle with the engine fully shielded. Unlike some it had front suspension, but this was simply a pivot below the bottom crown with rubber blocks to control the fork movement, which was essentially to and fro at the wheel.

A range was announced for 1940 and was unchanged in content. The Powerbike had a modified latch for its back-pedalling rear brake and the Cruiser K39 was now available only with petroil lubrication. A month later a Powerbike de luxe was added, which had the Villiers 98 cc Junior engine in its new form with detachable alloy head.

Post-war it was the only model to continue, but Plover, Falcon, Cruiser and Kestrel all returned in new forms.

Gloria

It would seem that Triumph were so ashamed of their cut price lightweight that they used a marque name derived from their car side for it. The Gloria name went on a number of cars over the years, some rather nice, but the motorcycle was the real bottom of the range.

The machine was for the 1932 season and was powered by a 98 cc Villiers engine which drove a two-speed Albion gearbox. The cylinder was inclined and exhausted into a cylindrical expansion box set in front of the crankcase with a long, small-bore tailpipe on the left. Ignition was by flywheel magneto, which also provided current for the direct lighting, and the mixture was supplied by a Villiers carburettor.

The engine and gearbox were assembled as one unit in engine plates and the whole to a simple open diamond frame. Tubular girders went at the front and the petroil tank was hung from the top

1932 Gloria with 98 cc Villiers engine, a Triumph model that they preferred not to be known for

tube, so was not of the saddle type. Small drum brakes were provided along with saddle, toolbox and centre stand. It amounted to 124 lb and was priced at 16 guineas.

For 1933, two machines were offered, one the 98 cc model and the other fitted with a 147 cc engine. This was equally simple, had the Villiers engine mounted upright and was available with a two- or three-speed gearbox. It had a saddle tank finished in black and cream and was supplied with legshields and a rear carrier as standard.

That year the Triumph range included their own

148 cc ohv model and for 1934 this was joined by the 148 cc Villiers-powered model XV/1. With these two there was no need for the larger Gloria any more and with a new range of their own four-strokes it was perhaps beneath their dignity to continue with a 98 cc pip-squeak. So the Gloria vanished as quickly as it had appeared, after two brief seasons.

The larger 147 cc Gloria of 1933, the final year of production

Below **1930 Grindlay-Peerless built in 680 and 750 cc sizes**

Grindlay-Peerless

This firm first built sidecars and added motorcycles to their product range in 1923. In the late 1920s their fame was boosted when Bill Lacey used one of their machines to take the world one-hour record to over 103 mph. This was the first time that over 100 mph had been held for the hour in England, and in 1929 Lacey raised the record again to over 105 mph.

There were other successes at Brooklands, but then Lacey moved on to Norton and the firm entered the new decade with a range powered by Villiers and JAP engines. In common with most small manufacturers they offered great variety. As the machines were hand-built so changes were easy to accommodate.

The Villiers engines used were of 172, 196 and 247 cc, while side-valve JAP units were the 490 cc single and 680 and 750 cc V-twins. With ohv the singles came in 245, two versions of 346 and three versions of 490 cc. This gave standard, sports and, for the largest, a TT model. There was also a 680 cc ohv V-twin. Diamond and loop frames and Brampton bottom link forks were used for the 350 and 500 twin-port models.

In 1931 the Villiers and V-twin engines were no longer listed and there were just four JAP-powered models, all with ohv. Two were standard and two sports, each in 346 and 490 cc sizes. In addition there were three models powered by Rudge Python engines, one of 348 cc and the others 499 cc. One of the larger had an Ulster engine and the other was a cut-price job with coil ignition and three-speed, handchange gearbox. It had the engine set vertically and dry sump lubrication.

There were only Python-powered models for 1932 and these numbered three. The low-cost 499 cc model continued as the Tiger with its three speeds and coil ignition, but a magneto could be specified for an extra £2.

The second machine was also of 499 cc, but had its engine inclined forward a little in a semi-loop frame whose downtube ran under the crankcase to the rear engine plates. The engine was either the Ulster or racing Python with magneto ignition and front-mounted dynamo. The gearbox had four speeds and, as the brake pedal went on the right, its change had a crossover linkage. This took the form of a rod running forward from the positive-stop mechanism on the right of the gearbox to a lever and cross-shaft set in the top of the front engine plates. On the left end of the shaft was splined a rear-facing pedal for the rider to operate. This machine was called the Special or the Tiger Chief.

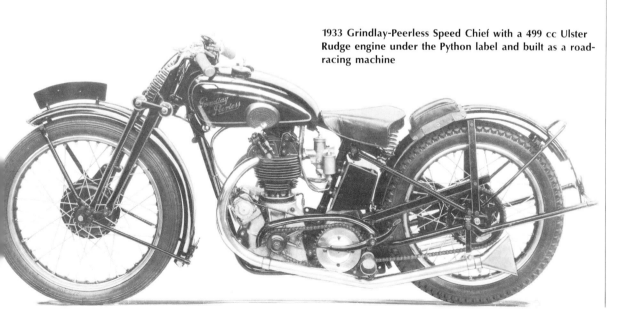

1933 Grindlay-Peerless Speed Chief with a 499 cc Ulster Rudge engine under the Python label and built as a road-racing machine

The third one was the Tiger Cub and had a 248 cc radial four-valve Python engine included in its frame, which was of the open diamond form. Its four-speed gearbox was hand controlled and it had coil ignition or the option of the Maglita unit. All models had chrome-plated petrol tanks with a black top panel, and all were fitted with a centre stand.

These three models continued for 1933 and were joined by two more based on them. One was the Speed Cub, which was as the Tiger Cub except that it had magneto ignition for its TT replica engine and a loop frame. The other new model was the Speed Chief, which had the Ulster engine set vertically in the frame, waist-level exhausts and came very fully equipped.

In January 1933 a road-racing version of the Speed Chief was announced fitted with a Replica engine. It had a four-speed gearbox with rocking pedal on the left, Brampton Monarch bottom link forks, racing fitments and Avon racing tyres.

All except the Speed Cub continued with little alteration for 1934, so there was one 248 and four 499 cc models. All the Tigers could have waist- or low-level exhaust systems and those with coil ignition had the option of a magneto.

This was their last season, for during the year motorcycle production ceased, although the company continued with other lines.

GroseSpur

This machine was made by the Carlton company for George Grose, a large retail dealer at Ludgate Circus in London. Like the Carlton it had a 122 cc Villiers engine with three-speed gearbox built in unit with it, ran on petroil and had a flywheel magneto for ignition and lights.

It appeared first in 1938 and had the engine unit installed in a simple tubular frame with blade girders. As standard it came with lights, legshields and rear carrier and ran quietly thanks to a large expansion box with single tailpipe on the left. It was sold as the model Superb.

The machine continued to be offered in 1939 and into 1940 without change, along with the Carlton, until their production ceased. Neither was revived after the war.

The 1939 GroseSpur Superb with 122 cc Villiers engine as made by the Carlton company for the London dealer

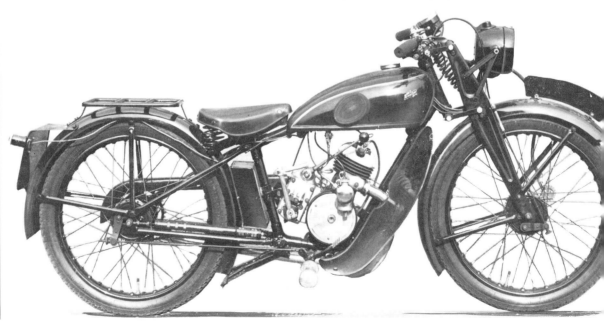

HEC

This autocycle first appeared at the Earls Court Show late in 1938 and was made by the Hepburn Engineering Company of King's Cross, London. It differed in a good many ways from the usual autocycle and not least in that it used an 80 cc engine of its own design but manufactured for them by Levis. Also, while the frame was the open bicycle type, the engine sat above the bottom bracket and not ahead of it as was more usual.

The engine was a single-cylinder two-stroke with separate alloy head and iron barrel. The crankcase was die-cast and also formed a housing for the clutch, which was driven by a chain on the right. A flywheel magneto on the left provided both ignition and direct lighting and an Amal carburettor supplied the petroil mixture. The exhaust comprised an alloy expansion chamber with a tailpipe on the left.

The fuel tank went between the frame members above the engine and the final drive was on the left under a top guard. The rest of the machine was heavy-duty bicycle with rigid forks and drum brakes. The rear was of the back-pedalling type, but could be hand operated if desired, and the clutch lever had a latch to hold it in the disengaged position.

The whole engine unit was held at three points and could be quickly and easily removed to leave the basic bicycle should this be needed.

By May 1939 (by which time the makers had moved to Birmingham) the exhaust tailpipe had become a short silencer with alloy front and rear parts and a cylindrical centre section. It was easy to dismantle to clean the baffles.

For 1940 the engine was fitted with ball-bearing mains, modifications to the clutch and changes to the flywheel magneto. On the cycle side the fuel tank was enlarged, stronger hubs and brakes were fitted and the rear stand changed from a clip-fitting to a spring-up type. During the war, HEC merged with Levis and turned to making air compressors, which they still do.

HEC Power Cycle of 1939 with 80 cc engine and a little different to the usual autocycle

Humber

Ixion

The Humber concern had its roots in the bicycle industry and was involved with two-, three- and four-wheeled-powered transport from the earliest days. They had their moment of glory in the TT, when P. J. Evans won the 1911 Junior, and some success at Brooklands, but were not a dominant make in the twenties.

In 1928 they introduced a 349 cc ohc engine and this was still in production in 1930. It was not unlike some more famous ohc units and had the camshaft driven by a vertical shaft and bevels on the right. Outboard of the lower bevel box a drive was taken by chain to the rear-mounted magneto, while the Pilgrim oil pump was driven from the right end of the camshaft. This resulted in rather a lot of oil pipes in the cylinder head area.

The engine was a twin-port unit with low-level exhaust systems and it and the gearbox were housed in a tubular frame with girder forks. The oil tank was a compartment in the saddle petrol tank and the machine came with rear stand, rear carrier and toolbox. It was advertised without lights and listed as the OCS model.

There were two other models for 1930 and both were also of 349 cc. One was the OHV and the other the SV with valve gear to suit. The ohv model had a single-port engine and twin pushrod

The Ixion company folded in the late 1920s, but the name was revived for 1930 only by New Hudson, just to clear stocks of a slow-selling model.

The machine had a simple 249 cc side-valve engine set vertically in an open diamond frame. It drove a three-speed Sturmey-Archer gearbox which had an integral handchange lever and thus no gate on the tank side. The magneto location was between the engine and gearbox, so was well protected but none too accessible.

Tubular girder forks went at the front and the cycle parts were conventional in form. Lighting was by acetylene or could be by dynamo, which was an option.

Once the existing stock was sold, the operation closed down and the Ixion name returned to oblivion.

---

tubes, but was otherwise as the ohc except that it did come with lights. The side-valve model was similar.

That really was it, for during the year the firm decided to concentrate on cars, so they stopped making motorcycles and later sold the bicycle side to Raleigh.

The 1930 Humber machine with 349 cc ohc engine and listed as the OCS model. The sv and ohv ones were very similar

James

To post-World War 2 riders the James was a utility two-stroke, but to earlier enthusiasts it was a Jimmy James V-twin or four-stroke single. The firm had its origins in 1880 and built its first motorcycle in 1902. From the start it was innovative and successful, although in 1920 it received a setback when the factory burnt down.

It took two years to get back on the market, but during the rest of the 1920s a succession of well-designed and well-made singles and V-twins left the premises. They were not built in large numbers for they lacked the *cachet* of a TT win or the bark of a tuned exhaust, but those that bought them were very pleased.

The range for 1930 included machines with James and Villiers engines, for the firm had seen the way business was drifting and the small machines were a hedge for the future. Smallest was the 172 cc model B11, then came the 196 cc B10 and B9 with lights and, last of the Villiers models, the 247 cc B8. All were conventional models with tubular frames, girder forks and well enough equipped for a utility model of the times.

The rest of the range had James four-stroke engines, starting with the B7 with an inclined 249 cc side-valve with front-mounted magneto. Next came the 349 cc sv B5 and ohv B4 with vertical cylinders, while the 499 cc machines all had V-twin engines. The B2 and B3 had side valves, the B1 was an ohv unit, while the B6 was a dirt-track model with its exhausts on the right and twin carburettors with an air pressure balancer. While the 1929 twins had fitted four-speed gearboxes as standard it was back to three for 1930 and 1931 with four speeds an option.

At the end of the year James bought the Baker firm and began to use that marque's frame for some of its models. It was of a bolted-up design with all straight tubes.

There was a rearrangement among the Villiers-powered machines for 1931 with the 172 cc becoming the C10, the existing 196 cc ones C9 and C11, and a Utility 196 appearing as the C12. The 247 cc model became the C8.

Among the four-strokes the 249 cc sv became the C7 and was joined by the C5 of the same capacity but with ohv. The sv 349 cc went from the list, but the ohv version stayed as the C4 and was joined by a new one of 499 cc with a four-valve Rudge Python engine and listed as the C3.

There were just two twins left and the 499 cc sv was given a light grey finish with blue lining and tank-top panel. It was called the Grey Ghost model C2, while the C1 took the name Flying Ace.

Both continued for 1932 as the D2 and D1 with oil bath chaincases and were joined by a new 347 cc sv with inclined engine and, like the others, a three-speed gearbox. It became the model D4. The 196 cc Villiers machines continued as the D11 with auto-lube and the D12 with petroil, as did the 247 cc D8 and the side-valve 249 cc D7. The ohv model of this size ran on as the D5.

This left two new models, both with 148 cc James two-stroke engines and loop frames. The D15 had a two-speed gearbox and the D14 a three-speed.

They continued into 1933 as the E15 Utility and E16 Comet, while the single petroil-lubricated 196 cc became the E12 Terrier but with a James-designed-and-built engine fitted with a four-speed gearbox. The 250 changed to the long-stroke Villiers engine as the E8, while the 249 sv became the E7 Mercury, which seems to strain the buyer's credulity. The 249 cc ohv was called the E5 Shooting Star and it and the E7 also had four speeds. The sv twin became the E2 Flying Ghost, so the range was smaller and less exciting than in the past.

For 1934 the whole range continued with a letter F prefix and a chrome tank with green panels, except on the F15, which had an all-green tank. It was the same for 1935 with just the model names listed in one place and numbers with a G prefix in another. The G12 continued to fit the James engine, but only the G5 had four speeds, although the G15 finally got three gears. It was H for 1936, and that year had no four-strokes in the line-up, so the delightful V-twin was no more and the firm concentrated on its range of two-strokes from then on.

There were five with the H15 and H16 of 148 cc, but both now with three speeds and the choice of direct or dynamo lighting. The 196 cc was the H12 and there were two of 249 cc, the H8 with auto-

93

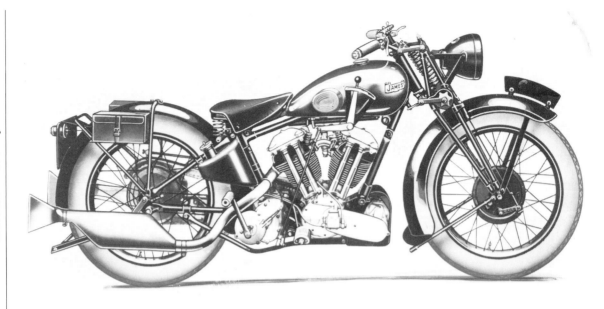

lube and the H9 on petroil but with a flat-topped piston. In June 1936 they were joined by the H17, a 122 cc machine of very simple design with tubular frame, blade girders and a cast-alloy expansion box in front of the crankcase. Its frame top tube ran above the tank.

For 1937 it was acknowledged that all the power units came from Villiers and the range adopted a black and gold finish along with the year letter I. It comprised the 122, two 148s, a 196 and two 249s.

There was no change for 1938 except that the J17 adopted a saddle tank, but there was an additional model in the form of an autocycle. This was much as many others of the same type with 98 cc Villiers engine and strengthened bicycle frame with rigid forks. It was very basic transport.

1939 brought a number of changes with all models, except the autocycle K18, having a new simple loop frame and a new tank finished in black and silver with gold lining. The K18 had many detail changes brought in from experience with the J18. The utility 122 cc K17 was also offered with a 98 cc engine to suit some countries' tax laws and the two 148s continued as the K15 and K16.

Above **1939 James 122 cc model K17 which went to war as the Military Lightweight officially and the 'clockwork mouse' by popular vote**
Top **The 1936 H9 James model with petroil-lubricated 249 cc Villiers engine**
Top left **1931 James Flying Ace C1 with 499 cc James twin**
Left **1931 James C3 single with 499 cc Python engine**

The K9 retained its 249 cc engine, but the K8 returned to the 247 cc unit and petroil lubrication. There was one new model, the K12, which used the new 197 cc Villiers 3E engine in the loop frame.

The whole range was listed for 1940 with an L year letter and was joined by the L20, which was a de luxe edition of the autocycle. It had the new Villiers engine of the same name, rubber-mounted handlebars and engine shields among its improvements over the standard model.

Then Jimmy James went to war using the 122 cc model as the basis of a light machine for the airborne forces. It was known as the Clockwork Mouse (officially, the Military Lightweight) and did sterling service to continue into post-war production as the ML.

Jones

This was a prototype autocycle designed by G. H. Jones around 1936 and built in conjunction with the Villiers company. The engine was of 98 cc, single-geared and with auxiliary pedalling gear. Cylinder head and barrel were one piece, with angled finning, the flywheel magneto went on the left and the expansion box below.

The engine drove back to a clutch, contained within an extension of the crankcase casting, and the clutch shaft was hollow to allow the pedal shaft to pass through it. In this way the whole unit could then be bolted as one to a frame with a special bottom bracket which it in effect replaced.

In other respects the frame was a strengthened bicycle type but had sprung forks. Caliper brakes were used on the prototype, but drums were intended for production.

The design was offered to a number of the smaller manufacturers and was taken up en-thusiastically, at first by Raynal Auto and Excelsior, and followed quickly by half a dozen more. However, in the production versions the engine (which became known as the Villiers Junior) omitted the concentric clutch and pedal shaft, and instead the pedalling mechanism passed through a cycle-type bottom bracket on the frame—much to designer George Jones' disgust. He considered that this was much too uncomfortable should the machine have to be pedalled.

Above **Engine unit of the Jones was bolted to the frame**
Below **Jones machine, the forerunner of the autocycle**

Levis

This firm dated from 1911 and in its early years was best known for its two-strokes. They had great success with them in the early 1920s with victories in the 250TT in 1920 and 1922 as well as in Europe, in France and Belgium, in the latter year. At that time these three events were thought the most important in the calendar, although the Germans and Italians might well have disagreed.

By the end of the decade the effects of this were wearing off, but for 1930 the range still included the 247 cc six-port model. It had a vertical engine and rear magneto as did the same-sized model Z, which was similar but with fewer holes in its barrel.

There were also four-strokes listed with vertical engine, rear magneto and total loss lubrication. The model C was a 247 cc side-valve, while the B had ohv with a single tube to enclose the pushrods. The final machine was a 346 cc ohv which came as the single-port A1 and twin-port A2.

The range reduced for 1931 to the Z, C, B and A2, all with a footchange gearbox for the three speeds, while four were listed as an extra. For 1932 the firm concentrated on the A2 and B models and the first was fitted with a crankcase shield that extended to include the front-mounted dynamo. There were also internal engine improvements, but the inlet port continued to be well offset to the left. In April a Popular A2 was added and this had a reduced price reached by deleting some features, although engine and frame were the same.

For 1933 the 247 cc continued as the B33 with the option of a four-speed gearbox but otherwise unchanged. The 346 cc became the A33 and had options of tuned engine parts available. It took the smaller-diameter exhaust pipes and tubular silencers of the Popular A2 as these had been found to improve performance. It also had a new frame and the four-speed option.

There was one more model and this was the D33, a 498 cc ohv on the lines of the A33 but all new. Its general layout was the same with vertical cylinder, single pushrod tube and total loss lubrication. A mag-dyno went to the rear with chain drive and there were rocker return springs in the top of the rocker box. The cycle side included a new frame, centre spring Druid forks and good-sized drum brakes, the front 7 in. and the rear 8 in. diameter.

These three models continued for 1934 with a 34 suffix number and little alteration and were joined by two of 247 cc but very different construction. The first was a revival from the past

Levis model Z from 1931 with 247 cc engine

97

1935 model D Special Levis of 498 cc. The engine has ohv although the pushrod tunnel gives the appearance of ohc

The real overhead camshaft Levis, the 247 cc model CB from 1935

and was simply called the Two-stroke. It used the B model cycle parts and had a mechanical oil pump. The second was much more interesting, for it had an overhead camshaft which was chain driven on the right from a half-time gear. The chain was Weller blade tensioned with an oil damper behind this and lubrication was the still-effective total loss with a duplex pump bolted to the outside of the timing chain cover. Levis advertised the use of fresh, clean oil as a benefit to reduce wear, which is borne out by the condition of engines half a century later—provided the owner remembered

to keep the oil tank topped up. Both rear magneto and front dynamo were driven by chain from the left end of the crankshaft so there were three sprockets there in all. The cycle side was neat and conventional with a four-speed, footchange gearbox and Druid forks.

The ohc machine did not reach production for nearly a year and so became more of a 1935 model than a 1934 one. For 1935 the four-strokes took the name Special after their letter B, A or D and received detail changes for that year and 1936 as well. By then the ohc engine had become an option for the model B, so its life was short. Changes were details mainly, but noticeable was that the footrests were now fixed to the lower frame rails and not through the chaincase and gave a considerable range of adjustment to the riding position. A loss was the knee-grips, which ceased to be shaped like a bird's wing and became flat and boring.

In addition to the three Special ohv machines a trio of Light models were added. These had a useful amount of weight shaved off them plus a reduced price, and the 250 went to coil ignition. This last failed to make the 1937 list, but the others did, as the LA37 and LD37, along with the three Specials. The Two-stroke was still there and was joined by the 247 cc Baby model, which had coil ignition.

The final 1937 model was new and called the 600. It had a 591 cc ohv engine much on the lines of the D and both had fully enclosed valves. The 600 frame had duplex downtubes and these ran to the base of the crankcase, where they joined the lower frame rails.

It was back to the one two-stroke for 1938 with the 600, three Specials and the two lighter editions now typed SP3 and SP5. The A and B specials had their valves enclosed and there were detail improvements, although lubrication continued to be total loss on the four-strokes and mechanical for the two-strokes. The B Special valve enclosure was further altered in March.

The range expanded further for 1939, when the

two-strokes were two in number and listed as the Master Two-stroke, a slogan Levis had used in advertising since before World War 1. One retained the mechanical oil pump while the other relied on petroil. The three Specials were still there along with the 600, but the rest were new to the list.

Two were competition versions of the A and D and these had single-port engines with the choice of full electrical equipment or a racing magneto and battery lights. The cycle parts were altered in detail to suit the application.

New was a 346 cc model with side-valve engine, Levis's first and only model with this configuration, and this had an alloy head and an exhaust lift cable that ran through the middle of the tappet cover at an odd angle. A new but orthodox frame was used and a neat machine resulted.

Also new were the SF350 and SF500 models, which used the A and D engines, modified, in a new frame with plunger rear suspension. This was unusual in that the two sides were connected by a hydraulic pipe leading to the top of each plunger column and the pipe also went to load a friction pad that bore against the sliding member on each side. This design was evolved to balance the spring loads and provide some damping and the pipes were filled with grease, not oil. The engine of the SF350 was reduced in height compared with the A, while the 500 had modified valve gear.

The range was the same for 1940 with little or no change, but that year saw the end of the marque.

1939 Levis SF500 of 498 cc with plunger frame. The two sides were linked by hydraulic pipe and to friction damping pads

LGC

Majestic

Another small Birmingham company that used others' engines to build its machines. For 1930 there was one model with a 247 cc Villiers engine and this was listed as the TS/1. The other three had JAP engines and were the 300 cc sv S1, the 346 cc ohv single-port 0/1 and the twin-port version of the same which was the 0/2.

All except the last continued into 1931, but that was their last year. Len Gundle, the owner, went back to making butchers' cycles and ice-cream trikes.

This make was a second string of the OK Supreme company and came about when the AJS concern was sold in 1931. While the bulk of the equipment moved south some parts stock was bought up by OK.

Three models were announced in January 1933 with 249, 348 or 499 cc inclined ohv engines. All had dry sump lubrication and rear-mounted mag-dyno, while the transmission included four speeds and a cast-alloy chaincase. The cycle side was conventional.

A week after the description, price and photo had appeared there was a note to say that the company would operate separately from OK Supreme. From then on there was no mention of them in the Press, so it would seem that this venture failed to get off the ground.

Left **The 346 cc LGC model 0/1, in this case from 1928**

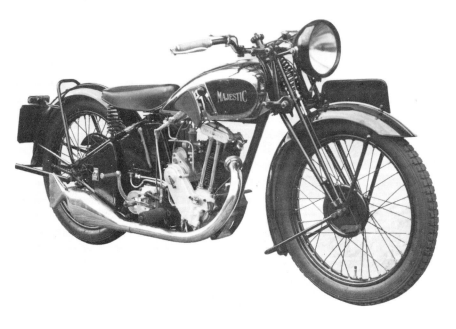

Right **The Majestic of 1933 which went as quickly as it came**

100

Martin-Comerford

When dirt-track racing came to England in 1928 few had much idea as to the best machine for the job. At first all manner of models were pressed into service and many firms listed a dirt-track model, but within a year or so two makes dominated. These were Rudge and Douglas, although many others scored some successes.

The Douglas had the acceleration and its noise and spectacular cornering made it a favourite with the crowds, but by 1930 the riders were moving towards the Rudge. Its short wheelbase made it faster for the lap and it was easier to maintain.

Then late in 1930 the JAP factory produced an engine designed just for speedway and George Wallis came up with a frame for it. This combination won on its debut and the JAP engine went on to totally dominate speedway racing for four decades.

The engine ran in a number of different frames, but the Wallis design was taken up by Comerfords, the big dealers at Thames Ditton in Surrey. It was one of the successful ones and sold in good numbers during the 1930s, at first as the Comerford-Wallis.

It followed the same lines as others, with short wheelbase, engine well forward, curved downtube and strutted forks. There were variations over the years, but no real change in the essence of the machine. In time it became known as the Martin-Comerford as it developed, but most alterations were carried out to improve reliability or to aid the riders in their dash from meeting to meeting.

Thus the rear-wheel spindle slots were lengthened to enable the wheelbase to be altered to suit the circuit. Frames were made with the headstock set round a little as they twisted in use and worked better when bent. Forks were normally Webb and in effect bridged telescopics with only about 1 in. of travel.

When the JAP engine took over, the speedway machine became standardized to the point where the make of machine was no longer listed in the programme. It may have taken something away that existed briefly in the early exciting years when experimentation raged, but its simple efficiency was what won races.

A Martin-Rudge from 1939 fitted with the usual JAP engine and set up for speedway

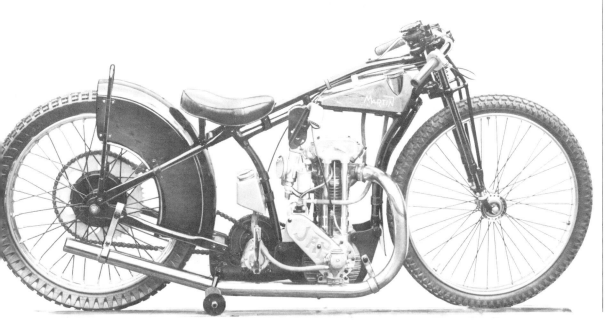

Matchless

For a time Matchless were the largest British motorcycle maker and from the turn of the century the Collier brothers were involved in powered two-wheelers. Both Harry and Charlie believed in competition, and it was the latter who won the single-cylinder class of the first TT in 1907 and again in 1910, while Harry took the prize in 1909. Coupled with this was success on the board tracks of the Edwardian period and at Brooklands, so that well before World War 1 the marque was well established.

The firm's premises were in Plumstead, to the south-east of London, and so well removed from the Midlands centre of the industry, but this seemed to have little effect on their prosperity in those days. They continued in the 1920s, during which time they also built cars for a short while.

At the start of the 1930s Matchless had a range of singles much as others, plus a big V-twin for sidecar work. For 1930 they also had their all-new

Silver Arrow, which was kept under wraps up to the last moment. It was one more attempt to provide the touring rider with the fully equipped, sophisticated machine it was said he wanted. A common trap.

The Silver Arrow, listed as the model A, was a side-valve V-twin of 54 × 86 mm dimensions and 394 cc. Its two cylinders were set at 26 degrees within a single casting under a single head. The result looked odd, rather like a single that was too long for its width, and with the exhaust emerging from the manifold at its right front corner and the carburettor in the middle of the block on the left the odd appearance was accentuated.

The skew gear-driven camshaft lay along the machine in the right crankcase and was extended to the rear to drive the mag-dyno. It suggested shaft drive, but this was an illusion, for chains conveyed the power to the three-speed gearbox and then on to the rear wheel. Lubrication was dry sump with the oil tank bolted to the front of the crankcase, so there were no external oil pipes.

The engine and gearbox were carried in a tubular frame with pivoted rear suspension controlled by coil springs and friction dampers mounted under the saddle. At the front went girder forks. Both wheels had drum brakes interconnected to a foot pedal on the right, while the front brake could also be operated independently by its handlebar lever.

The whole ensemble was topped off by an instrument panel mounted above the bars and

carrying both dials and switches. This was to provide the final touch to a machine sold to the discerning as quiet, smooth running and as comfortable as a car. In truth it was quiet, other than for timing-gear rattle, but this was to be expected from a low output side-valve twin. The same attribute also meant a restricted performance and steady acceleration all of which spelt death to sales.

As others had found and would again in the future, the enthusiast might clamour for advance and sophistication but never bought it. Such a machine could not readily be used for weekend sporting events and few could run to more than a single machine in those days. Also the clubman felt that buying quiet and comfort could signify that he was over the hill. For the mythical man-in-the-street the machine was still too much of a motorcycle to be attractive.

Fortunately for Matchless they continued with their line of straightforward singles and twins, which sold well and kept them solvent. The singles all had a vertical cylinder with the magneto tucked in behind it and the smallest were of 245 cc and comprised the side-valve R/4 and ohv R/6. Next came the twin-port model T/S2 of 348 cc, while in the largest class there were three models, with the 497 cc T/5 having side valves and the 491 cc V3

overhead. There were two versions of the latter, one with twin ports and the other, called the Special, with one. The latter was guaranteed to be capable of 85 mph. Finally there was the 583 cc side-valve model V/6 to complete the singles.

There were two versions of the big V-twin and both used the same 982 cc engine with side valves. The basic model was the X/2 and the other the X/R2, which had chrome-plated rims and nickel-plated cylinders.

All models had dry sump lubrication using the rotating and reciprocating plunger set in the crankcase below the timing chest and worm driven from the crankshaft. This system was to last them several decades. The cycle parts were much as others of that period with tubular frames, girder forks and saddle tanks.

The Silver Arrow had been a focus of interest when first shown to the public, but was too small in capacity and too placid in performance to excite. Only 12 months later this situation changed when Matchless unveiled a machine with a four-cylinder overhead camshaft engine at Olympia. It was called the Silver Hawk, listed as the Model B.

Equally new, an aisle or two away, was the Ariel Square Four, and either model would have been a show-stopper, but for two such machines, with dissimilar engine layouts, to appear during the Depression was remarkable.

The Hawk engine was in essence two Silver Arrows placed side by side. Dimensions became 50.8 × 73 mm and the capacity 592 cc, but the 26-

Below **1930 Matchless Silver Arrow model A of 394 cc with its narrow V-twin engine**
Below left **1930 Matchless T/5 with 497 cc engine set vertically in the frame**

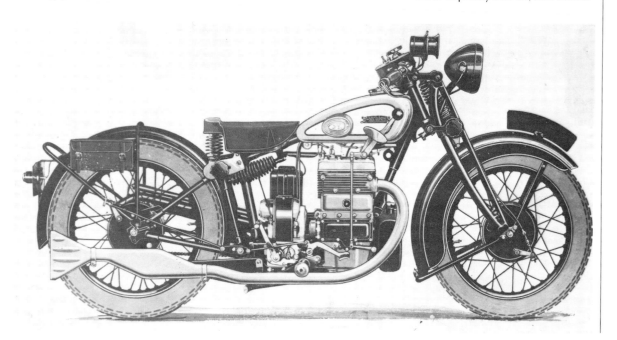

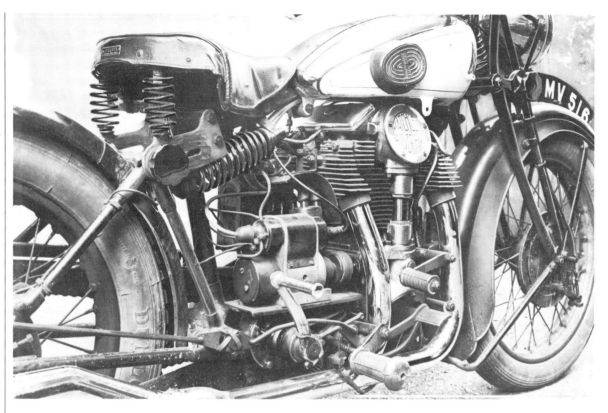

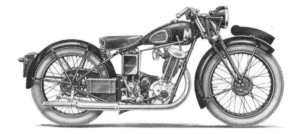

Above **Inclined 245 cc engine for the 1934 Matchless model 34/F**
Above left **The 1934 Matchless 982 cc 34/X2 V-twin**
Top **Engine of the Matchless Silver Hawk from 1934. Listed as the ohc 34/B with 592 cc in its V-four cylinders**

degree vee angle remained. It had a three-bearing, two-throw crankshaft set across the frame, one-piece block and one-piece head. The single camshaft was driven by shaft and bevels on the right and from that side the engine looked like a massively finned ohc single, which, for some reason, had twin exhaust pipes. From the left it was much less impressive with just the carburettor.

A skew gear on the vertical camshaft drove a shaft with a coupling at its rear end which connected to the dynamo and distributor unit for the coil ignition system. As on the Arrow the oil tank was bolted to the front of the crankcase, so no oil pipes were needed to connect it, but there was a feed up to the top bevel box.

The Hawk had a duplex primary chain with Weller spring tensioner, so the four-speed, handchange gearbox could run at a fixed centre.

For the rest the four was much as the twin, with spring frame, coupled brakes and an instrument panel.

Like the twin it failed to achieve much success, for it was expensive at a time when the world was hard-up. It also paralleled the Ariel in running into head joint problems if pressed too hard, while the bevels either whined or rattled—all right for a near-racer, but not really acceptable for a de luxe sports model.

So the customers stuck with the singles and for them Matchless had some new models with

348 cc Matchless G3 Clubman of 1935 with upright cylinder

inclined cylinders in the trend for the time. In fact only the 245 cc sv model continued from the 1930 single range with a new typing as the R/7. The big twins also ran on as the X/3 and X/R3, while the Silver Arrow was fitted with a four-speed gearbox and became the A2.

There were four new singles and all had inclined engines in the current fashion, while all models in the range had a large, chrome-plated letter M on each side of the petrol tank. Two of the new models had side valves, these being the 348 cc D and 583 cc C, while the other two were ohv. These were the 245 cc D/S and 491 cc C/S, both with twin-port heads.

In May 1931 a Light 500 was added to the range as the D/5 and took its name from its low weight, which just came under the tax barrier. This was quite an achievement, for the machine was equipped with electric lighting powered by a Maglita unit. The engine had an inclined cylinder, side valves and a 497 cc capacity. Dry sump lubrication was employed and a three-speed, handchange gearbox fitted.

For 1932 the D/5 was joined by the single-port D/6 and twin-port D/3, each fitted with a 348 cc ohv engine. The 348 sv model D, 583 cc sv model C, 491 cc ohv model C/S and 245 cc models R/7 with sv and D/S with ohv all continued, as did the Hawk, the Arrow and the two versions of the big V-twin.

All models had a new fabric oil filter fitted into the oil tank that year and a face cam engine shock absorber. Most had a very clean handlebar design with built-in lever pivots and throttle control by a lever beneath the right bar. A common pivot was used by front brake, air and throttle levers, all of which lay in accessible positions.

From 1933 the firm began its practice of prefixing each model designation with the last two digits of the year, so the D6 became 33/D6. This was continued for the rest of the decade, but is omitted in this text to avoid tedium.

The 1933 range continued to list the D, D/5 and D/6, as up to the end of 1932 they continued to qualify for a low road tax due to their light weight.

The other models were generally made sturdier

as an extra pound or so was no longer so vital and at the same time the finish was changed. Out went the tank with chrome-plating and white panels to be replaced by a black, gold-lined finish enhanced by the large letter M.

The range was thus much as before, but with all models except the Hawk and the old trio of lightweights listed in standard and de luxe forms. Other than the detail changes the D3, CS, C, X3 and XR3 models were as before, the 245 cc sv became the D7, the 245 cc ohv the D2 and two of the low-tax-weight models were joined by heavier versions as the 497 cc sv D5 and 348 cc ohv D6. Both the Silver Hawk and Silver Arrow remained in the list despite low sales.

In March 1933 a further 497 cc model joined the range. This was the D80 with inclined engine, ohv, light weight and good performance. It had a twin-port head with the option of high- or low-level exhaust systems and a four-speed footchange Burman gearbox.

Two months later the Silver Hawk received an amendment in the form of an optional footchange for its gearbox. A parts kit allowed existing machines to be converted.

The 1934 range was thinned down a little, and among the casualties was the Silver Arrow and the D, D/5, D/6, D6 and D7. This left the ohv D2, D3, CS and D80, the side-valve C and D5 plus the two versions of the V-twin, which became the X4 and XR4, topped off by the Silver Hawk.

The most obvious change was the adoption of chrome-plated brass beading around the edges of the mudguards, this having first been seen on the D series in 1933. Otherwise it was a case of detail improvements, with the V-twin acquiring the engine shock absorber and oil bath chaincase as used by the rest of the range.

The range was added to before the New Year with a pair of 245 cc models. These were the ohv F and the sv F7, both of which had inclined engines, coil ignition and three-speed, handchange gearboxes. The rest of the range had four speeds and all bar the V-twin the option of hand or footchange.

The mudguard beading was changed to a gold line for 1935 and a change to chrome-plated wheel rims reflected the move away from the economies of the Depression years. A further indication of better times was the appearance of the D90, a super sports 497 cc ohv with raised compression ratio and polished internals. The other models again showed detail improvements, but this steady progression was what the era demanded,

for it brought stable prices and ease of spares supply.

The D range ran on with the D3, D5 and D80, as did the C, CS, X4 and Silver Hawk. The XR4 and D2 went, but the F7 stayed and the ohv version became the F4.

In April 1935 a most important new model was announced by Matchless which was to set the style and format for the range from then on. All the existing models had inclined engines, which was a style that had come in fashion in the late 1920s but was no longer what the buyers wanted.

The new machine was the G3 and was known as the Clubman. It had a vertical cylinder and used the tried and trusted 69 × 93 mm dimensions to obtain its 348 cc. It had ohv, a magneto tucked in behind the engine and a dynamo beneath that, where it was chain driven from the crankshaft. The engine design was similar to the existing ohv models, but hairpin valve springs were used and dry sump lubrication with the usual oil pump.

A four-speed footchange Burman gearbox was used and it and the engine housed in a cradle frame with twin downtubes. The remainder of the machine follwed company lines and a single high-level exhaust system was fitted. In addition to the basic model a Clubman Special was also listed, this being a trials version with suitable tyres, gear ratios and fitments and typed the G3C.

The Matchless range underwent a major revision for 1936 with only the side-valve F7, D5 and X4 remaining from the past. Out went the Silver Hawk and in came a range of singles to supplement the G3 and G3C. All were built on very similar lines and many features were common to all the models.

The smaller ones were both of 245 cc and the G2 had coil ignition, whereas the G2M used a magneto. The bigger machines were the G80 Clubman and G90 Super Clubman, both of which were supported by special models listed as the G80C and G90C. All were of 497 cc capacity and fitted out to match their names and tasks. As in 1935 the 90 model was a tuned version of the 80.

1937 saw the end of the inclined engines as the 245 cc sv became the G7 and the 497 cc sv the G5. Both had new engines with vertical cylinders and dwarf tappet chests. Both had coil ignition and like all models that year were equipped with cvc

Above right **1937 Matchless 497 cc G80 Clubman with the magneto tucked in behind the engine**
Right **Engine of the 1940 497 cc Matchless G5 with coil ignition. Note flying M on tank**

control for the dynamo and a four-speed foot-change gearbox.

The V-twin became the model X with a shorter frame and new petrol tank and the magneto went back in front of the engine but more tucked in than before. For the singles the 348 and 497 cc models continued as they were, but in the 245 cc class one new model was added in the form of the competition G2MC. This took the same style as its larger brothers.

During 1937 Matchless decided to stop supplying machines to the technical press for road tests and this action was maintained for many years. The company also bought the rights to the Sunbeam motorcycle and this led to the formation of the AMC group, although the Sunbeam name was sold on to BSA in 1943.

There were still 12 models in the line-up for 1938, but the G90C had gone, and to make the number up was the 348 cc ohv G4. This was the 350 equivalent of the G90 and these two models were finished with red panels to their chrome-plated tanks with the same colour for the wheel rim centres. The two models also had hairpin valve springs, but otherwise it was the range as before with detail improvements. The visual change for the year was the adoption of the flying M with wings on the petrol tanks, while the X now had dwarf tappet chests.

It was the same for 1939 with the models divided into three groups. The Clubman machines were the G2, G2M, G3, G4, G80 and G90. The Clubman Specials were the G2MC, G3C and G90C in place of the 80 of the year before. In the Tourist range were the G7, G5 and model X. Changes for all were to details only.

Most of the range was still listed for 1940 and except for the side-valve singles had the tank finished in red and chrome. The competition models were out, but the G2M, G3, G4, G80 and G90 all remained from the ohv range. All three side-valve models were still listed.

All the singles had a new frame with single downtube and it was this that was adopted for the forces' favourite, the 41/G3L, with its telescopic front forks. Post-war the models were to continue.

In the mid- to late-1930s Matchless supplied engines to other firms, including Brough Superior, Calthorpe, Coventry Eagle, OEC and OK Supreme. The V-twins also went into the Morgan three-wheeler, so to an extent AMC began to take over the mantle worn by JAP and Blackburne in earlier years.

Mercury

Many motorcycle enthusiasts carry out modifications in a small way to improve their machines and some go further to bigger changes. From this a few move on to construct specials, which may consist of fitting one make of engine into another make of frame or a major change to a basic road model which could entail only keeping the original engine, and that in a far from original form.

Alterations on a grand scale were not so usual in the 1930s and most were simply engine changes, which many marques of the period were well adapted to allow. Against this background the Mercury was unusual, for it was a special built for grand touring and, unlike the rest, went into limited production, a notion not repeated until the Triton came along in post-war years.

The Mercury was the result of the dissatisfaction that a group in Croydon, Surrey, had with what was available to them at the start of the thirties. The instigators were Laurie Jenks and a Mr Swabey, who together ran a small Scott tuning shop, and in time they were joined by three others.

The original aim was to accommodate any engine, but inevitably the choice fell on the Scott units they had to hand. These were not new but secondhand, rebuilt with some areas modified.

The prototype was built in 1933 with a tubular frame and provided a useful amount of information. The next step was to move on to a more radical design and lay down some limited production. In the end there were five made and the first took to the road in 1937.

It was unusual to say the least. The engine was essentially a 596 cc Scott fed by a single Amal and with mag-dyno electrics. A three-speed gearbox was fitted. The frame was constructed from I-section Duralumin extrusions which were mainly straight or with slight bends. They bolted together to make a duplex structure of triangular form from the side. There was suspension for both wheels, but neither end was conventional.

At first sight the front forks were telescopics, but this was not so. Each fork tube was slotted along its lower length and this slot faced forward. A plunger slid inside the tube under spring control and from it a plate protruded through to support one end of the wheel spindle.

The fork turned in the manner of the OEC duplex steering. It differed in that at the steering head the fork tubes were joined by a crown which turned on a large-diameter ball set in the front of the main frame. The lower ends of the fork tubes were each attached by a link to a large casting. This was in bronze for strength and shaped like a wishbone to bolt to the main frame at the base of the down beams. As with the OEC the steering was very self-centring and once on the move not easy to divert.

The rear suspension was supposed to keep the chain tension constant, as the wheel moved, and did this with short pivoted plates and steel guide flanges. The springs lay along the top of the frame members that ran from rear wheel to headstock and were linked by bellcranks to the movement. Neither suspension system was damped.

To fit the machine for its purpose the two sides were enclosed within the frame area. The panels had access holes and could be readily detached. Comfort was further helped by the fitting of 4 in. section tyres to both wheels, which had alloy hubs

and 8 in. diameter brakes. At that time such a tyre size was only used for competition and big V-twin rear wheels and at the front for sidecar use or by the Americans.

There was also a stepped-level dualseat, a rarity among a sea of saddles, and a five-gallon petrol tank mounted on rubber and with a toolbox plus glove compartment set in its top panel.

The tuning shop became Mercury Motors for 1938 and the other sets of parts were organized. Only three were finished pre-war and the final fifth alloy-framed Mercury did not reach the road until 1959. All varied to some degree, and that owned by Laurie Jenks had rotary valves fitted to the engine and pannier bags either side of the front wheel.

All five and the prototypes were found to still be in existence in 1984, which must be a unique survival record.

The Mercury with its Scott engine and built-up frame. Shown with the side panels removed while the forks and seat are also of interest along with many of the detail fittings

Montgomery

This was another fringe make that relied on proprietary parts, although they also made frames and forks for other firms, including Brough Superior in that concern's early days. Like many others they found the 1930s hard going for there were few customers for the expensive hand-built machine, and lower down the scale it was hard to compete with BSA or the many similar models using the same bought-in parts.

For 1930 Montgomery offered a range which used just two frames, but had each model in standard or de luxe form. Most basic was the 250TS with a 247 cc Villiers engine, while the rest of the range was JAP powered. With side valves were engines of 300, 346, 490 and 600 cc and a single cylinder plus a 750 cc V-twin. The ohv engines came in 245, 346 and 490 cc sizes.

In 1931 the range extended with Greyhound models in 245, 346 and 490 cc sizes, these being sporting versions of the basic models. They were of orthodox design but well finished and the 346 cc example had an inclined engine. There was also a 677 cc ohv V-twin Greyhound model and a 994 cc side-valve for hauling sidecars along.

There were no Montgomery models in the buyers' guide published late in 1931 as they were involved in a change of premises. It was not until March 1932 that their range was announced and it was greatly curtailed to two models in 346 and 490 cc sizes. The Greyhounds had two-port engines and four speeds while the standard models had three, and the 346 cc a single-port engine.

This got them under way and while the standard 350 was dropped for 1933 the other models were joined by 245 cc standard and Greyhound ohv machines. The standard 500 became the Bulldog and the two V-twins with 680 ohv and 750 sv engines were back in the list. There were also two two-strokes with Villiers engines of 148 or 247 cc in a simple frame with blade girders and a single pressing formed as leg and undershield.

The two twins continued for 1934 along with the Greyhound in 245 and 346 cc sizes. There was only one two-stroke, the 250, but the 490 cc Bulldog was joined by a 600 cc ohv version. New was a 550 cc side-valve model and the 499 cc Super Greyhound. This had an inclined single-port JAP engine with dry sump lubrication, a cast-alloy chaincase, four-speed Albion gearbox with foot-change and the usual strong Montgomery frame.

For 1935 this became the model 46 Greyhound, and was joined by the model 41, which had coil ignition and only three speeds. There was a third 499 cc model, the 50 Sports Greyhound, which was for competition use. The smaller models were given the name Terrier and came in 245 and 346 cc sizes. The smaller were the 32 with coil ignition and three speeds and the 36 with magneto and four speeds. The larger equivalents were the 36-350 and the 39.

The range was the same for 1936 but without the model numbers, so the machines were listed as Terrier or Greyhound in standard and de luxe form. The 498 cc model alone was also listed in Sports form with a tuned engine. In January a

122 cc Terrier was added with Villiers engine and simple loop frame. It had a massive cast-alloy expansion chamber in front of the crankcase and a long tailpipe on the left with a small fishtail end. A de luxe model was also available with legshields and a well-valanced rear mudguard.

Both 122 cc two-strokes continued for 1937, as did all except the Sports machines. The standard models with coil ignition and three speeds were now all called Terrier in 245, 346 and 498 cc sizes, while the de luxe machines were all now Greyhounds.

The 1938 range was longer and had a new name, Retriever, for the top-of-the-range versions of the 245, 346 and 498 cc ohv models. At the other end of the scale the 122 cc two-stroke became the Standard and the Standard de luxe. In between, the standard 245 and 346 cc ohv models stayed as they were, but the ones with magneto and four speeds reverted to their Terrier de luxe name. Both 498 cc ohv machines were now Greyhounds and the range was completed by three side-valve models—the Terrier of 245 cc, the Terrier Sports of 490 cc and the Terrier Standard of 600 cc. This added up to 14 models, which did cover most bases except the big V-twin market.

The range shrank again for 1939 to the models that actually sold, and these numbered eight. There was just one 122 cc two-stroke, but it was joined by a version with a 98 cc engine. The other models were two each in 245, 346 and 499 cc sizes, one standard and the other the MDL model with plunger rear suspension. This was of the simplest form with a compression spring and rebound rubber. The largest models, the Greyhounds, were fitted with a new type of JAP engine, with fully enclosed valve gear and horizontal fins running to the top of the cylinder head. This engine retained the usual near-square dimensions and the mag-dyno was tucked in behind the cylinder, where it was driven from the timing chest.

The smaller machines continued with their Terrier name.

A 1940 range was announced as for 1939 plus a 122 cc Terrier MDL with extra equipment and another Terrier with a 197 cc Villiers engine. With the advent of war, production ceased, not to start again.

Above **1937 Montgomery Terrier de luxe with 122 cc Villiers engine and simple cycle parts**
Left **The Montgomery Greyhound of 1931 with 680 ohv JAP engine and a nice line to its exhaust systems**
Right **The Greyhound model MDL Montgomery of 1939 with 499 cc JAP engine with continuous fins all the way up both barrel and head**

New Comet

New Gerrard

This marque had its roots in supplying components and was first built in Edwardian times in Birmingham. Production was spasmodic, but began again in 1930 with a single lightweight.

The engine was a 172 cc Villiers unit which went into conventional cycle parts with a three-speed gearbox. For 1931 it was replaced by a 196 cc unit and called the Super Sports, but from then on the firm found it better business to be suppliers to the trade. Thus they returned to just making components.

Jock Porter won the 1923 250 cc, the 1924 175 cc and was third in the 1925 175 cc TT races on New Gerrard machines, so in the mid-1920s the name was not unknown. They hailed from Edinburgh and the firm was Jock Porter, who ran a motor business and designed, built and rode the motorcycles as well.

The machines were built up from bought-in parts aside from the frame and by 1930 the range had become a single model. This had a 346 cc ohv JAP engine and little else to distinguish it from a dozen others, except that it came from Scotland. The same model was offered for 1931 and continued as the range for some years. By 1935 its Burman gearbox had the option of four speeds in place of the usual three plus the second option of hand or footchange.

For 1936 it was four speeds and footchange without the option and in this form the one model continued to be offered right up to 1940, when production ceased.

Jock Porter at the 1930 Junior TT with his New Gerrard. He built them in Scotland and his single model remained in production throughout the decade

New Henley

This was another small firm who assembled machines using bought-in parts. Engines were Villiers or JAP by 1930 and these went into a variety of frames with Burman or Albion three-speed gearboxes and fittings much as many others.

One model was called the Bryn and this had a 247 cc Villiers engine installed with its cylinder inclined forward in a channel steel frame. It had the Burman gearbox and Brampton forks. The other Villiers-powered models were the 172 cc V1 and 196 cc V2, which went into loop frames with Albion boxes.

The rest of the range used JAP engines and the singles were the 346 cc ohv model 3, 490 cc ohv model 5 and the same size model 6 with side valves. The final model was the 8 with a 750 cc sv V-twin engine. These all went into the duplex frame that the firm had used for their entries in the 1929 TT.

A slightly larger range was listed for 1931, but did not include the 172 cc machine. The V1 became a 196 cc model with two speeds while the V2 had the super sports engine. The Bryn continued, as did models 3, 5, 6 and 8, but they were joined by three more. Of these the 4 had a TT version of the 346 cc ohv engine, but was otherwise as the 3. The model 4A had a 490 cc ohv engine and really took the place of the 5, which became the super sports model. The 7 was a de luxe version of the 490 cc sv model 6.

During the year the make ceased trading and became one more victim of the Depression.

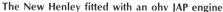

The New Henley fitted with an ohv JAP engine

New Hudson

New Hudson's moment of glory in the TT came when Jimmy Guthrie finished second in the 1927 Senior; they also saw some success at Brooklands during the twenties.

They made their own engines or used proprietary ones over the years from their beginning in 1903 and in 1930 had a good line of conventional singles on offer. These all had model numbers, vertical cylinders, dry sump lubrication, saddle tanks and a high standard of finish and equipment.

There was an sv and ohv model in each traditional capacity with the 249 cc numbered 80 and 91, the 346 cc as 83 and 85, and the 496 cc as 84 and 86. There were also three models with Power Plus-tuned engines and these were the 346 cc ohv 87 and the 496 cc ohv 88 and 89.

The range was totally revised for 1931 with four basic models, each produced in standard or de luxe form, and all with inclined engines and partial enclosure. This last took the form of side panels that ran from the front of the crankcase to the rear of the gearbox and from crankcase top level to the underside of the duplex frame. On top of the panel at the rear stood the battery and toolbox.

Other features were a tank-top instrument panel, hand gear lever moving within the right knee-grip, a centre stand and a kickstart lever that doubled as a prop-stand. The forks were tubular girders and carried a large headlamp and the horn on the top crown.

The engines were 346 cc sv or ohv, 496 cc ohv and 548 cc sv. Lubrication was from a sump cast into the front section of the crankcase and ignition was by magneto, while the dynamo was clamped to the rear of the crankcase. The magneto sat just above it and the two were driven from the crankshaft by a chain mounted inboard of the primary drive. The valves were fully enclosed.

During May 1931 New Hudson used the 548 cc model hitched to a large Watsonian sidecar in a non-stop reliability run. This was from Brooklands to Land's End and back and the intention was to complete this journey ten times, a distance of 5560 miles, without stopping the engine. It very nearly managed this, but on the last leg back to Brooklands a garage overfilled the petrol tank and the engine was cut for safety reasons. It was mopped and restarted in short order to complete its run and the engine stripped perfectly. For all this

Below **In 1940 the New Hudson name reappeared on a 98 cc autocycle**
Right **A 1931 496 cc New Hudson with enclosure panels**

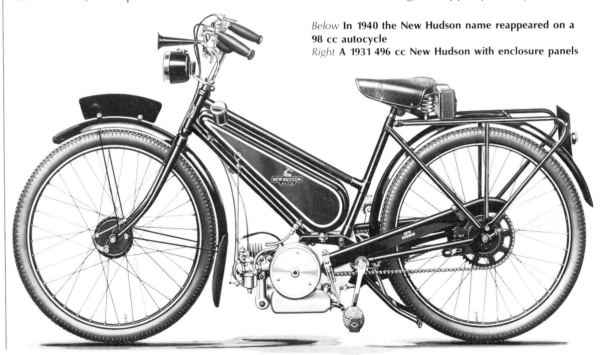

the ACU gave them a certificate, but not the Maudes Trophy they were after.

Had they gained this it could have helped the company over a bad patch. The new engines had run into a few problems and the public had not gone for enclosure in the way predicted and as totally as New Hudson had. A major trophy could have helped them to regain confidence, but as it was they were now stuck with their range.

For 1932 the 500 was revamped with revised dimensions, new cylinder head, new and separate rocker boxes and new valve gear from the camshaft up. A fair amount of weight was also carved off, but the appearance was much as before with inclined engines and enclosed nether regions. The models were the 346 cc sv 32 and ohv 34. The equivalent 493 cc ones were models 01 and 3, but in addition to the standard ohv 3 there was the de luxe 4, which had legshields and a form of panniers, plus the Bronze Wing. This was a super sports version with special engine, golden-bronze tank finish, more ground clearance and nail catchers for both studded tyres.

The final models were both of 548 cc with side valves and were the standard model 1 and de luxe 2 which had legshields and panniers. For all models there was a controlled oil feed to the primary chain, various detail changes and the finish was as before except for the lining, which went from white to gold.

The whole range went forward as it was into 1933, but sales continued to be depressed as few were prepared to risk scarce pennies on a model with a whisper of a problem. The troubles were no longer there, but the firm could not ride forever on future hopes. That year they were approached to make Girling brakes and suspension parts, which is precisely what they did from then on.

In March 1940 the name reappeared on the side of an autocycle. The engine unit was the usual Villiers 98 cc Junior de luxe and sat under the usual bicycle-type frame with rigid forks but rubber-mounted handlebars. Both wheels had drum brakes and the fittings were typical of the type. The name and the autocycle were revived post-war, but by this time manufacture had been taken over by BSA.

New Imperial

In their time New Imperial won six TT races, all in the 250 class, except in 1924, when they did the double and took the 350 as well. Their last TT win came in 1936 and that year their works models came 1–2 in Ulster in a side-by-side finish. The company start date is often taken as 1900, when Norman Downs took over, but was really 1892. During the 1930s they built some innovative machines.

For 1930 the range was simple, with six models all with vertically mounted engines, rear magneto, Pilgrim oil pump and three-speed gearbox. There were two of 344 cc with side valves, and the first was the model 2, which had a single loop frame and qualified for the lower tax rate thanks to its light weight. The other model was the DL2 and like the rest of the range it had a duplex loop frame and was fitted as standard with a tank-mounted speedometer. There was a third side-valve in the form of the 499 cc model 7 and three with ohv, which were the 245 cc 9, 346 cc 10 and 499 cc 7B.

All six continued for 1931 plus Blue Prince models of 344 and 499 cc with twin-port heads and dry sump lubrication, but only a couple went on into 1932. It was that year that the firm took their first step along the road to unit construction, then something held to impede servicing and not to be encouraged. Before then there were competition versions of the Blue Prince models and a new lightweight 245 cc ohv with single-port head, waist-level silencer on the left and loop frame. The latter was also offered with Miller coil ignition in place of a magneto and Lucas M-L lighting set.

The unit construction models were announced in August 1931 and had a remarkably modern specification. In addition to a common base for both engine and gearbox they also had wet sump lubrication with the oil carried within a compartment formed in the crankcase. On the cycle side there was rear suspension with a pivoted rear fork and the springs under the saddle in monoshock style.

The models were built in 344 and 499 cc sizes and both had twin-port heads, inclined cylinders and fully enclosed valve gear. While the concept was novel the actual construction followed the ways of the period. Primary transmission was by chain with a Weller tensioner on both chain runs which connected to a three-plate cork clutch. A cast-alloy case enclosed the chain. The gearbox had three ratios and final drive was by chain.

The frame had duplex tubes which bolted to the front of the crankcase, twin tank rails and two seat tubes to form a rigid structure with the engine. The rear fork pivoted on taper roller bearings and was triangulated by a link from the upper chainstay to the seat tube. Wheel movement was controlled by

two compression springs and friction dampers. For the rest it was girder forks, 7 in. drum brakes and full equipment with many rider features. The model numbers were 16 and 17.

The remainder of the range was little altered and the smallest machine was the 245 cc ohv 8. This was also available with a close-ratio, footchange gearbox as the 20 and as a special racing model as the 22. In the 350 class the models 15, 19 and 21 were built on the same lines, along with the F10, which was the dry sump Blue Prince machine. The 344 cc sv 2 was the other model to retain its number from the previous year. In the 500 class there was the side-valve 18 and ohv F11 Blue Prince, and both Blue Prince models continued to be offered in competition trim.

A third unit construction model appeared at the show late in 1931 and for all its small size was of great interest. The prototype as shown was a 150 cc ohv single with inclined engine and fully enclosed valve gear. The camshaft ran across the engine behind the crankshaft, so the pushrod tubes were to the rear of the cylinder and the valves set in a transverse vee in the head.

The camshaft was gear driven on the right and this gear pair formed part of the primary transmission and went on to gear drive the clutch. Straight-cut spur gears were used with ample bearings to support them. The gearbox was of a crossover design, so the final drive chain went on the left and the box had three speeds. They were

selected by a car-type gear lever working in a tower casting on top of the box.

The lubrication was by Pilgrim pump, which was bolted to the outside of the timing cover and driven by the camshaft end. Ignition was by a flywheel magneto on the left end of the crankshaft and this also provided the current for the lights. The cycle side was simple and basic, as expected of any low-tax 150 in 1932.

The prototype design failed to make it into production, but in March 1932 a revised model appeared and was built for many years. The new design was more conventional in one way in that the timing gear went on the right, as did the pushrods and oil pump. Less usual was the continued use of unit construction and helical gear primary drive.

Ignition was now by coil with the points in the end of the dynamo, which was mounted above the gearbox and gear driven from the clutch. From this layout came the triangular chaincase shape that was to characterize the model series from then on. Due to the gear drive the engine rotated in the opposite direction to usual, and many were they to set the ignition timing the wrong side of top dead centre. Other than when tdc was the required mark.

The gearbox still had three ratios, but was now controlled by a conventional lever working in a gate bolted to the petrol tank side. The cycle parts remained much as before with a simple loop frame, blade girders and neat leather toolbox.

The move to unit construction continued for 1933 with only the side-valve models 2 and 18 and ohv Blue Princes in the old style. The 499 cc engine

Below **The Blue Prince 344 cc model F10 New Imperial of 1931 with ohv and partly-exposed clutch**
Below left **A 1931 model 7 New Imperial of 499 cc with side-valve engine**

of the 18 was altered to dry sump lubrication and its valves were fully enclosed.

New was the 30, a 247 cc edition of the 148 cc model 23 and built along the same lines, plus a rear-wheel shock absorber, which the smaller machine lacked. Also new were the models 16A and 17A, which were rigid-frame versions of the larger unit machines. The others in the range were dropped.

Both unit and non-unit lines extended for 1934 with de luxe versions of the 23 and 30 plus a new 344 cc model 40. This was similar to the smaller models but made to a larger scale, while retaining the loop frame and rigid rear end. It had gear primary drive as the others and took its place alongside the unit models with chain drive, which continued in both rigid- and spring-frame forms.

These last were named Unit Major, while the 150 was the Unit Minor and the 250 the Unit Super. The Major continued in both 344 and 499 cc sizes. The two Blue Prince models also ran on, as did the model 18, which was now the only side-valve left in the range.

New and exciting were two Grand Prix models of 245 and 344 cc. These were replicas of the works racers and were built for fast road work or road racing. Engines were set vertical and separate from the gearbox, which had four speeds and foot-change. The engine internals were polished and compression plates went under the barrel to allow the ratio to be adjusted.

Ignition was by rear-mounted magneto and lubrication dry sump with the oil tank combined with the petrol one. Both had a pistol-grip shape that was distinctive and attractive. A rigid frame was used and both models, numbered 50 and 60, were listed with the option of a bronze cylinder head.

1934 saw a very special New Imperial appear for the works to race. It was fitted with a 491 cc V-twin engine and two were entered for the TT. One managed to climb to 6th, but both retired on the fifth lap. The twin was also eligible to run for *The Motor Cycle* cup for the first British multi to cover 100 miles in one hour on British soil. This was only possible at Brooklands and on 1 August Ginger Wood duly ran the New Imp, complete with its Brooklands can, for the hour and covered over 102 miles to take the cup.

The twin engine was based on the 245 cc Grand Prix with two barrels mounted at 60 degrees on a massive crankcase. Both exhausts were thus at the front and the whole machine was little larger than

Above **The prototype 150 cc New Imperial of 1932 with valve gear behind the cylinder**
Top **A unit construction New Imperial of 1933 with oil bath chaincase and pivoted fork rear suspension**
Above right **1933 New Imperial model 30 of 247 cc**
Right **The 1933 TT New Imperial which led to the models 50 and 60 the following year**

the 250. Unfortunately it did not handle at all well, unlike the smaller single, and riding it was hard work.

Two models based on the twin were listed for 1935 with the 90 the tourer and the 100 the sports machine. Unlike the racer both were to have unit construction, but details were not finalized when the range was announced. In the end they never did appear.

Also new and real were two new singles of 496 cc with inclined cylinder and unit construction. The 70 had ohv and the 80 side valves, but otherwise they were the same machine and followed the lines of the earlier models. These all ran on with the addition of the models 27, 37 and

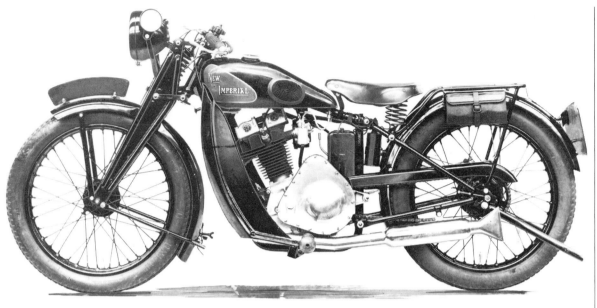

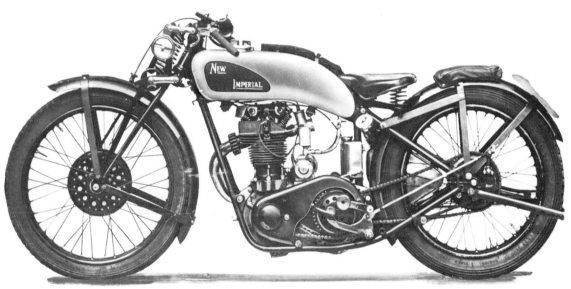

47 in the three capacities, fitted with a Maglita in place of coil ignition. The 23, 30 and 40 continued, along with their de luxe versions, and were joined by the sports 25, 35 and 45. There was also the 49, which was a 350 supplied complete with a Watsonian sidecar.

The original unit models with chain primary went, so there were no models with spring frames, but the Blue Princes, Grand Prix and the 18 all remained. Changes were minimal aside from development for the racing models.

The new unit 500 model 70 was modified early in 1935 when new head and barrel castings were introduced. These included tunnels for the pushrods to operate in rather than the tubes used

by the other models, and the valve gear was positively lubricated.

The Blue Prince and old side-valve models did not figure in the 1936 lists and neither did the 500 twin, which had not made it on to the stage. From the unit models the 23, 30, 40, 49 and 70 ran on and were joined by a pair of Unidyno machines. These were the 247 cc 36 and 344 cc 46, which were similar to but not the same as the others. The changes were to the shock absorber, which moved from the rear hub to the engine gear, and to the mag-dyno drive. This was taken from the inlet camshaft by chain in a light alloy casing on the right. In other respects the machines were much as before and both models had a four-

119

The 344 cc 1935 model 49 was supplied complete with Watsonian sidecar

speed, handchange gearbox and a new cradle frame.

The remaining unit models were the 76, which was a sports version of the 70, and the side-valve 80, which was stretched to 554 cc. Non-unit machines were the 245 cc 90 and 346 cc 100, which had vertical cylinders, four-speed foot-change gearboxes and power units based on the works engines from the year before.

The Grand Prix models became pure racing machines fitted out accordingly as regards equipment, magneto and carburettor. A bronze head with coil valve springs was fitted as standard, but as an option a bimetal aluminium and bronze skull head was available. This had hairpin springs and rocker return springs. The cycle parts were much as the works models and for the fast road rider a silencer was available. The oil tank filler was on the left to suit the pits at the TT, but there was no mention of lighting equipment.

The spring frame was back again for 1937 and available for all models except the 148 cc 23. All retained gear drive, which now just had two gears in the alloy chaincase as all the magnetos were driven from the inlet camshaft. Except for the 150 all shared a common rigid or sprung frame and had a two-port head. There were no side-valve engines.

Each of the basic models 36, 46 and 76 were available with mag-dyno, Maglita or coil ignition, and all had hand gearchange and low-level

exhausts. These machines also came in de luxe form with mag-dyno only, footchange, valanced mudguards and more chrome-plate.

The Clubman models were also based on the unit construction theme, but were well modified internally to increase their power and fitted with double helical primary gears to transmit it. Models were the 245 cc 90 and 346 cc 100, which thus differed from 1936 in having inclined cylinders. At the top of the scale was the 496 cc model 110, and it stayed there for 1938.

The whole range continued for that year with an improved gearchange mechanism which went on all models except the 150, as that alone had only three speeds and hand selection of them. Also new and fitted on the Standard and Clubman models was a single-port cylinder head, which increased the power output. The de luxe machines continued with the two-port but with the option of the single. There was a new silencer with opposing cone baffles and the petrol tanks were decorated with a large NI transfer in place of the earlier full name surmounted by a lion.

In January 1938 one more machine joined the range in the form of the 247 cc 36L. This was in the form of the earlier unit construction models with the triangular primary chaincase and gear-driven dynamo. Coil ignition, a single-port head and a three-speed handchange gearbox were used, the transmission shock absorber went into the rear hub and only the rigid frame was offered. In truth it was a stores spares special and comprised assemblies from earlier models, some up to six years earlier, and built as a means of obtaining sales for minimal outlay while cleaning out some of the old stock. It was not to do much to stave off impending financial trouble.

Most of the range continued to be listed for 1939 and the de luxe models were fitted in the spring frame as standard. This feature was no longer available for any other of the machines and the rather over-large tank initials of the year before gave way to a small neat name transfer on deep blue panels.

The unit construction machines were the 23, 36, 46 and 76 in the various capacities, plus the 110 as the sports 500. New were two Grand Prix models of 245 and 346 cc and these revived the 50 and 60 numbers of the past and were cast in the same mould. Thus their engines were vertical, the specification sporting and the gearboxes separate.

However, the company had run into problems due to the death of the founder, Norman Downs, and had to be sold. Once again it was Jack Sangster who came to the rescue and by early 1939 he was in control of the firm. Due to this change-over the new Grand Prix models never did make it into production, but the rest of the range continued to be made at Hall Green in Birmingham.

Sangster then planned to move the New Imperials to the Triumph works in Coventry, where there was some empty space. This happened in August and from then on the two firms did have the same address. The range shrank to four basic unit construction machines for 1940 and then just faded away. Like many others it was not revived after the war.

Left **Engine unit of the 1935 New Imperial 496 cc model 80 with full train of gears on the timing side running up to the magneto**

Below **New Imperial model 60 of 1939, a 346 cc ohv listed as the Grand Prix**

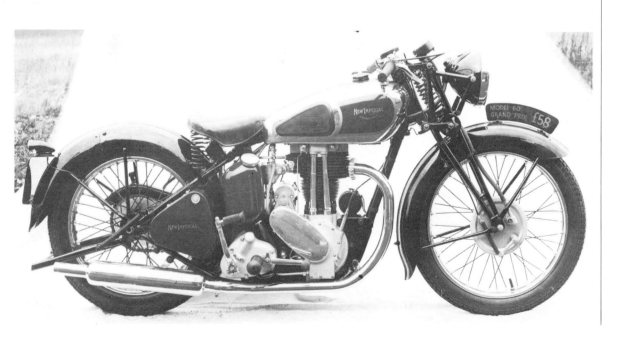

Newmount

This was not really an English machine at all but a German Zundapp with new tank badges. It was the model S200 with a 198 cc two-stroke engine inclined forward a little and based on 60 × 70 mm dimensions. It had a magneto mounted behind the cylinder and a large outside flywheel on the left with the primary drive outboard of this.

The engine was petroil lubricated and drove a three-speed gearbox with hand or foot control. The exhaust system was extensive, with a single pipe leading to a transverse box which fed two pipes beneath the engine, which led to a second transverse container, which had a single outlet on the right with a fishtail exhaust.

The frame was built up and its backbone a steel forging which included the headstock and an attachment for the tank rails. The same point also supported twin I-section beams that ran down under the engine and up again to the backbone at the saddle nose. Further beams bolted on to form the chainstays.

In 1931 this machine became the 200 standard and was joined by the 200 Lightweight, which had its engine installed with the cylinder vertical. They were both available with the option of coil ignition in place of the magneto and were listed with other machines. One similar was the 300 with a two-stroke engine of this size inclined forward in the frame and lubricated by pump.

As well as the two-strokes the firm added four-strokes using Rudge Python engines. There were three models in this list and all had four speeds and coil ignition. The smallest used the 348 cc ohv engine and the other two had 499 cc units and were listed in standard and special forms. All these models continued to be offered for 1932 and 1933, after which the make was no longer available.

Below **A 198 cc Newmount from 1931, really a German Zundapp in disguise**
Right **The 1939 Norman Motobyk with 98 cc Villiers engine**

Norman

This company was sited in Ashford, Kent, where they made bicycles, and they came into the motorcycle field with two models for 1939. One was an autocycle called a Motobyke and the other of 122 cc and called a Lightweight. The autocycle was much as many others with a 98 cc Villiers Junior engine, petroil lubrication and a flywheel magneto to provide ignition and direct lighting. It had an open frame with the fuel tank just above the engine, rigid forks and cable-operated drum brakes with the option of back-pedalling for the rear. A rear carrier and centre stand were included in the specification and the price was with full equipment.

The motorcycle had a unit construction 122 cc Villiers engine with three-speed gearbox housed in a simple loop frame. The cylinder was upright and the twin exhausts ran straight back and then dipped down a little to a waist-level silencer on each side. Oil and electrics were as on the autocycle. Blade girders were fitted and the machine had a cylindrical toolbox under the saddle and a rear stand. It also came with legshields as standard.

The Lightweight motorcycle was listed for 1940 along with three versions of the Motobyke. The original machine became the standard model and had cable brakes without any option. Next came the de luxe with Webb blade girder sprung forks and the option of compensated coupled brakes. Finally there was the carrier, which was as the de luxe but lower geared. All the autocycles now fitted the Junior De Luxe Villiers engine with detachable cylinder head and flat-top piston.

One final model was created by fitting a 98 cc engine into the motorcycle frame, and on this note production ceased until 1946, when the same two basic models were made.

Norton

At the end of the 1920s the range of Norton road models was looking very vintage in appearance, having altered little during the decade. The machines had a frame that was long and tall, a crude gearchange, vague lubrication and the magneto stuck out in front of the engine, albeit under a large polished cover for 1930. The format was truly much as had been laid down by the firm's founder with solid engineering and upright cylinders. Never was a Norton to incline its barrel even at the height of such fashion, for that was just not Bracebridge Street style.

While the road models were dated the competition side had brightened up no end in the twenties. Following their lone TT win in 1907 the ohv engine had brought them two TT victories in 1924 and the camshaft engine had taken over in 1927. Along with these had come success in Europe and both race wins and prestigious records at Brooklands.

Thus 1930 saw Norton poised for a decade of success based on their achievements of the 1920s, but this was not to come in that opening year. For that the old range was still listed with all the familiar model numbers. The more basic machines had diamond frames, three-speed gearbox, total loss lubrication, saddle tank and front-mounted magneto. Machines were the 490 cc sv 16H and model 2 with semi-TT handlebars and footboards, the 634 cc Big 4 model 1 and model 14, which had a four-speed gearbox, the 490 cc ohv model 18, the model 20 which was simply a twin-port 18 and the 588 cc ohv model 19. There was also the 24, which was a 19 with four-speed gearbox, and the 21, an 18 with semi-dry sump lubrication. Optional features listed were dated in many cases, but included the four-speed gearbox and a form of foot gearchange.

The next class of machines used the cradle frame and were characterized by having the magneto sited behind the engine, where it was chain driven from the left end of the crankshaft. These models, three in number, also had polished alloy chainguards. Smallest was the 348 cc ohv JE and the others the 490 cc ES2 and its twin-port variant the model 22.

To complete the line there were the two camshaft models, the CS1 of 490 cc and CJ of 348 cc. Both had the early Moore design of engine with the blister on the right of the crankcase for the camshaft drive and the magneto as on the ES2. The larger machine used a three-stay cradle frame, but the CJ used a lighter one with only two stays. Both models had dry sump lubrication and three-speed gearboxes with normal or close ratios being available.

Outside the road range there was one short-lived special model for dirt-track use, as speedway racing was then called. This used the twin-port model 20 engine in an abbreviated frame with a Webb speedway fork. The fixtures and fittings were to suit the track cinders and it worked well on its initial outings. It did not last, for the firm was far more involved in road racing, and the dirt-track model was swept away by the JAP engine within a season or two.

1930 was a year in the doldrums for Norton, both on the race circuits and in the showrooms, but 1931 changed all that. Moore had left the firm and taken his camshaft design with him, but in his place came Arthur Carroll, who redesigned the engine into the form that was to run to 1963. At first it had teething problems, but by late 1930 it was winning races and ready for the decade.

1931 brought a radical change to the side- and overhead-valve models, which assumed what was in effect their final form for the next three decades. The engine changes were straightforward and simple. The magneto went behind the engine, where it was chain driven from the inlet camshaft and had the dynamo strapped to its back. The lubrication became dry sump with a simple gear pump in the timing chest.

The model numbers and engine dimensions remained the same, so the 500s still used the famous 79 × 100 mm sizes. 350s were 71 × 88 mm as always, the model 19 was 79 × 120 mm and 588 cc, while the Big 4 was 82 × 120 mm and 634 cc. The frame usage also stayed as it was, so the 16H, Big 4, 18, 19 and 20 continued with a diamond frame, as did the footboard-equipped model 2 version of the 490 cc sv machine.

For the JE, ES2, 22, CJ and CS1 it was the cradle frame with the smaller camshaft model still in the

Above **A 1932 Norton International with famous Carroll camshaft design**

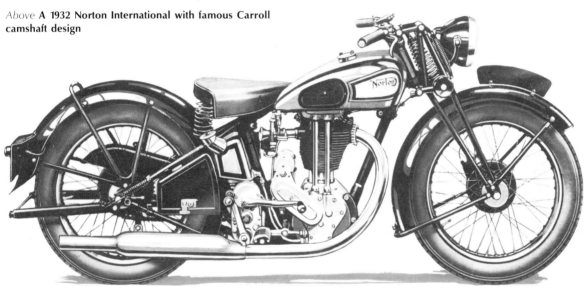

Above **Typical ohv model 50 Norton of 348 cc from 1935**
Below **This 1937 348 cc Norton CJ has the same transmission as the ohv models**

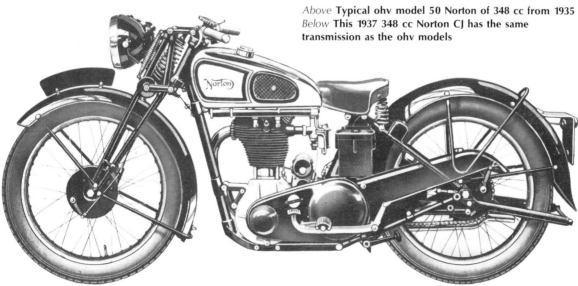

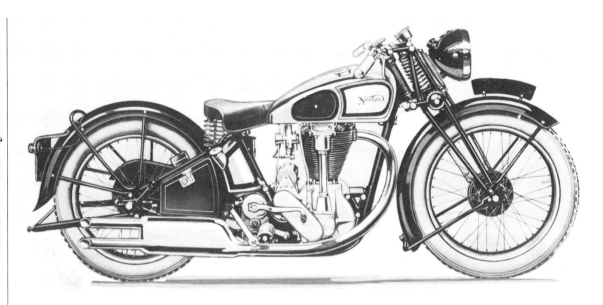

Norton 490 cc CS1 fitted with the strange silencer common to all models in 1938 including the trials one

two-stay type. The camshaft engines were the Carroll type with its bottom bevel box, outboard magneto drive and new look that was to become very familiar. All models other than the CJ had their exhaust pipe on the left and there was a four-speed gearbox option.

Norton had a most successful 1931 racing season and this was reflected by the appearance of the new International models in 1932. There were two of these based on the existing camshaft machines but built with racing magneto, tuned engine, option of silencer or straight open-pipe and fitted with a four-speed gearbox. They were listed without lights, although a mag-dyno could be had as an option and came as the 348 cc model 40 and 490 cc model 30. Equipment included a large wrapround oil tank which occupied the space normally taken by both the standard tank and the battery, quick-filler caps for the tanks, TT mudguards and a Moseley 'Float-on-air' pad for the rear one. Both tanks had scalloped edges and the oil tank filler was on the left to suit the pits at the TT.

The idea was for the Inter to be for racing while the CS1 and CJ continued for road work, but in practice it did not work quite that way. The fast road men wanted the Inter's four-speed gearbox and that big seductive petrol tank, so they ordered a model 30 with mag-dyno and quickly fixed it up with lights. Touring riders avoided the CS1 with its bevels and oil leaks to buy the cheaper ES2 and add a few extras.

The road range of sv and ohv models was as before except that the JE and 22 faded from the

scene. Exhaust pipes moved to the right on the 16H, Big 4 and CS1, where they were from the start on the 30 and 40. Norton wheels with three-stud fixing of hub to brake drum were also adopted that year.

Their design seemed complex, for the wheel bearings went into a sleeve with a large T-bar end and this screwed into the back of the brake drum. A cone next to the T end matched one in the hub so that the latter was held against the drum and located on the three studs. Three nuts made sure it stayed in place and the assembly turned on the wheel spindle. The wheels were thus qd and interchangeable.

The arrangement was altered for 1933, when it was simplified to three long nuts which held the hub to brake drum. A drum and an end cap hid them from view but also were prone to hold water, and this led to corrosion.

For 1933 there were Norton forks with check springs for the Inters and a four-speed box for the CS1 and CJ, although a positive stop remained an option. The model 19 changed its dimensions to 82×113 mm, which made the capacity 597 cc, and two new 350s appeared. These were the model 50 and twin-port 55, which kept to the traditional 71×88 mm and 348 cc. Both were ohv engines and much as the models 18 and 20 as regards cycle parts. All ohv models were fitted with the four-speed gearbox, which remained an option for the sv ones.

The side-valve 16H built by Norton for many years and seen here in 1939 form with enclosed valve gear

For all models in 1933 there was an option of a tank-top instrument panel and suitable petrol tank to allow it to be fitted flush. It carried the speedometer, ammeter and light switch, while a further option was a blanking disc to cover the hole left should the speedometer be removed. High-level exhaust systems and raised frames continued to be listed for Colonial use, as it was termed, and found favour with competition riders.

1934 saw the works racing Nortons continue to dominate European and TT racing as they had since 1931, while the road models ticked on with detail improvements. Norton forks with check springs went on to all models, as did a Norton clutch with shock absorber which deleted that item from the crankshaft end. An oil bath primary case and neater positive stop mechanism was adopted and in the sv and ohv engines the camshaft gears were moved to become a train which reversed the direction of magneto rotation. On the Inters only a narrower one-piece front hub and drum came into use. The road model range was as the year before and remained the same from then on up to 1939 and the war.

The famous Norton four-speed, footchange gearbox went on to all models for 1935. It was a major step forward and was accompanied by a move to the right by the remaining exhaust systems and the appearance of hairpin valve springs on the Inters as standard and aluminium-bronze heads as an option. The latter were intended for racing and not best suited to road use.

In 1936 the ohv models lost the spindly look about the engines as the pushrod tubes were made fatter. The Inters gained the option of bi-metal, aluminium-finned, bronze skull heads and light alloy barrels plus a change to 14 mm plugs, which went on to the ohv machines the following year.

For road use 1937 saw the adoption of the two-brush dynamo and separate regulator box for all models. At the same time the light switch moved from the rear of the headlamp shell to join the ammeter in a small top panel where a tank-top panel was not fitted.

1938 brought noticeable changes to most models with the option of plunger rear suspension for the Inters. For the ohv machines the pushrod tubes were angled in at the top and the valve gear fully enclosed, as it was on the sv ones. All were fitted with a strange silencer with twin rear outlets that found favour with no one.

The odd fitment was even used on the trials Norton. This format dated from 1935 and had taken over from the old Colonial specification for competition-orientated riders. In theory at least it could apply to any model in the range and really was a factory kit of options fitted on the assembly line. Items used included special gear ratios, raised exhaust system, high-clearance frame, narrow front fork and hub, folding kickstarter and chrome-plated mudguards, chaincase and chainguard.

Also rather special but not in the catalogues

was the big banger camshaft model. This first appeared around 1936/37 with the model 19 dimensions and 597 cc capacity. It was based on the CS1, but was only intended for sidecar use and then for road racing or ISDT work. To suit the former, some were built with bimetal heads and to get the tall engine into the frame the top tube had to be kinked. There were not many of them, but they dominated sidecar racing in the early post-war years.

The last year of the decade saw a return to a tubular silencer and two options for the ES2. The first was the plunger frame and the second the International type of petrol tank which transformed the appearance. The CS1 and CJ were also given the option of the plunger frame.

The Inters were listed in two forms. The first was a road machine much as the C models, but with bigger petrol and oil tanks plus more highly tuned engine. For them a light alloy head and barrel were listed as an option. To supplement the road machines there were a pair of Racing International models, referred to also as the Manx Grand Prix and the forerunners of the post-war Manx model. These machines were built for racing with bench-tested alloy engines, racing magneto and carburettor, close-ratio gearbox, megaphone exhaust, plunger frame and conical hubs.

It was a fine model on which to finish off, for ahead lay the war, many thousands of 16H models and then peacetime austerity. The signs were there at the end of 1938, when the firm announced that it would not be competing in road racing the following year. The reasons given were the disruption it caused and the amount of production work that had to be done. Much of this was of course for the services to deal with the contracts the firm had won.

The full range was listed for 1940 and should have included revised engines and frames for many models. These never came, for post-war the need was for immediate production rather than innovation.

NUT

Newcastle upon Tyne was the home-town of this marque, hence the initials for the name. It was a small company, founded in 1911, but in 1913 a NUT, ridden by Hugh Mason, won the Junior TT. He more or less ran the firm and in the early 1920s had to find fresh backing when the original finance was withdrawn.

He managed this, but then moved on, and the firm struggled to keep going building V-twins of quality and, inevitably, high price. They moved more than once and this created gaps in production, so no models were listed for 1930, but later in the year a range became available.

The power units were JAP, but the V-twins were all specially prepared for NUT and came in 500 cc ohv, 700 cc ohv and 750 cc side-valve form. There were also a pair of singles, both of 350 cc, one sv and one ohv. The cycle parts were conventional and the machines were fully equipped to a high standard. Front forks were Brampton, gearboxes from Burman and on some of the twins a Bowden carburettor was fitted.

The same range was offered for 1932 and one 700 was fitted with disc wheels for a Rhodesian customer. For 1933 the range listed was extended to add 500 and 700 cc ohc V-twins and a 250 cc ohv single, while the 350 cc models were dropped. It is unlikely any of these ever came about, for production was by then minimal and during the year came to a final halt.

Big NUT 700 ohv twin of 1933, their last year. A machine with style and line, high quality but equally high price

OEC

The Osborn Engineering Company were far removed from the centre of the motorcycle industry, for their works was at Gosport in Hampshire. In spite of, or maybe because of, this they produced some unusual machines, with the design work going into the steering and suspension systems, while the power units remained the same as those used by many other small companies.

They went in for record breaking in the 1920s and in 1925 Claude Temple used an OEC to set the one-hour world record over 100 miles for the first time. He was also the first to set the world's maximum over 120 mph and did this in 1926. In 1930 Joe Wright broke this record twice, but the second record, when the figure went over 150 mph for the first time, became the subject of a scandal. An OEC went on show as the record breaker, but then someone realized that it was not the correct machine and that Wright had used his own Zenith for the run that counted.

The difference was important, for the OEC had their duplex steering system with the inference

that it had played its part, whereas the Zenith had a normal frame and girder forks.

The duplex steering system dated from 1927 and went on the firm's duplex cradle frame which was first used late in 1924. By 1930 it had evolved into a design with single downtube and twin lower engine rails. These extended forward of the crankcase nearly to the wheel centre and were bowed out for tyre clearance on full lock, although that was rather limited.

The front end of each extended lower rail was joined to a tube that ran up and back at an angle akin to a steering head one. At the top the two tubes were joined by a cross-member which was part of the main frame. In each tube went races and a spindle which had links attached to it top and bottom.

The links pointed ahead and in and were joined by two more spindles. On these were two further tubes which thus lay parallel to the first, fixed pair but were closer together. They held the front wheel and could move on their spindles against springs. The total effect was what is known to engineers as a four-bar chain and viewed from above was much as Ackermann car steering but turned round.

The effect when riding was odd, as any movement of the bars, which were clamped to the top junction between the front tube pair, raised the machine relative to the front end. This induced a massive self-centring effect, heavy steering, no feedback from the road and the ability to withstand heavy blows on the bars without deviation from the set course.

A couple of years later OEC added rear

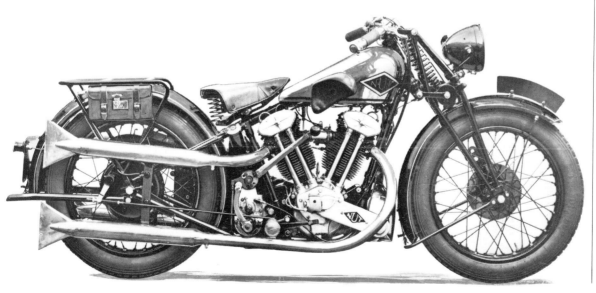

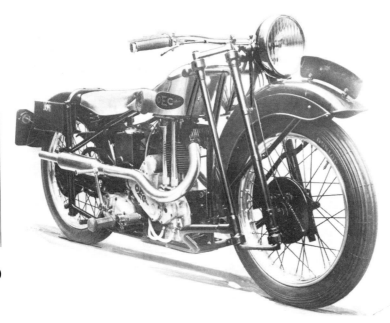

Top 1931 OEC Flying Squad model with 980 cc ohv JAP engine in the duplex frame with rear suspension and duplex front end
Centre 148 cc OEC model 34/1 of 1934 with rear suspension, an unusual feature for a small machine at that time
Left A view of the front end of an OEC model 36/2 with 497 cc Matchless engine and odd rear suspension. A 1936 model

suspension as an option for their machines. This was slightly more conventional in that the wheel was carried in a pivoted fork, but the springs that controlled it went into plunger units. Links joined the two, but while the system was common in Europe in the late 1930s it was not in England.

In 1930 when you bought an OEC you received the duplex steering, but the rear suspension was still an option. A range of engines were offered in 350 and 500 sizes, in sv and ohv and made by Blackburne or JAP, except for the 350 cc side-valve, which came with Blackburne or Sturmey-Archer units.

These both went for 1931 when all models had the spring frame as well as the duplex steering and all were JAP powered. The singles had 346 and 490 cc sv or ohv engines and there were twins with ohv units of 498, 680 and 980 cc plus side-valve ones of 750 and 1000 cc.

The whole range continued for 1932 plus models with 600 cc sv or ohv JAP engines, and as befitted a small firm just about any model could be had with a sports engine and many of the ohv ones with a racing unit. Gearboxes were all Burman footchange and all except the 500 ohv single had three speeds, the exception having four. All models continued with the special frame.

1933 brought a model with a 245 cc ohv JAP engine and this too had a four-speed gearbox. The other singles all continued, but not the two smallest V-twins. The ones left were the 980 cc ohv and the 750 and 1000 cc side-valves.

The whole range changed to new engines for 1934, but all models had rear suspension to the same design as before and all had the option of the duplex steering. As standard the frames were of conventional form with tubular girder forks.

The smaller machines had Villiers engines and the 34/1 was fitted with a 148 cc unit and the 34/2 with a 249 cc one. Both had petroil lubrication, flywheel magneto ignition and three-speed Burman gearboxes with footchange. The larger model was also available with a 346 cc engine or a 249 cc water-cooled unit. The other models all used Matchless engines with ohv singles of 245, 348 and 497 cc plus one with a 497 cc sv single and another with a 982 cc sv V-twin. The top of the range was the 34/8, which had the 592 cc ohc Matchless Silver Hawk V-4 engine fitted.

In July 1934 the Press carried details of a novel OEC which was enclosed to form a two-wheeled car. This was a prototype and when it reached production it was listed as a Whitwood as a

separate make and will be treated as such here.

When the 1935 range was announced it was seen to be smaller and without the Villiers-powered models, the sv 497 or the ohc V4. Left were five singles and the 982 cc V-twin. The 245 and 348 cc ohv models were listed in standard and de luxe forms, the first with coil ignition and three speeds, the second with magneto and four-speed. The 497 cc model was only listed in de luxe form and all models continued to have rear suspension and the duplex steering option.

Aside from the Whitwood, OEC themselves introduced an innovative design on rather similar lines for 1936. They called the result the Atlanta Duo and its major features were a 21 in. seat height allied to footboards that positioned the rider's feet well forward.

To achieve the low seat level the engine was tilted well forward and its combined fuel and oil tank positioned above the gearbox. The mechanics went into a frame comprising four tubes running along the machine with the normal OEC rear suspension modified to plunger and simply attached to the rear of the tubes. At the front went the duplex steering and the dualseat sat above the frame with a cowl ahead of it and a very wide mudguard with backrest at the rear. The footboards were long and at the front ran into legshields which extended well back on their inner sides.

Three of these models were listed with the choice of 245 or 500 cc ohv single cylinder or 750 cc V-twin JAP engines. The first two had coil ignition and the twin a magneto, while all had a four-speed Burman gearbox with the option of foot or handchange. A windscreen was available as an extra and the machines were fully equipped.

Only three other models ran on and these had the Matchless engines and were in the same configuration of 245 and 497 cc ohv singles and the 982 cc sv V-twin. The smallest had coil ignition and all had the footchange, four-speed Burman gearbox. The duplex steering was fitted as standard and the conventional system with girder fork became the option.

In October 1936 the 1937 range was listed as six models, all de luxe with rear springing and girder forks, the duplex steering reverting to being optional. Engines were Matchless singles of 245, 348 or 497 cc with ohv and there were three V-twins of 750, 1000 and 1100 cc and side-valves.

Then in February 1937 the range was revised to four models and the engine type changed to AJS,

The very strange OEC Atlanta Duo of 1936 with feet-forward riding stance and the usual duplex steering

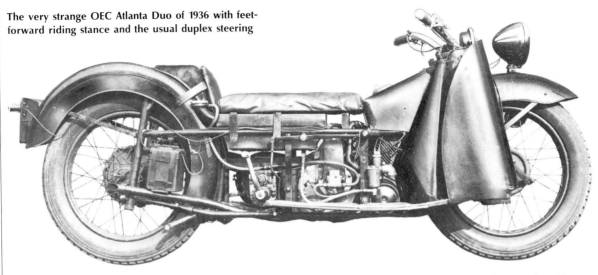

Above OEC Atlanta Duo viewed from the saddle to show the odd steering linkage and instrument panel detail

with the forward magneto on the singles. These were in 245, 348 and 497 cc sizes and all had twin-port heads and exhausts terminating in megaphone-style silencers. The fourth model had the 982 cc sv V-twin engine.

New was the rear suspension, although it still used the same principle. The difference was that the rear wheel was held in short arms that pivoted in bearings formed in the front of the spring box forgings. They were thus half their previous length and no longer connected together. The arms were linked to spring-controlled plungers as before and friction dampers were built into their main pivot.

Below 1939 OEC Commodore with short rear suspension arms, megaphone exhaust and Girling wedge action brakes. The engine is an AJS of 497 cc

Any variation between setting would have aggravated the tendency for the wheel to lay over. At the front went Druid girder forks or the OEC duplex steering.

There were five models listed for 1938 and all had the revised rear suspension and names in place of type numbers. Engines continued to be of the AJS pattern and capacities were 245, 348 and 497 cc, all singles and all with ohv. The smallest model was called the Ensign and only built with girder forks, but the 348 cc Cadet and 497 cc Commander could be had with the Druids or duplex steering as distinct models to produce the five listed. In the latter guise they became the Cadet- or Commander-Duplex.

The 1939 list stretched to six, with three each with girder or duplex front end. There were only two capacities, with the 497 cc Commander continuing and being joined by the same-sized Commodore. This had a tuned version of the engine with crossover hairpin valve springs fully enclosed, unlike those of the Commander, which were exposed and not crossed. The remaining model was the 348 cc Cadet.

On all models the rear suspension movement was increased, the petrol tank redesigned, the exhaust systems reshaped and Girling brakes adopted. These were cable operated with a wedge action and a similar design at the other end of the shoe enabled them to be adjusted. On the Commodore each hub had two drums with a ribbed alloy muff between them and this aided cooling and hub rigidity. The rear brakes were operated by cables from the two ends of a cross-over shaft which also carried the pedal, and each cable had an adjuster. The front brakes had a balance beam compensator to work them both. The twin drum brakes were available as an option for the other models.

In March 1939 the firm added two lightweights to its list with 98 or 122 cc Villiers engines in a simple rigid frame with blade girders. It is likely that few were built, as they were not in the 1940 list, which just had the three basic ohv models. Then production stopped and did not restart until 1949, when OEC built Villiers-powered models up to 1954.

OK Supreme

1928 was the year that OK won their solitary TT, the 250, although they were placed for the next two years. They dated from the turn of the century and up to 1926 were simply the OK. The partners then split and Ernie Humphries added the Supreme part of the title and went on to produce some interesting but hardly profitable models. Such men enlivened the scene in the 1930s and we all owe them a debt, for it would have been a drab time without them.

The range for 1930 was prosaic enough, with vertical JAP engines in conventional cycle parts. The model B had a 300 cc sv engine with front magneto, but the others had that item behind the cylinder. There was a 245 cc ohv, a twin-port 490 cc and three of 346 cc, all with ohv and listed as one-port, two-port and super sports. There was a further model with a 344 cc engine and listed as a light ohv model. With side valves were two of 490 cc, one a roadster and the other a sports model.

In May 1930 this range was joined by the M/30 with a 747 cc sv JAP V-twin engine, but a little later came a much more interesting machine. Designed by George H. Jones, this was the one that became known as the Lighthouse and was based on the design raced by the firm from 1930.

The new model was of 248 cc capacity with an inclined cylinder on top of a very substantial crankcase. This was partly because the oil tank for the dry sump system was included in it but also because it rose well up the cylinder, which was short with few fins. This aspect was emphasized by the use of a short stroke for the engine.

The camshaft drive went on the right with a vertical shaft driven by bevel gears. It ran in a tunnel and carried bronze cams at the top end so was in effect the camshaft. The cams moved short tappets that lay across the engine and these moved rockers to open the valves. The top of the shaft tunnel had a small glass window in it for checking the oil supply and it was from this that the model gained its nickname.

The drive side of the engine was also quite impressive with crankcase, short stubby barrel and a large cast-alloy chaincase which enclosed the transmission and the magneto drive. This went behind the engine and a mag-dyno was fitted on the road models. A three-speed gearbox with hand control was used and the rest was standard industry but with a neat shape of knee-grip fitted to the tank.

There was also a new 245 cc dry sump ohv JAP-powered model for 1931 as well as the one from the previous year. All models now had a /31 suffix and amounted to the 300, 490 and 747 cc side-valve machines plus one each of 346 and 490 ohv.

There were eight models for 1932 with two new ones and no V-twin. The first newcomer was one of many that appeared to fall in the 150 cc tax bracket and was the model P/32 with 148 cc side-valve JAP engine. This had an inclined cylinder, coil ignition and the points mounted on the end of the dynamo. The gearbox was a Burman three-speed and the cycle parts of the simplest, which kept the weight to 172 lb. The second was the 490 cc racing model R fitted with a JAP engine.

The rest of the range was much as before, for it was the time to keep costs to a minimum. All models took a /32 suffix and there was the 248 cc ohc, 245, 346 and 490 cc ohv, and the 300 and 490 cc sv. From early in the New Year the ohc and ohv models were also listed in competition form with footchange and raised exhaust systems.

The 150 failed to make it into 1933, but in its place there were two light models both with JAP engines. One was of 346 cc and was called the Coeur de Lion and the other was the 245 cc Flying Cloud. Both had three speeds, a duplex frame and the option of coil or magneto ignition. The smaller was also listed as the G33 de luxe when it had four speeds and extra equipment. A shield covered the right side of the engine and gearbox while a second one went ahead of the crankcase.

The camshaft engine was still listed as the A/33 but now had a four-speed gearbox with the option of foot control. Finally, the two 490 cc models continued with detail improvements as the sv N33 and ohv L33, but were joined by the LB33 in July 1933. This had a new single-port ohv head, special cams and piston to make a de luxe model which was named Britannia.

All the models had names for 1934 with the LB 34 as above, the L/34 as the Phantom and the side-valve N/34 as the Hood. There were three 245 cc

ohv Flying Clouds in standard G34, de luxe GDL34 and sports G2/34 versions. For all, the frame was modified to move the engine forward and this allowed the dynamo to go in the engine plates directly behind the crankcase. The metal shield on the right was made neater and for the de luxe there were covers on both sides. A very neat feature was the battery mounting, which allowed this component to be easily swung out for servicing.

There were two 346 cc Coeur de Lion models with ohv JAP engines. The GS/34 was the standard and the GS2/34 the de luxe with four speeds, mag-dyno and the engine shields.

There was a new ohc design for 1935 built in 248 and 346 cc sizes and called the Silver Cloud. Each came in standard or racing forms and the same engines were also used for a pair of trials models. The engines were more conventional than the Lighthouse with a straightforward vertical shaft and bevels layout for the single-camshaft design. The rockers were two-piece with an external valve arm which helped to keep the oil inside. Ignition was by magneto and lubrication dry sump.

On the cycle side went four speeds, footchange and a straight-through exhaust on the racer, which also had a much larger oil tank. For the rest it was as expected for sports or racing use.

Among the ohv models the 245 cc ones ran on as the Flying Cloud in standard and de luxe forms and were joined by a low-cost version named the V35 Dauntless with coil ignition. The two 346 cc ohv machines continued, as did the sv and ohv 490 cc ones. The final model was the Road Knight, which had a 600 cc side-valve engine and was only sold complete with a Hughes sidecar.

The six Silver Clouds continued with no real changes for 1936, as did the 490 cc side-valve Hood. The rest were new and there was a 346, two of 498 cc and no fewer than five 245 cc models. All had ohv and the largest a camshaft mounted high in the timing chest, where it was chain driven. The pushrods splayed out from this point with the two tubes forming a vee and this allowed the use of straight rockers across the head. This OK engine powered both the R/36 Sports and S/36 Special model, with the first having a tuned power unit and high-level exhaust.

The other machines had new JAP engines of 245 and 346 cc and these were developed from earlier models. Lubrication was total loss and the base model was the GT/36 with three speeds and coil ignition. Next came the G/36 with four speeds and

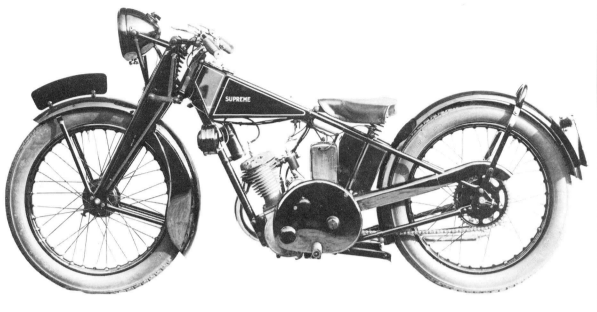

Top **Very basic 1932 model P/32 OK Supreme fitted with a 148 cc side-valve JAP engine and built to fall into the 150 cc tax bracket**

Centre **The famous Lighthouse model OK Supreme with 248 cc ohc engine that had the cams at the top of the vertical shaft and window to inspect them by. 1932 model**

Left **1934 OK Supreme with 490 cc side-valve JAP engine, listed as the model N/34**

Left **The 1935 Silver Cloud model WS/35 OK Supreme with more conventional 346 cc ohc engine**
Above right **One of the Flying Clouds, the 1935 245 cc GDL/35 OK Supreme with partial enclosure of the engine and gearbox**
Below right **The 1938 OK Supreme AC/38 with high camshaft 245 cc JAP engine which was only used for one season**

magneto and then the GDL/36 with better forks and equipment. All three retained the Flying Cloud name. The other two of 245 cc were the higher-tuned Sports 70 in three- or four-speed form (G70 or GT70) and finally came the 346 cc GH/36 Grand Sports.

The range was thinned out a little for 1937 with only four ohc models listed, two of each size for road or track use. The 248 cc road model took the name Pilot, but the 346 cc remained a Silver Cloud. From the ohv 250s of the year before three continued, as the G/37, GDL/37 and G70/37, all with the Flying Cloud name. The 346 cc model also continued and this lighter end of the range was joined by the SV/37, which had a 245 cc side-valve engine.

The two models with 496 cc engines with splayed pushrod tubes were no longer in the lists and in their place was the L/37 Phantom. This had a single-port 490 cc JAP engine with dry sump lubrication and magneto ignition.

There were 14 models for 1938, including three new ones with high-camshaft JAP engines. These had a most distinctive line with a single pushrod tube that gave an air of ohc and an outer chaincase to enclose the drive to the mag-dyno. The camshaft was also driven by a short chain and it was from this that the second chain was turned. Both had tensioners and the valve gear was fully enclosed. The new engines were in 245, 346 and

498 cc sizes and the models they went in were the AC/38, BC/38 and HC/38.

Most of the other machines came from the previous year, except the N/38, which had slipped from the list for 1937 but was now back again. Ones that ran on were the 245 cc G/38, GDL/38, G70/38 and SV/38. The four camshaft machines were still there plus the 490 cc ohv L/38.

The high-camshaft and ohc models could be obtained in trials trim as an option, but the last model in the list was a pure competition one. It was the GT Special /38 and built for grass-track racing with a 344 cc JAP engine set up to run on alcohol fuel, with the rest of the machine constructed to suit its purpose.

In May 1938 the ohc engines had their valve gear fully enclosed and the valve spring design changed. In place of the normal arrangement there were four springs laid side by side to lie fore and aft along the engine. The rear end of each went under the inlet valve collet and the front under the exhaust one. Each spring had two coils formed in its length, so these lay in between the rocker spindles near the centreline and on that line went a cross-pin over which the centre of the spring ran.

For 1939 the high-camshaft JAP engines were dropped and six models with Matchless single power units appeared. Left from the past were the 245 cc side-valve SV/39 and the ohv G/39, GD7/39

and G70/39, all known as Flying Clouds. The ohc road models were still listed as the 248 cc CG/39 Pilot and 346 cc WS/39 Silver Cloud, while the grass-track machine became the GTS/39 Alcohol Special and was also listed in a suitable form for Brooklands.

Two sizes of Matchless ohv engine were used but in various forms. The basic 348 cc model was the BA/39 Snowden Ranger, which used the G3 engine with coil ignition. It was also listed in de luxe form as the CA/39 and in this case was fitted with a magneto. Third came the JA/39 Utility, which was only sold as a sidecar outfit with the G3 coil ignition motor, while fourth was the GA/39 Gladiator which had the sports G4 engine.

The 497 cc HA/39 was equally sporting and had the same name and the G90 engine, while the DA/39 Dominion used the G80. All these models

had dry sump lubrication, four-speed gearboxes and conventional cycle parts.

In April 1939 a further special 348 cc model was added to the list in the form of the RRS/39. This was a road-racing version of the grass model, but was supplied with full road equipment. It could thus be ridden to meetings and was similar to one being campaigned by Les Graham. Suitable options and extras helped it in its task.

The whole range less the racer and the camshaft models was listed for 1940 and in November 1939 a big V-twin was added to it. This had a 750 cc side-valve JAP engine and was first shown in a matt service finish. In a later listing it no longer appeared, although the RRS/40 did, but by then the firm was engaged on more vital work.

Post-war they were rumoured to have assembled a small batch of GTS models, but then turned to making accessories.

OMC

P&P

This 1930 make was marketed by C. G. Vale-Onslow, brother of Len Vale-Onslow, who manufactured the SOS, and indeed the OMC was built at the SOS works. It was a typical lightweight and powered by a 172 cc Villiers super sports engine which had auto-lube and a flywheel magneto for ignition and direct lighting.

A three-speed Burman gearbox was specified with handchange in a gate on the side of the tank. The engine and gearbox went into a pin joint frame with twin downtubes and two pairs of seat tubes. The latter all ran from the saddle nose to either side of the gearbox. Webb tubular girders were fitted and the brakes came from the same company. Equipment included a Lycett Aero saddle, Dunlop tyres, a rear carrier and an oil tank that tucked between the four seat tubes. A saddle petrol tank was fitted and finished in French grey with a red panel and lining.

Few of these machines seem to have been built and the make was not listed for 1931.

Packmann & Poppe machines were built at the Montgomery works in the early 1920s and their best-known model was one called the Silent Three. This had a Barr and Stroud sleeve-valve engine and the designers went to considerable trouble to reduce the noise level of the complete machine.

Their machines ceased to be listed from around the mid-1920s due to a fire at the Montgomery works and a little later P&P linked up with the Wooler concern. The make was then revived and for 1930 was listed with four rather different models, three with spring frames and four-speed gearboxes.

The odd man out was the model 90, which had a 500 cc ohv engine. Of the same capacity but with ohc was the Silent 500, while there were two models for the smaller-size end of the market. One had a 245 cc ohv JAP engine and was the model 80 and the other, the 60, was a 199 cc two-stroke.

During 1930 production of these machines ceased and the marque withdrew from the market.

Rare 1930 OMC fitted with 172 cc Villiers engine

Panther

Mention of this make brings one of two images to mind for most people. Either it is of a massive sidecar outfit propelled by a machine with sloping engine in place of its downtube and turning over slowly but with great finality, or it is the incredibly cheap Red Panther in the line-up at Pride & Clarke's emporium in Stockwell Road, Brixton.

The firm's name was Phelon & Moore and it was founded in 1904, but Joah Phelon was involved with powered transport as early as 1895. In 1901 he took out a patent covering the use of the engine in place of the downtube and the idea of long bolts to hold the main bearings, cylinder and head as one unit to contain the stress.

The Panther name came in the 1920s and at first applied to one model, but in time became the range, although the company was still P&M at the end. There was also a Panthette, which was a 250 cc transverse V-twin with unit construction built between 1926 and 1928, but it did not sell well and led in time to a small range of Villiers-powered models.

These were still listed in 1930 and made use of the Panthette frame members to house 147, 196 and 247 cc Villiers engines. The machines were simple but inexpensive, so sold well. The other models in the range had the traditional inclined engine and were the 499 cc model 50 and 594 cc models 60 and 85 Redwing. They were very easy to spot on the road with the engine laid in as the downtube and the timing cover at right angles to it and stretching far up to the dynamo. With a saddle tank they had nice lines and a style of the 1930s rather than of the decade before. As with all good Panthers they carried their oil in the crankcase for the dry sump system, had ohv and the pushrods enclosed in a single tube.

For 1931 the 85 was dropped, but there were two Redwings in its place as the models 90 and 95 with a new 490 cc engine and three- or four-speed gearboxes. There was also a 499 cc model 55 and a 594 cc 65, as well as the three with Villiers engines as the 15, 20 and 25. The big engines were available with magneto or coil ignition and the machines had a novel headlamp dip system. In this there were two shells side by side with the right turned off on dip and the left swung down and left by a cable. A left twistgrip activated the cable and acted as the switch for the right lamp. A small instrument panel went above the lamps and carried a clock and the speedometer.

The most important model listed in the 1932 range was the new 249 cc single. This had the engine inclined in the frame, ohv and the oil tank formed in the front section of the crankcase. Ignition was by magneto, which went to the rear of the cylinder and was gear driven. The pushrods were enclosed within a single tube and the rocker

Also rare is this 1930 P&P model 90 with 500 cc ohv engine

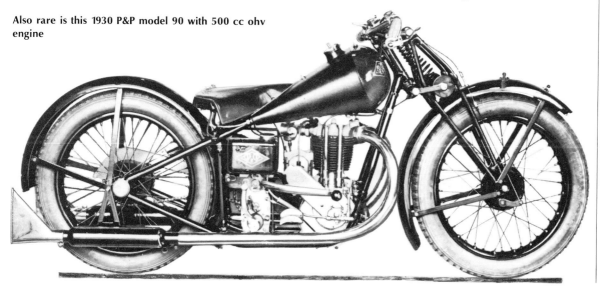

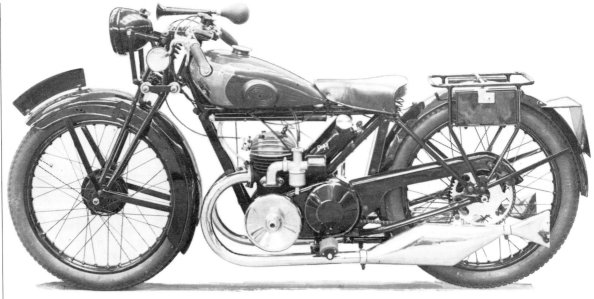

Above **Panther 25 with 247 cc Villiers engine as in 1931**
Below **Famous Panther sloper, this being a 1932 Redwing 90 of 490 cc**

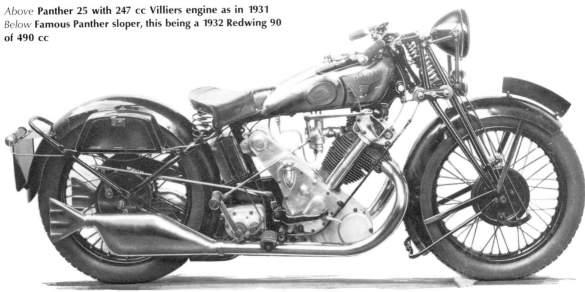

box was bolted to the right side of the cylinder head.

The frame was conventional with a downtube and the rest of the machine the same with a three-speed gearbox, although there was the option of four. Either were hand controlled and the model had centre spring girder forks, saddle tank and a centre stand. With a two-port head it was the model 40, but was also listed with a single port as the 30, when it scraped under the weight limit.

There were four larger ohv models in two sizes with the 50 and 60 as before and the Redwing 90 being joined by the 594 cc Redwing 100. All changed to a duplex primary chain and continued with interconnected brakes, while the Redwing

engines had the same rocker box side mounting as the 30 and 40. Lighting options included the twin headlamp system again. The range was completed by two Villiers-powered machines, the 147 cc 10 and 247 cc 20. It was joined by the Express model in March 1932, being a cut-price version of the 50.

For 1933 Panther bored out the 249 cc single to create the 348 cc ohv model 45. It had a new and stronger frame, bigger brakes, bigger tank and options of three or four speeds and hand or foot gearchange. In appearance it was very much as the smaller model, which continued in two-port model 40 form.

The big singles had new frames and their engines were modified to use two long U-bolts to

on the 250 but with a red panelled tank instead of the normal green one and whose price was cut to the bone by bulk buying. There were two models with acetylene or electric lighting and the low price brought plenty of customers, which kept the factory very busy. The model 40 remained, but there were few buyers, for the price difference was significant.

The firm got round this for 1934 by calling their own models the Redwing 70 and 80 and fitting four-speed footchange gearboxes and twin-port heads. The Red Panther's price was kept down with three speeds, one exhaust system, hand-change and coil ignition. This applied to the basic 249 cc model 20 and the new 348 cc model 30 which joined it. There was also a 10, which did have four gears but was otherwise as the 20.

Above **Dipping system with the left shell moved by cable**
Below **The 1935 249 cc model 20 Red Panther sold by Pride & Clarke**

clamp crankcase, barrel, head, rocker box and steering head as one. The forks were a new type of Webb girder and a roll-on rear stand was fitted. The primary chain reverted to the single pitch type and the four models in two capacities and Special and Redwing builds continued. New petrol tanks were fitted, and where handchange was supplied the lever worked in a slot in the tank top. This allowed large, soft knee-grips to be used and these were set into the tank sides. The two-strokes were no longer listed.

Early in 1933 Panther reached an agreement with Pride & Clarke of Stockwell Road, London, which helped both in those hard times. The outcome was the Red Panther, which was based

The four big singles were little changed and retained their coupled brakes and twin headlamp option. New were the Stroud trials models, which were based on the 70 and 80 but fully prepared for their specialized use. They thus had competition tyres, narrow mudguards, raised exhaust for the one-port head and a crankcase shield. Each engine was prepared to suit and the clutch had special fabric inserts.

Just how good the Red Panther could be was shown to all when the firm won the Maudes Trophy late in 1934 for tests carried out a year earlier. These had been at Brooklands and were to highlight economy, speed, safety and easy servicing.

1935 saw the Red Panthers with a new cylinder head with fully enclosed valves. Adjustment was by eccentric rocker spindles and there were now four models. Base was the 20 with coil ignition and three speeds and next came the de luxe 10 with four speeds and magneto but still with hand-change. The third 250 was the 70 with footchange and fourth the 348 cc model 30.

The four big singles had new crankcases with a bigger and well-finned oil tank section, and modified timing gears as an aid to quiet running. Tappets appeared between the cams and pushrods, while there were a number of detail improvements. The final model was the 348 cc Redwing 80, much as the year before, while the Stroud trials models continued but to special order only and in very small numbers.

The Red Panthers were three in number for 1936 with the 249 cc 20 and de luxe 71, a revised 70, plus the 348 cc 30. All had a revised cylinder head with screw tappet adjustment and a new, well-ribbed crankcase with improved lubrication system. Ignition was still by coil, transmission three speeds and exhaust systems single for the basic model, but the 71 had a Maglita, four speeds and

two exhausts respectively.

The bigger singles were down to the Redwings 90 and 100 with full valve enclosure, a fibre coupling between the magneto and its drive, and a duplex chain to drive the dynamo. The clutch now ran dry, so the inserts became fabric and a four-speed footchange gearbox was used.

The range was again completed by the 348 cc model 80, which was joined by the Redwing 85 of the same size but designed for sidecar work. It had a single-port version of the engine, a four-speed gearbox and lugs to take the chair connections.

It was detail changes only and fewer models for 1937 with just two Red Panthers, as the 20 and 30, and three Redwings, as the 85, 90 and 100. For the latter there was a new colour scheme in place of the green panels and leaping panther transfer. The chrome tanks now had ivory panels with a panther's head transfer below the name, all lined out in red and black. The wheel rims were to match, which enhanced the effect.

The same applied to 1938, when the cylinder head and rocker box of the engines was modifed and the Redwing 90 was listed as the 100 but fitted with the 490 cc engine. This changed early in 1938

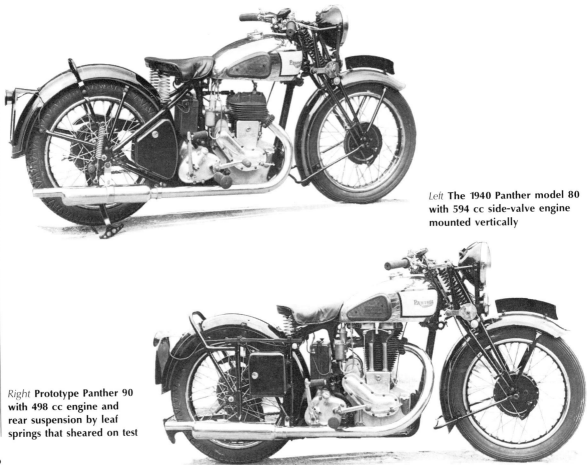

Left **The 1940 Panther model 80 with 594 cc side-valve engine mounted vertically**

Right **Prototype Panther 90 with 498 cc engine and rear suspension by leaf springs that sheared on test**

when the Redwing 95 appeared in its place, based on the design of the 85 with inclined engine and frame downtube. The capacity was 498 cc and the engine had a single port and fully enclosed valves and valve gear.

It was much the same for 1939 with the 20 still the cheapest, fully equipped 250 on the market. Quite an achievement and one that benefited both P&C and P&M. There were lubrication changes and other details altered for both the 20 and 30, and they were joined by the 40, which was a de luxe edition of the 249 cc model. On the larger models the 100 had a new frame and rear hub, which also went on the 95. Both, and the 85, had a new pressed-steel primary chaincase.

During 1939 Panther ran another test to enter for the Maudes Trophy, which was now with BSA. For this they chose to run a model 100 from London to Leeds until 10,000 miles had been covered. It took just over ten days, despite some vile March weather, and demonstrated the capabilities of the machine very well, but in the end the trophy went to Triumph.

For 1940 there was to have been a spring frame of novel design for the big Panthers. It used four leaf springs with two on each side running back to the top and bottom of a vertical tube. The two tubes were linked by a stay over the wheel and carried the spindle lugs. It worked well until one spring sheared on test, and then its cost and the advent of war removed it from the scene before it reached production.

Aside from the frame Panther had other surprises for 1940 with a trio of Redwing models with vertical engines, one of which had side valves. This was the 594 cc 80 and it continued the feature of a large crankcase with the oil tank cast into it. The frame was all new with a single downtube and duplex cradle beneath the engine and four-speed gearbox.

The ohv model 90 was built along the same lines, but was of 498 cc, and there was also a vertical twin with in-line cylinders, but this only reached the prototype stage. The range was completed by the inclined engine models, which were the Redwing 60, 70 and 100 of 249, 348 and 594 cc. There were no Red Panthers so the ultra-cheap 250 was no more and the 80, 90 and 100 were listed with the spring frame.

Panther then turned to war contracts, although motorcycles continued to be built well into 1940 for export but only in the inclined-engine form.

Pouncy

This marque came from Dorset and emerged in March 1931 with a single model called the Cob. It was a conventional machine powered by an upright 346 cc Villiers engine coupled to a three-speed Albion gearbox. Lubrication was by petroil as standard, but auto-lube was available as an extra. Ignition was by flywheel magneto, which also supplied the direct lighting.

A simple frame carried the mechanics and had tubular girders and a centre stand. A saddle tank was used, the brakes were 6 in. diameter and the finish black with a red panel on the tank nose. Footchange was an extra 10s. while the hand-change gate was bolted to the frame just below the front of the tank. It cannot have been very convenient and maybe persuaded buyers to go for the foot option.

For 1932 the range was expanded to three models, including the original, which continued to be called the Cob. Footchange became standard on this model, which was also available with four speeds, a tuned engine or a run-in engine, the last costing an extra 25s. The model was also fitted with a larger fuel tank with knee-grips and a quick-action filler cap, while the rear brake pedal was moved to the left side of the machine.

A second 346 cc model was listed as the Triple S and this was fashioned on A. J. Pouncy's own competition machine. It was as the Cob but had a tuned engine which was run in before delivery, four speeds, automatic chain oiling and a special exhaust system. The third model in the range was the 148 cc Kid with Villiers engine and three-speed gearbox.

1933 saw the range down to three models with new names, but all continued with Villiers engines. The Triple S became the Mate and the Kid the Pup, but they remained with 346 and 148 cc engines. New was the Pal with a 249 cc engine and four-speed, footchange gearbox. All were petroil lubricated and had flywheel magnetos.

During 1933 the firm moved to Hampshire and only the two larger machines continued for 1934 as the 249 cc Pal and 346 cc Mate. After an announcement late in 1933 they faded from sight and no 1935 range was listed. News of the firm came in February 1935, when a new 249 cc model was launched, it having made its debut in the London to Exeter trial.

The machine was still known as the Pal and the engine was the Villiers with flat-top piston. Less usual was the exhaust system with a pipe from each side of the cylinder running straight back to a large, cast-alloy expansion box above the gearbox. From this two waist-level outlets connected to a tubular Burgess silencer on each side. The carburettor went in front of the cylinder and faced forwards.

The frame was unusual and of duplex cradle construction with twin downtubes. It incorporated the OEC form of rear suspension with a pivoted rear fork, plunger spring boxes and a link to join the two. This was rare for a lightweight at that time. The remainder of the machine was normal with tubular girders, four speeds and a large toolbox on top of the expansion chamber. A super sports version with tuned engine was also available.

The single model went forward for 1936, but during that year production stopped.

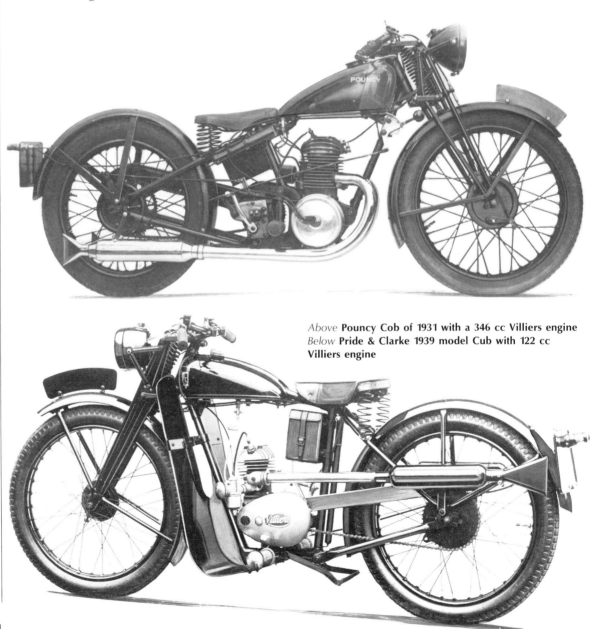

Above **Pouncy Cob of 1931 with a 346 cc Villiers engine**
Below **Pride & Clarke 1939 model Cub with 122 cc Villiers engine**

Pride & Clarke

Radco

158 Stockwell Road, London SW9, was a very well-known motorcycle address and P&C had their premises along both sides for quite a length of the road. For years they were associated with Panther, but were always ready to do deals to fill their showrooms with machines at cut prices, a practice they were to continue for many post-war years as well.

In the 1930s they sold their own brand of sidecar for many seasons, but early in 1939 they added a lightweight motorcycle sold as the Cub. It used the 122 cc Villiers unit construction engine with three-speed gearbox and twin exhaust pipes that ran straight back from the cylinder to black tubular silencers with fishtails.

The engine unit went into a simple loop frame with blade girder forks, drum brakes, Lycett saddle and centre stand. Ignition was by flywheel magneto and this supplied the direct lighting, while lubrication was by petroil.

Legshields were fitted and extended back to the footrests and a toolkit went into a box mounted up under the saddle. A tyre pump was clipped to the seat tube and a bulb horn was fitted.

The model was only listed for that one short season and from then on Pride & Clarke kept to selling other firms' wares, which they did very successfully.

This firm dated from just before World War 1 and their range was powered by Villiers, JAP and their own engines.

By 1930 their machines were conventional, sturdy, well finished but perhaps rather old-fashioned in looks. The range ran to nine models and most were two-strokes. Smallest were the 147 cc Villiers-powered L and M models, the first with two speeds and the second with three, but otherwise the same with petroil lubrication, flywheel magneto ignition and simple frame and forks.

Next in size were a pair with 196 cc Villiers engines and labelled O, with two speeds, and N with three, both having auto-lube and the flywheel magneto. The last pair of two-strokes were the two-speed P and three-speed R, which had Radco 247 cc engines with mechanical lubrication. The three four-strokes were all JAP powered and comprised the 245 cc ohv E and the 490 cc side-valve H and ohv K.

For 1931 there was one more model, the S, which had the 196 cc Villiers engine with three speeds but petroil lubrication. Otherwise the range was as before.

The 1930 Radco model K with 490 cc JAP engine

The 1932 range lacked the JAP-powered models, but the petroil-lubricated model S became the U and was joined by a two-speed model-T version. The other models all ran on as the 147 cc L and M, 196 cc O and N, and 247 cc P and R, all with two- and three-speed gearboxes.

The range was the same for 1933, but that was their last year and they halted motorcycle production to concentrate on components such as handlebars and control levers. Twice in the 1950s Radco made a tentative move towards re-entering the motorcycle field, only to think better of it and withdraw.

Above **1932 Raleigh MO32 with 297 cc side-valve engine**
Below **98 cc Villiers engined Raynal Auto in 1938 form**

Raleigh

Raynal

This name is better known for its bicycles, but they dabbled in powered machines in Victorian times, left them during Edwardian days and returned to them after World War 1. They also sold engines and gearboxes to other firms under the Sturmey-Archer label and continued until 1934. Their gearbox design was then taken over by Norton and used by them in various forms from then on.

The 1930 range of Raleigh models had vertical engines and were of conventional design with dry sump lubrication. There were four with side valves, which were the MG30 of 225 cc, the export-only MJ30 of 248 cc, the MO30 of 297 cc and the MA30 of 495 cc. The ohv models were the MT30 of 348 cc and the MH30 of 495 cc and both had two-port engines, forward-mounted magnetos, a diamond frame and Raleigh girder forks. The fuel tank was formed in two halves, joined by a top strip to give the desired saddle appearance. With cream tank panels they were handsome machines.

On the face of it the 1931 range was much as before, with the MO, MA, MT and MH all present but with a 31 suffix. In fact it was all change to inclined engines with rear magneto, a new frame and forks to accommodate this and more modern lines with chrome-plated tanks. The 225 and 248 cc sv were dropped from the list but in their place came the MG31, a second 348 cc ohv model with twin ports and exhaust systems, cradle frame, one-piece tank and a four-speed gearbox with the choice of foot or hand control.

For 1932 the MG32 became the only 348 cc model, but there were still five models in the range. The MO, MA, and MH continued and were joined by the 598 cc side-valve MB32 while all five continued for 1933 with a new suffix.

By the end of 1933 the company had turned to only building three-wheeler cars and vans, which they had begun in 1930, so the motorcycles were no longer available. In 1935 the three-wheelers also ceased and the firm returned to bicycles only.

Raynal came on the motorcycle scene late in 1937 with a production version of the prototype Jones autocycle, powered by the usual 98 cc Villiers engine. It was called the Auto and its lines were much as others of the type. The frame was of the open bicycle type with simple sprung front fork, but both wheels did have drum brakes.

The petroil tank went between the frame members, a rear carrier was supplied and also a rear stand which clipped up when not in use. The lighting was included and direct, with the current supplied from the flywheel magneto. Unlike some similar machines the rear brake was rod operated by the pedals and not the back-pedalling type, which was prone to rapid lining wear if the rider rested on the pedals enough to hold it on.

For 1939 the Auto with sprung front forks was renamed the De Luxe and joined by the Popular, which had rigid forks but was otherwise the same. Both were available in a choice of finishes. They continued as they were into 1940 until production ceased for the duration. The make reappeared with the Popular in 1946 and continued until 1950, when the company was acquired by the Raleigh group. Throughout their autocycle period they also made bicycles, as they did before and after the powered versions.

Rex-Acme

The company was formed in 1922 by the amalgamation of the two makes, the Rex, which dated from 1900, and the Acme which appeared a little later in 1902. During the Edwardian era the Rex became well known and was quite successful in competition, but the Acme was a very minor make.

Once joined they soon had success in the TT with places in 1922 and 1923, but in 1925 Walter Handley became the first man to win two events in one race week. The races were the 350 and 175 cc and in both Handley rode a Rex-Acme. 1926 brought him placings in both the Senior and Junior, while he won the 250 TT in 1927.

The marque also had success at other racing circuits and at Brooklands, but this was all during the twenties. By 1930 their best days were behind them and in the chill winds of the Depression they became one of many using bought-in parts to assemble their own machine.

For that year they gave the prospective customer plenty of choice from small two-strokes to a V-twin. The range began with four models with Villiers engines, all in diamond frames, and these were the 147 cc V10C, the 172 cc V10S, the 247 cc V10A and the 343 cc V10B. The 172 cc motor was the super sports version with auto-lube and carried its oil tank under the saddle.

Above **Early 147 cc Rex-Acme from 1929**
Below **1932 Rex-Acme model R12 with 500 cc twin-port JAP engine**

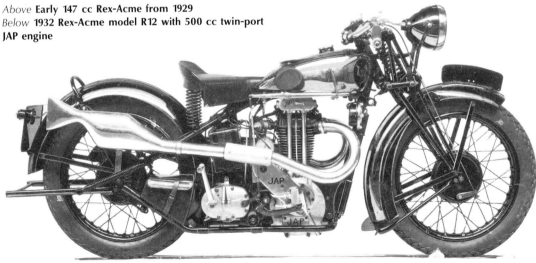

All the other machines had cradle frames in which the engines sat upright. There were five models with Blackburne units and the smallest was the B10 with a 295 cc sv engine. Next came the 348 cc sv K10 and two of the same size with ohv, the one-port M101 and two-port M102. Last was the D10, which had a 596 cc sv engine.

Four more models had JAP engines and came as the 346 cc sv U10, 340 cc ohv O10, 490 cc sv C10 and 747 cc sv V-twin E10. All conventional but well built and in the style of the time. The final model took care of the 500 cc ohv class and this alone had a 495 cc Sturmey-Archer engine. In addition there was a speedway model available with a JAP or Blackburne engine, this machine having been first listed in 1928.

A range was announced for 1931 but was smaller. There was just one Villiers-powered model, the 147 cc V11C and only two Blackburnes, the one- and two-port 348 cc ohv models listed as the M111 and M112. Three machines had JAP engines and one, the 300 cc sv J11, was new. The others were the 346 cc ohv O11 and the 490 cc sv C11. The Sturmey-Archer 495 cc ohv model remained as the SA11 and was joined by the P11, which had a 499 cc Python engine. New was the option of a Python engine for the speedway machine which continued to be offered with the JAP or Blackburne units as well.

Although a range was listed, production came to a halt soon after and that seemed to be the end of the company. However, the name was taken over by the Mills-Fulford sidecar company and reappeared in May 1932. Two models were listed and both had two-port ohv JAP engines set upright in cradle frames. The 346 cc O12 had a three-speed Burman gearbox and the 500 cc R12 a four-speed one, but in most other respects they were the same. Stainless steel tank sides were used and the tank top carried a rain gutter with its own drain hole. Lubrication was dry sump and a Lucas mag-dyno went aft of the cylinder. The exhausts ran at waist level.

For 1933 these two models continued as the O13 and R13 and were joined by two more. One had a 249 cc long-stroke Villiers engine running on petroil, while the other had a 250 cc ohv two-port JAP. The latter was very similar to the 350 cc model and had the same finish.

During 1933 the new company ceased making Rex-Acme motorcycles and another well-known name fell victim to the difficult times.

Reynolds

Albert E. Reynolds was a Scott dealer based in Liverpool and a fan of the marque. He had specialized in it through the 1920s and early on had begun to market his own accessories and parts designed to improve the standard product. As would be expected, while most would fit any Scott they could not be used on anything else. Reynolds also built up a good workshop that could tackle any Scott job at a competitive cost.

When the Scott company ran into money troubles in 1931 they raised some cash by selling a showroom and area distributorship to Reynolds and agreed to supply him with machines prepared to his own specification. With his initials of AER they were known at first as Aero Specials.

The first was launched in May 1931 with the TT engine, in either capacity, Brampton bottom link forks, Velocette-type foot gearchange, concealed cables and twin headlamps. It was built to a very high standard and was very fully equipped. It was also a good deal more expensive and was promoted as a Scott for connoisseurs.

In 1932 the machines became the Reynolds Special and now had a new radiator and plunger rear suspension as an alternative to the rigid frame which continued to be offered. Many of the detail fittings were items that Reynolds had been selling to Scott owners over the years and they added to the luxurious specification and individual appearance of the machines.

For 1933 only the larger engine was listed, as it was for 1934, when it was joined by a second model with a 249 cc water-cooled Villiers engine. This was a conventional design with auto-lube, magneto ignition, four-speed footchange Burman gearbox and it came with legshields.

Reynolds was keen to use the 747 cc Scott triple as the basis of a really de luxe model, but this plan was thwarted by the lack of engines. The same problem arose when the larger triple was shown and in the end he had to accept that the best days of the Scott were in the past and as a dealer he needed another marque.

So his showrooms began to hold motorcycles without twin-cylinder, two-stroke engines and then cars, but he did not give up his ideas and in time these surfaced as the AER.

Above **The Reynolds 1931 Scott special with its many extras built to provide a machine of the highest standard for any enthusiast of the marque**

Right **A 1933 export model K built with the 1140 cc engine for the President of a South American republic**

Below **1930 Royal Enfield model C of 346 cc with outside oil pump, oil tank formed with petrol one and rear magneto**

Royal Enfield

The Redditch firm never quite managed to acquire the charisma of some others, but for all that they remained in business for a long time. In the main they kept to basic machines that customers would buy and this policy must have served them well in the Depression years. Their slogan 'made like a gun' could perhaps have lost the suggestion of weight if it had changed to 'precise as a rifle', but at least customers knew it and used it.

For all that the firm kept clear of exotic designs that would not sell, and they were often at the forefront of improvements that did. Thus in 1928 they adopted saddle tanks and centre spring girders, while in post-war years they were one of the first to adopt pivoted fork rear suspension.

During the 1920s the models were given type numbers, but from 1930 on letters were used. Logically the range for the first year ran from A to K and in time was to stretch to Z, with a few omissions. The model A was also the smallest at 225 cc and a two-stroke with a mechanical oil pump, an advanced feature for the time. As with the whole of the range, it was fitted with girder forks with twin tension springs. It had a three-speed, handchange gearbox and the usual Enfield detachable rear mudguard and carrier.

The model B had a 225 cc side-valve engine, while the C had an inclined 346 cc unit, also with side valves. This was based on dimensions of 70 × 90 mm, which the company retained for its 350s to the end. This continuity helped production and occurred with many other models over the years. Model D was a 488 cc sv and E its ohv counterpart and again three-speed gearboxes were fitted, although four speeds were available as options.

The next batch of models were new and all had inclined engines and dry sump lubrication. The oil was circulated by twin plunger pumps driven by a

shaft in the timing cover, itself turned by a worm on the crankshaft. The oil was carried within a compartment cast into the front of the crankcase and the system was to be used by the firm for many years. The models were the F with 346 cc side-valve engine, G with the same capacity but ohv, H with 488 cc sv and J with the ohv version of the bigger engine.

The range was completed by the 976 cc model K, which had a V-twin engine with side valves and was an old stager meant for sidecar use. While old-fashioned in some respects it did have the new-type forks, easy access to the rear wheel and good-sized brakes.

Early in the year the model CO joined the range with an inclined 346 cc ohv engine. Lubrication was by adjustable pump and the oil was carried in a section of the petrol tank. Later in April it was joined by two more machines, the HA and JA, which were much as the H and J models. It was a case of varying the details to produce a greater range with minimum expense to attract every

Left **The 1934 LF model four-valve Royal Enfield 488 cc engine with crankcase oil tank**
Below **The Royal Enfield 148 cc Cycar model Z on show late in 1934 at Olympia**

possible customer into the showroom. All were thus available in standard or de luxe forms, the latter with suffix L added to their type letter.

For 1931 the two-stroke was redesigned, so at first the two 225 cc models were left off the list, as were the old-style models D and E. The 350 class was covered by the old side-valve C31 and the newer F31, while with ohv the machines became the CO31 and G31. The larger singles received more changes with just the HA31 and JA31 continuing as they were. The model J apparently continued as the J31, but this was modified to a longer-stroke engine and 499 cc with a twin-port head. It continued to have an inclined cylinder, as did all the range.

The H31 used the same stroke but was bored out to the old 488 cc dimension, which gave its side valves 570 cc to deal with. The most exciting new model was the JF31, which used the J dimensions fitted with a four-valve head. The valves were laid in pent-roof form so the rocker gear was little more complex than usual. Finally came the big V-twin as the K31.

In February 1931 a further 350 appeared as the single-port CS31, very much on the lines of the CO model and under the 224 lb weight bar, although it carried full electrical equipment powered by a Maglita. In April the 225 cc two-stroke returned with inclined cylinder, alloy cylinder head, the old bore and stroke, the mechanical oil pump and outside flywheel on the right. A dynamo was clamped into the engine plates behind the crankcase and driven by chain. It carried the points for the coil ignition in its end and the whole machine was finished in maroon.

The range went down to ten for 1932 with the F, HA and JA models out. New was the L, which had a 499 cc side-valve engine, coil ignition with the points housing in the timing cover and the dynamo gear driven from the cam gear train. It was also offered with a sidecar as the LC. The A, C, G, H, J, K and CS all ran on with duplex frames and cleaned-up handlebars as neater looks had become a theme. The CO also continued and the JF became the LF but retained the four-valve head.

New on the 500s was a centre stand that doubled as a prop-stand. If pushed to the ground it was held down by a catch on the rear brake pedal and a touch on this released it. This gave the prop facility on either side and from this the machine could be pulled on to the stand in the normal way.

The advent of the 15s. tax for up to 150 cc machines saw many new models to take advantage of it, but few were as radical as the Enfield Cycar model Z. This was announced in March 1932 and was a machine with the works fully enclosed and equipped with legshields for the rider.

The frame acted as the enclosure and was formed from sheet steel as an inverted U. At the front the steering head was welded in and from this the frame pressing ran back to the rear wheel spindle. Depressions and flanges stiffened the structure, as did the forward part of the rear mudguard. The left side was taken in to form one side of the primary chaincase and a cover completed that aspect. A similar technique was used to enclose the flywheel magneto on the right and the legshields bolted into place.

The petrol tank went up into the channel section of the frame, where it was supported against rubber packing and held by a ring nut round the filler cap and a single bolt at the rear. The left side of the chassis was smooth except for the chaincase, while on the right only the end of the gearbox with the kickstarter was exposed. The hand gear lever protruded through a slot on this side. The entire rear mudguard was quickly detachable in typical Enfield style and was fully closed in from the frame to the vertical wheel line.

Within this remarkable frame went a neat 148 cc two-stroke engine with inclined cylinder with non-detachable head. To facilitate its removal the two rear fixings were long bolts which ran up from the underside of the crankcase. The carburettor clipped to the right front corner and the exhaust pipe to the left one. Lubrication was by petroil and ignition by the flywheel magneto, which supplied the direct lighting of the basic model or the battery where this was fitted.

A three-speed gearbox was fitted and driven by chain and simple clutch. The rear chain was on the left. The front forks were girders with pressed steel blades and small drum brakes were used. A most enterprising effort to build a cheap ride-to-work model but not one with any pretence to styling.

The Cycar was given a black-with-gold-lining finish for 1933 and the model A was also little altered that year. The below-224 lb C and CS model of 346 cc continued in the lists to catch the last of the tax advantage and the L and K ran on. The 499 cc single had little change, but the V-twin now had a four-speed gearbox as standard and a neat ratchet to hold the front brake lever on when parked.

The other models were, in part, new. Smallest

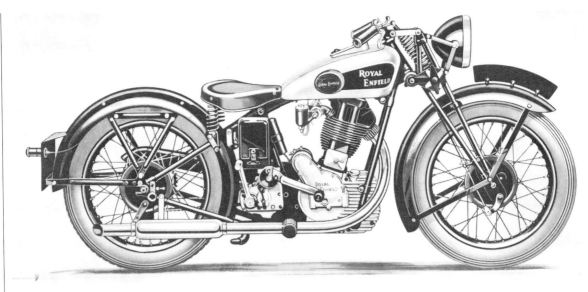

Top **The three-valve 488 cc model LO of 1935**
Centre **1936 Royal Enfield 346 cc model C**
Right **Similar, but heavier model J of 499 cc seen from the drive side**

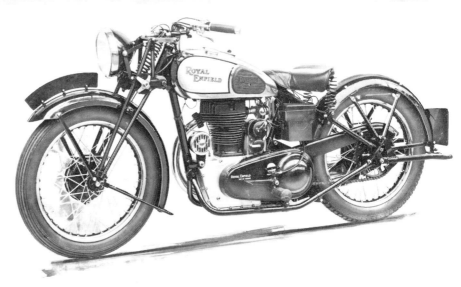

was the model B, which now had a 248 cc side-valve engine, rear magneto and a mechanical oiling system supplied from a tank cast as a forward part of the crankcase. A four-speed gearbox with handchange and a cast-alloy primary chaincase were fitted.

This left three ohv models called Bullets for the sporting rider. All had four speeds, footchange, upswept exhaust and high-compression pistons. The smallest was of 248 cc and built on the lines of the model B. The others had dry sump lubrication and were derived from existing machines to produce the 346 cc Bullet and the 488 cc four-valve one which continued with the special centre stand from the year before.

In January 1933 the V-twin became available with a larger engine for export only. This came by extending the stroke to 99.25 mm and the capacity to 1140 cc. There were some detail improvements to cope with the extra power, which also helped the looks of the model. A three-speed gearbox was fitted with its handchange lever on the left side of the petrol tank and the machine came with footboards, pan saddle, American-style handle-bars and hand or foot clutch operation.

Three months later in April another two-stroke went onto the lists as the 148 cc model X. In essence it was the Cycar engine located with its cylinder vertical in a light duplex tubular frame. A dynamo went in the engine plates behind the crankcase, although the flywheel magneto was retained, but in other respects the Z and X were mechanically very similar. Thus the X had three speeds, blade girders and small drum brakes.

There were more revisions and changes for 1934. There was nearly a new model A as this machine went over to petroil lubrication and a one-piece head and barrel and single exhaust system, although it retained coil ignition, dynamo and blade girders. The X amd Z continued as they were, as did the V-twin in its two sizes.

The six four-stroke singles all had dry sump lubrication and this was modified to improve its operation. All three Bullets now had their pushrods concealed in tunnels cast in head, barrel and rocker box as had been done on the 488 cc one the year before. This engine continued with its four valves. The side-valve machines were the B and C, with the change to dry sump oiling, and the L, which was stretched out to 570 cc by changing both bore and stroke.

The final model in the range came along late and had a smaller engine to suit the tax rules. It was the model T of 148 cc with ohv and inclined cylinder, very much as its bigger brothers. Valve gear was fully enclosed and a four-speed gearbox fitted with handchange as standard or foot selection as an option.

In May 1934 it was joined by a very similar 248 cc ohv, which copied its engine features, duplex frame and blade girders. This was the model S and for 1935 the 248 cc Bullet became a tuned version of it as the S2.

The bulk of the range remained as it was for 1935 as the models Z, T, A, B, S, C, L, K and export KX. The 148 cc two-stroke was dropped, as was the 346 cc Bullet, whose place was taken by the model G. This left the 488 cc Bullet and this had a major engine change to become the three-valve model LO. Vertical valves were used in place of the pent-roof arrangement of the older four-valve unit and there were two inlets and a single exhaust. The rockers lay across the head and the inlet one carried a bridge beam which spanned both inlets and was free to pivot the open both to the same spring loading. For the rest it was the cycle parts much as before with minor changes, and in April 1935 a cheaper version of the three-valve model typed the LO2.

1936 brought the first machines in a new style with vertical cylinders. The general construction followed the usual Enfield lines with a gear train to drive the camshafts and rear-mounted dynamo or mag-dyno, dry sump lubrication, with the oil carried in a forward extension of the crankcase, and fully enclosed valve gear.

There were two standard models, the 346 cc G and 499 cc J, with coil ignition and four-speed, footchange gearboxes. The frame had single top and downtubes with duplex rails under the engine and pressed-steel blade girder forks were fitted along with full equipment. The 499 cc engine had new 84 × 90 mm dimensions. The third model in the new style was the JF Bullet, which represented a return to the four-valve head in the manner of the older LF model. It alone had tubular forks, but all models had a new absorption silencer. The rest of the range continued as it was with its inclined engines and side or overhead valves plus the two-stroke Z and A models.

April 1936 brought two more versions of the G and J in the form of competition models. These were not really that much altered but did have the silencer tilted up, more ground clearance, competition tyres and narrow, chrome-plated mudguards. The finish of the petrol tank was in

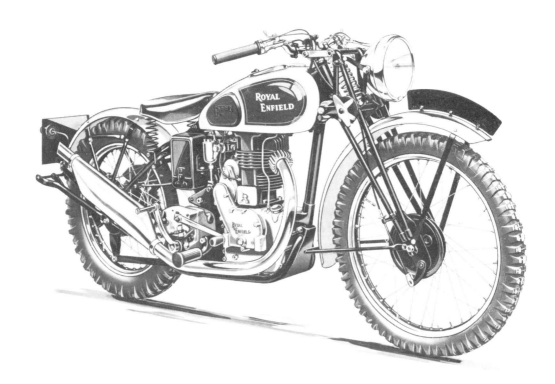

chrome with scarlet panels as was that of the wheel rims. For the less successful rider there was a lifting handle on each side of the rear wheel.

In July 1936 the trend to vertical engines continued with the appearance of two more models in this style. One was the 248 cc ohv S2, which replaced the inclined-engine Bullet, and the other the 346 cc sv C in place of the older machine. Both had dry sump lubrication and four-speed gearboxes.

When the range for 1937 was announced it proved to be a lengthy one, a sign of the firm's coverage of the market and its willingness to build a model if there seemed to be buyers for it. It also highlighted the move to vertical cylinders, for only the A and T retained inclined ones. The latter was also listed as the TM with a mag-dyno.

Of the upright singles there were the sv B and ohv S and S2 of 248 cc, the sv C and ohv G plus a tuned de luxe G2 version of 346 cc, and the ohv J, de luxe J2 and four-valve JF Bullet of 499 cc. There was also the H, which was a 499 cc version of the 570 cc sv L and the two competition machines. Finally came the V-twin listed as the K and the KX de luxe. In either case the home market model was now fitted with the 1140 cc engine, which had dry sump lubrication and no fewer than four oil pumps.

In April 1937 it was announced that the 248 and

346 cc Bullets were back as modified versions of the S2 and G2. The range of options was large and the machines could be prepared for road racing, trials, scrambles or grass-track.

For 1938 the range stretched to 20 models and there were no fewer than six of 499 cc with ohv. They were all built to the same basic pattern and began with the model J. Next came the J2 Bullet with new twin-port cylinder head and assembled as a fast sports roadster. The J2 was also listed with a four-valve head, as was the Competition model, which came in two forms with two or four valves. Finally there was the JM, which was the basic model fitted with a mag-dyno in place of the coil.

In the smaller sizes the 248 cc ohv S, S2 and Bullet continued, as did the 346 cc ohv G and Bullet. The 148 cc ohv T and TM were still there, as was the two-stroke A and the side-valve singles as the models B, C, H and L plus the BM and SM with magneto. To complete the list there were the V-twin, 1140 cc side-valve K and KX models.

If all that was not enough a further 346 cc ohv appeared in May 1938 as the model CO. It was very much as the de luxe G but built on a lighter scale to reduce weight, so aside from that aspect followed Enfield practice.

There was more rearrangement for 1939 and some new model letters in addition to the continued confusing Enfield practice of using the

Left **Competition Royal Enfield from 1937 with 499 cc engine and tyres, mudguards and silencer to suit**
Right **Long-running 225 cc model A Royal Enfield in its 1938 form with large expansion box, outside flywheel and rear dynamo with points on the end**

same letter for totally different models from one year to another. Thus there was still a model A and it was still a 225 cc two-stroke, but it had a revised engine with vertical cylinder, a new frame, brake pedal moved over to the left, the option of tubular girders in place of the blades and covers for the dynamo and outside flywheel.

On the other hand the T was dropped in either form, while for the 248 cc sv there was even a new letter, for this model became the D. The top half of the engine was as before, but the crankcase lost its oil tank, which became a separate item tucked in between the rear engine plates. The D had coil ignition with a Miller dynamo driven from the timing chest and carrying the points at one end and its regulator on its back.

Just to confuse owners the model S was as the D with separate oil tank, but had the ohv top half, so was not as in 1938. It had a three-speed handchange gearbox and was also offered as the SF with four-speed and foot operation. The S2, however, continued as it was with the crankcase oil tank. At least all the models had a nice new green finish for the petrol tank, which helped to keep track of them.

In the 350 class the road range comprised the side-valve C, ohv CO with coil ignition and the ohv CM with a mag-dyno. The 499 cc J changed to tubular forks and also took to a mag-dyno, while

the side-valve L, K and KX were as before. Finally there was the H, which became a 570 cc machine but only sold complete with a sidecar. It used the L engine but with coil ignition in place of the magneto.

A month after the road range was announced came news of the sports models. These were the Bullets and the smaller of the two was the 346 cc G. It had an all-alloy engine, so the top half was new and included rocker box covers with cooling fins. This engine was also used by the Competition version, which was fitted out for trials use. The 499 cc J2 was the larger machine and this had an alloy barrel but kept to its iron head. Again a Competition model was listed alongside it and both were also offered fitted with the four-valve head.

This took the firm up to the war, but like most they announced a 1940 range. Included in this was one newcomer in the form of the 126 cc RE two-stroke, which came in response to a request from Holland. This was from a firm in Rotterdam that had been handling the 98 cc DKW and who had the concession removed in 1938 because it was Jewish owned. Their answer was to ask Enfield to make a copy but to enlarge it to 125 cc. By April 1939 prototypes were in Holland and production began about the time that the war did.

The result was that England had a fully

developed lightweight which served the para-troops during the conflict as the Flying Flea and the civilians after it for a good few years. The RE was a straightforward design with unit construction of engine and three-speed, handchange gearbox. Its odd capacity would seem to arise from a miscalculation, as the bore and stroke were given as 54 × 55 mm in service manuals which came to 126 cc. For insurance purposes, maybe, the bore was quoted in England as 53.79 mm, which brought the size to just under 125 cc.

That aside, the engine had flywheel magneto and points on the right, petroil lubrication and an alloy head. The unit was housed in a simple tubular loop frame and blade girders controlled by rubber bands provided the front suspension.

The rest of the range was based on the 1939 one and totalled seven machines. Smallest were the 248 cc sv D and ohv SF and next came the light 346 ohv CO and all-alloy Bullet model G of the same size. A new feature of the G was a plain bush big-end. This was something that Enfield had been experimenting with for some while and it used a mild steel bush lined with white metal. This ran in the rod eye and on the crankpin between thrust washers and required really good lubrication. Given this it lasted well and the same part also went into the 499 cc ohv J and J2 Bullet, plus the 570 cc sv L.

And so Enfield went to war, mainly with the RE, C and CO but with some of the others to use up stock and to provide D models for training.

Royal Ruby

In this case the RR initials did not confer the prestige they did on four wheels. The company was sited in Bolton, Lancashire, and built motorcycles from late Edwardian days using their own engines. By 1930 they had turned to using Villiers units and for that year had two models.

The first was of 247 cc with the engine upright and the second of 343 cc with it inclined forward. In both cases they drove a three-speed gearbox with handchange and went into a conventional set of cycle parts.

For 1931 the firm listed a single new model with a 346 cc long-stroke Villiers engine inclined in the frame. This was called the Red Shadow and had a dynamo as well as a flywheel magneto and auto-lube. It had its oil tank under the saddle as expected, but the battery was housed in front of

the crankcase and the frame downtube ran steeply in front of it to give protection. It was fitted with a three-speed gearbox.

1932 saw two 346 cc models as the range. The Standard had direct lighting and three speeds with handchange, but the Club had a dynamo, electric horn, four speeds and the option of hand or footchange.

The two 346 cc machines became the Sports models for 1933 and were available in standard and competition form. They were joined by similar 249 cc machines which were listed as Sports and Super-Sports models. The latter was also available with a water-cooled engine and in either form had a four-speed gearbox. The other models had three, although the 346 cc ones had the option of four as well as dynamo lighting. All models had a very wide chain line achieved by fitting the engine sprocket outboard of the flywheel, which in turn gave plenty of room by the final chain for the fitting of a larger-section tyre.

This, however, was the last year the make remained available.

Below **A 1933 Royal Ruby 346 cc Super Sports powered by a Villiers engine. Oil tank for auto-lube under saddle and battery hung out in front of engine**

Above left **1939 Royal Enfield 248 cc model SF with separate oil tank tucked between the crankcase and gearbox**
Below left **The 126 cc model RE of 1940 which became the wartime Flying Flea based on a 98 cc German DKW**

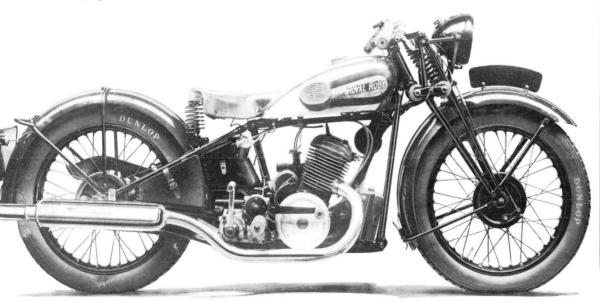

Rudge

Rudge began with the earliest of bicycles and returned to them in the end, but from 1910 to 1939 also made motorcycles. They were innovative from the start with the one-piece fork link, the variable gear for belt drive and the four-valve engines of later times.

By the 1930s their reputation was well established as makers of fine machines and their name was in the list of TT winners and among the record books at Brooklands. In 1928 success in the Ulster Grand Prix led to the 499 cc sports machine taking this name and in the same year they built their first dirt-track model.

1930 was a tremendous year for Rudge at the TT, when new radial, four-valve engines were used for the Junior and the machines took the first three places. The Senior was nearly as good with first and second spots, but in this case the better-known pent-roof four-valve head was used.

The road range at that time had three JAP-engined models with 248 and 300 cc side-valve units and a 245 cc ohv one. All were vertically mounted with four speeds and coupled brakes, a Rudge feature that dated from 1926 and was first applied to their rim brakes. In 1928 they adopted 8 in. drum brakes, so jumped from about last to first in this area but continued with the coupled system. In this, the foot pedal applied both brakes, but was designed to work the front progressively harder as more force went on the pedal. A hand lever could work the front brake separately.

The other models all had four-valve, single-cylinder engines and three were of 499 cc. The fourth was of 339 cc with smaller brakes, but all the road models had dry sump lubrication and four speeds. The larger machines were the Special and the Ulster, the latter the more sporting machine with raised compression ratio and a central plug.

The other 499 cc model was the Dirt Track, which had wet sump oiling and a countershaft in place of the gearbox. To gain ground clearance on the left the exhaust pipe was run up to a point well above the top of the chain runs.

Rudge aimed to cash in on their TT successes with the 1931 range and were unfortunate that this came at a time when the market was depressed. In addition they had incurred heavy costs in developing the radial valve engines and running a racing team, all of which had to be paid for in the machine price. To cap this the road models were redesigned to move the magneto from its vintage-style front mounting to the rear and this involved a good deal of expenditure.

The 1931 line-up looks entrancing when viewed from across the years, but in the depressed time it is not surprising that sales dropped well away. There was no longer a small JAP-powered model and the starting point was a new 348 cc ohv with full radial head with the six rockers. It had dry sump lubrication, oil tank under the saddle, front-mounted dynamo, pressed-steel chain cover and the Rudge four-speed gearbox with many needle roller bearings in it. None of this equated with a cheap machine, and from then on the specification improved. The Special stayed with the pent-roof head and the Ulster was the sports model with cast-alloy chaincase.

There were models that retained the front magneto, but these were 350 and 500 TT Replicas based on the 1930 works jobs. The smaller had the radial valve head, neither had lights but both had footchange. The Dirt Track model also had the front magneto.

In an attempt to offer a smaller model to the public a 248 cc machine was added to the range for 1931, but this too had a four-valve radial head. Unlike the other models it had coil ignition with the points set in the timing cover and smaller brakes.

For 1932 Rudge continued to work up to an ideal rather than down to a price and introduced a four-valve radial head for the Ulster and the TT Replica. The Special stayed with the pent-roof design and the road models had a new lever-operated centre stand. This lay along the chaincase and made it easy for anyone to raise the machine. Footchange became an option for the Ulster.

Both 248 and 348 cc radial-engined models were available and there was a TT replica in both sizes. All models bar the 250 now had the alloy chaincase, while there was the option of coil or magneto ignition for the 248 cc road machine.

An option added for 1932 was a handchange lever which coupled to the positive stop mechanism, so it only had to be pushed fore or aft to select gears. The speedway model was no longer listed.

The 250 was fitted with a cast-alloy chaincase for 1933 but not the hand-operated stand. All models continued with the coupled brakes and the range list was as for the previous year. Thus there were road and replica models in 248, 348 and 499 cc. The largest had a new head with semi-radial valves in which the inlets were parallel and the exhausts splayed out. The touring 500 became

the Silver Vase Special and retained the pent-roof head, while the magneto on the Ulster went back in front and that on the 250 was driven from the left with its chain within the primary case.

There were just four models for 1934: two of 248 cc with radial heads and two of 499 cc, one semi-radial and one pent-roof. This last was the Special, which gained a metal cover over the battery on the left to match the oil tank and another on the right to enclose the gearbox end and the gap from it to the back of the magneto drive cover. The alloy chaincase now had a large letter R on a black circle on the clutch dome. The

Left **The radial four-valve Rudge engine with its many rockers as seen on a 1933 model of 348 cc. The long lever is connected to the stand and raises the machine on to it**
Below **1937 Rudge Sports Special with 493 cc pent-roof four-valve head with rockers enclosed. Note gearbox enclosure also**

Rudge Rapid with 245 cc two-valve engine in 1938 form with the gearbox enclosure but exposed valves. Note coupled brakes

hand-operated centre stand continued to be fitted.

The Ulster was given an aluminium-bronze head and the same battery and gearbox panels as the Special, while both had an instrument panel which carried a Jaeger clock and speedometer on either side of the steering damper.

The smaller machines had their oil tank moved to a position in front of the crankcase and were offered in standard or sports models. The first had handchange and the second the same, or foot as an option, and a different tyre size.

The habit of road racing had died hard at Rudge, for despite the poor sales and financial problems they had in the early 1930s they could not stay away. Just to make it harder for them they were still successful with a 1-2 in the 1931 Lightweight TT, 2-3 in both Junior and Lightweight in 1932 and a 1-2-3 in the 1934 Lightweight.

To help the cash flow they had begun to sell engine and gearbox units under the name Python in 1931. Although not as prolific as JAP motors they can be found in a good number of the English marques in this book and also went into a number of European ones. This was not enough, so the firm withdrew their racing support for the 1933 season and then called in the receiver in March of that year.

The racing continued as a syndicate which borrowed the works machines with success before they began to fall behind the pace. The works carried on with its reduced range, but the market

for well-made but pricey machines was a limited one in those difficult times, so sales continued to be depressed.

As would be expected there was little change for 1935, but in fact more than many anticipated. The 499 cc models received a new clutch and the oil tank of the 248 cc ones moved back to the more normal position beneath the saddle. The Sports version was otherwise the same, but the other became the Tourist and was unusual for a Rudge in having a two-valve cylinder head. It also lacked the coupled brakes of the other models.

The company was still unable to improve sales and at the end of the year went into liquidation. This could have been the end of the Rudge, but they were bought up by the giant EMI concern at Hayes and continued with the same programme.

The Tourist became the Rapid with minimal alteration, but did get the coupled brakes, while the Sports was fitted with the big fuel tank as used by the larger models. Low-level exhausts became standard on the sports models and the two 499 cc machines were fitted with a Revulator in place of the clock. This went in a similar case but was simply a manually-set cursor which related machine speed to engine speed in each gear.

For 1937 the 499 cc Rudges finally had their valve gear enclosed and moved away from the vintage design with minimal lubrication and heavy

The 1940 Rudge Autocycle with 98 cc engine built by the Norman firm in Kent for a short time

wear. The radial engine with its extra rockers and pivots had been very prone to this and the new arrangement was a great improvement.

The Special still retained its pent-roof layout and the Ulster the semi-radial and the bronze material, but both were new and incorporated the rocker pillars. A simple alloy cover enclosed all the works. In addition to these two models there was also a Sports Special with the pent-roof engine, lighter mudguards, raised exhausts and other detail changes.

At the same time the gear pedal was moved to the right side of the machine and the brake pedal to the left along with the brake drum. This ended the feature of interchangeable wheels. The 250 continued to use the left pedal arrangement.

There was only one of these, the Rapid, as the four-valve model was no longer listed. There was a new cylinder head and fuel tank, but otherwise it was much as before.

Sales of the range improved, but not to a level to justify the size of the Coventry factory, while control from Hayes proved awkward, so the decision to move was made and carried out. The 1938 range included one more model in the form of a Sports 250, which had a tuned engine and waist-level exhaust. With the problems inherent in moving there were few other changes except where essential and the results were continued

sales at the same level despite the disruption.

The range stayed the same for 1939 and production continued to rise slowly, so, but for the war, the firm would have found its feet again. As it was, the main Hayes factory produced radar equipment and was desperate for space so motorcycle production ceased in December 1939 to make room.

Right to the end the 250s continued with the gear pedal on the left. A very late change on the Ulster came in that last year when a light alloy cylinder head was adopted in place of the heavy bronze one. It had inserted valve seats and screwed-in bushes in bronze for the head bolts.

With the move to Hayes it had been decided to investigate the autocycle market and a design was produced. This used the 98 cc Villiers engine in a strengthened cycle-type frame and was similar to many others.

It was announced in the two forms of Standard and De Luxe early in 1940 and the main difference was in the engine shields fitted to the latter model. They had drum brakes and rigid forks so were very typical of the type.

The autocycle was made by the Norman firm in Kent using the Rudge name, and this continued for a while. In 1943 EMI decided they would not be returning to motorcycles and the name was sold to Raleigh Industries to reappear post-war on one of their ranges of bicycles. Rudge spares became the provenance of Godfreys in London, who had them made by sub-contractors for many years.

Scott

The Scott motorcycle was a beloved anachronism by 1930, for the original light and rigid design had put on weight which stifled the performance from the Edwardian engine design. It was nearly two decades since the marque had won the Senior TT for two years in succession and since then there had been a war and in motorcycling a revolution.

In 1910 the Scott was an advanced design with a good engine and better frame and forks, but in two decades it had not really progressed at all. For the 1930s it deserved better than to remain in the mould of the past, but Alfred Angas Scott had been dead for seven years and had relinquished his connection with the company that bore his name in 1915. Sadly, those who came after lacked his vision and in the late 1920s were still building his original design when they should have been developing something newer.

As so often happens when a firm has a unique and innovative design, Scott ran into financial difficulties more than once. This had a considerable effect on the way the company was run and on the machines they produced.

The list of models seemed lengthy, but was based on one basic engine and one basic frame, both in two forms, put together with a variety of parts to produce the range. All true Scotts had a twin-cylinder, water-cooled engine, but from 1929 they also built an air-cooled single.

This was a means of producing a model for the smaller end of the market, but unlike nearly all their competitors they chose to make the 299 cc engine rather than buy from Villiers. The result was a crude design with iron barrel and alloy head. The 1930 head was held by six bolts as the three allocated for the year before had allowed it to warp badly. The crankcase was a round cup laid on its side with a lid carrying the second main, and thus the big-end and crankshaft had to be assembled when in position. The crankpin was clamped on each web and aligned by the lid with some access from the cylinder hole.

The case lid went on the right with a flywheel outside it and on the left sprockets and chains drove the magneto and three-speed gearbox. The magneto sprocket turned a Pilgrim oil pump, but this only fed the left main. The frame had duplex downtubes with Scott telescopic front forks, but the whole machine was rather long and heavy for its job.

The rest of the range had the unusual Scott twin-cylinder engine with its central flywheel, inaccessible primary chain, twin inboard mains, overhung crankpins and crankcase doors to allow big-end inspection or to take an oil pump drive. The mechanics went into a large alloy casting on which sat the block with non-detachable head. The alloy water jacket on top of the head could be removed to allow the water passages to be viewed.

The engine was made in 499 cc and 597 cc sizes for most models and known as 'Short Stroke units' with a common stroke and change in bore. However, for one model the engines were built in Power Plus form with a longer stroke, by just over 3 mm, and, again, two piston sizes to give 497 and 598 cc.

The engines drove either a two- or three-speed gearbox and the mechanics went into the triangulated frame with triple chainstays as used from the earliest Scott. The older style was without top tube and had an oval fuel tank fitted to the seat tube. The later type had a petrol tank with integral top tube bolted at each end to the frame.

The models all came in either engine size and the two-speed ones were the Sports Squirrel and Super Squirrel fitted with Short Stroke motors. With three speeds and the frame top tube were the Flying Squirrel Tourers in standard and de luxe form, while with the long-stroke Power Plus engines were the TT Replicas, based on the model that had finished third in the 1928 Senior.

In addition to the road models with long-stroke engines there was the Sprint Special, which was listed for grass-track and hillclimbs but could be used for any sporting occasions. Its options were numerous and each was hand-built in the competition department. Finally there was a dirt-track model built especially for that sport.

For 1931 the single changed to Webb girder forks, a shorter wheelbase and lost some weight, while the lubrication was improved. There were changes for the Flying Squirrels which featured single down and seat tube frames similar to the

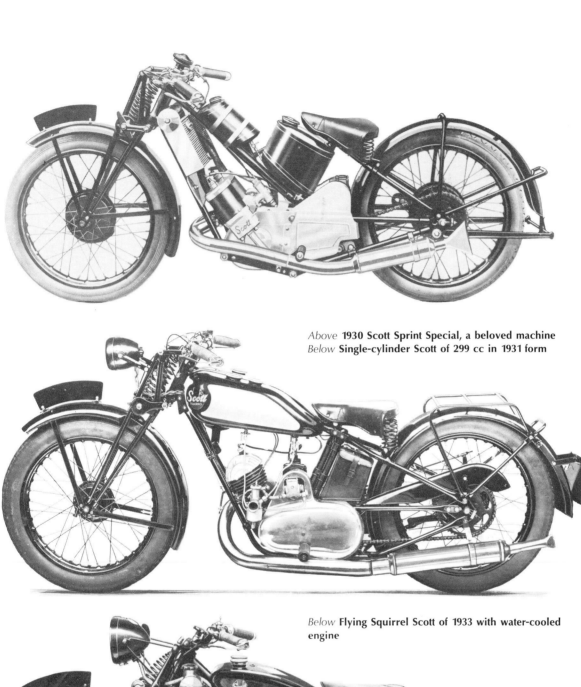

Above **1930 Scott Sprint Special, a beloved machine**
Below **Single-cylinder Scott of 299 cc in 1931 form**

Below **Flying Squirrel Scott of 1933 with water-cooled engine**

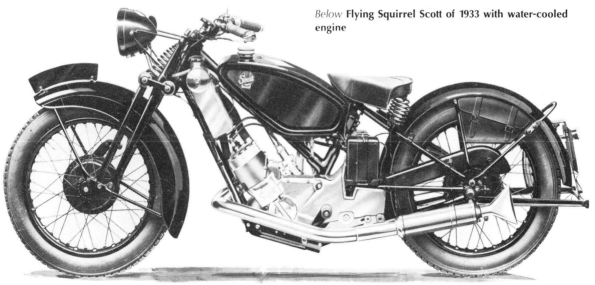

1930 Sprint Specials and these models could be fitted with the Power Plus engines. There was also talk of a new 650 cc vertical twin engine, but this soon lapsed as the company was in financial trouble and an Official Receiver was appointed. The 1931 range was revised without the 650 and the single was dropped, but the rest remained.

Production continued at a low ebb and for 1932 the firm offered its two engine sizes in the Flying Squirrel Tourer, the de luxe of the same name, the TT Replica and the new Sports Flying Squirrel, which was evolved from the Sprint Special. All except the first were fitted with Brampton bottom link forks in place of the Scott telescopics and the last had the Power Plus engine.

Further news for Scott enthusiasts in July 1932 was that the Liverpool firm of Hemmings were offering a replacement block with detachable cylinder head for the machine. This was only in the 597 cc size so could be used to convert the smaller model, and the one-piece, light alloy head was held down by nine studs. This made decarbonizing much easier, enabled the combustion chamber to be fully machined and allowed the compression ratio to be altered by varying the thickness of the copper head gasket. The same firm offered a good number of other items for the marque.

The Power Plus engines followed suit in 1933 with an alloy head secured by 16 bolts. They also had a new oil pump whose output was linked to the throttle and this was fitted into a body cast as part of the right crankcase door.

All the engines went to the Power Plus dimensions, although these units were only fitted to the Sports and Replica models. These models and the Tourer and de luxe were much as before

Engine of the Scott three with one side panel lifted, this being the 1934 986 cc version

except for the fitting of Brampton girder forks on the Tourer. The others continued with the bottom link type.

The range stayed much as it was for 1934 but with just the Tourer, de luxe and Replica in the two engine sizes. The Replica was also available with a four-speed gearbox.

There was a new machine being worked on and in February 1934 details were announced. The engine was an in-line triple of either 747 or 986 cc and water-cooled as any self-respecting Scott always was. It had an Elektron crankcase into which the built-up crankshaft was inserted from one end and this had case walls assembled to it carrying the mains. The assembly included the big-end roller bearing and its outer race, to which the alloy split rods were clamped. There was one Amal and a three-into-one exhaust on the left and two

1938 598 cc Clubman's Special Scott with plunger rear suspension

oil pumps linked to the throttle and supplied from a sump. Ignition was by coil and a four-speed gearbox went behind the engine. Final drive was by chain, the kickstarter doubled as a prop-stand and the cycle parts were conventional, with duplex frame and bottom link forks. The 747 cc prototype had been built early in 1934 and was later road tested by *The Motor Cycle* but never reached production.

The 1935 range was reduced to a single model, the Flying Squirrel, with the choice of 497 or 598 cc engines. Both these now had a detachable cylinder head. There was also a change to the frame and detail alterations with an option of footchange for the gearbox. Then at the last minute Scott wheeled a new triple into the show at Olympia just before it opened.

This was based on the earlier model but had a 986 cc engine, which now had a horizontally split crankcase. In many aspects it was as the prototype, but the radiator was blended into the front of the fuel tank and the whole machine had much more style. On the outside was a well-finned exhaust manifold with the inlet beneath it and recessed into the block. It caused quite a stir.

However, it was still not in production when the next show came round and Scott did not even have a stand at that one. They continued to just list the Flying Squirrel with either engine, while the three was said to be available to special order. The same statement and range held true for 1937 also, and at the end of that year the three was dropped with very few having been built. The two Flying Squirrels continued alone for 1938.

1939 saw a new model, the Clubman's Special, which had a tuned engine and a 90 mph guarantee. Both it and the Flying Squirrel were only available with the 598 cc engine, but both could be had with a plunger rear suspension that bolted on to the rigid frame. Wide- or close-ratio gearboxes were available but still with just three speeds, although the selection was by foot.

Less well advertised was the weight, which *The Motor Cycle* quoted as 490 lb in a 1939 test of the spring frame Clubman's model. In turn this made the brakes poor by any standards, for they just could not cope with the excess avoirdupois even in town. The light, lithe Scott was now suffering badly from middle-age spread and had become a dull machine.

On that note the Scott stopped production for the duration, but returned post-war for a few years.

Seal

The Seal was one of motorcycling's oddities, for it was a three-wheeler that fell into the type known as Sociable. In these the outfit was conceived as a motorcycle and sidecar but with the rider brought in from the cold.

To do this the sidecar body was extended to provide two seats, side by side, and the mechanics were left outside to get wet. From some angles it looked like an early Austin 7 until observed more closely or the wheels counted.

The Seal dated from 1912 and the design sold for most of the 1920s was laid out in sidecar fashion as a two-tracked vehicle. The engine was a large side-valve JAP which drove a three-speed gearbox, but the frame that supported them was unusual.

It was built up from straight tubes that were bolted or clamped together. There were no brazed lugs and the main frame was four tubes than ran along as two pairs on either side of the engine and extended from it back to the tail of the rear mudguard. The mechanics could be slid along them to adjust the chains.

The front suspension was also unusual, as the headstock, complete with the forks, all moved about a pivot point in front of the crankcase. The compression spring that took the load was attached to a braced point above and in front of the forward cylinder head.

The fork itself comprised two tubes, curved at the bottom, which were attached to the crowns, which turned in the headstock. A rear loop braced them and a link connected them to a steering wheel set in the sidecar body. The wheels, front and rear, turned on live spindles with the bearings in lugs clamped to the frame and forks.

All told it was an odd machine and in addition to the passenger model there was also a commercial design. For 1930 this placed the rider in a small, open-topped cabin on the machine in a normal riding position. This allowed the whole of the sidecar to be devoted to goods carriage and the standard body had a large platform, sides, roll-back canvas hood and a front locker. The rider's compartment included a windscreen and side screens and steering control remained with a wheel.

Engines offered for the machine were a choice of 343 cc Villiers, 680 cc JAP twin or 980 cc JAP twin. The outfit was sold under the name Progress.

For 1930 the passenger vehicle was extensively modified to three tracks and a central front wheel. To signify this the name was changed to New Progress and in July 1932 it was joined by a carrier version.

This was even more odd, for it had front-wheel drive with the 680 cc sv JAP engine carried above the wheel. It drove an Albion three-speed-and-reverse gearbox and sat in a structure of clamped-up tubes which somehow incorporated a headstock and a pair of fork springs.

The chassis continued to comprise four long tubes with an unsprung rear axle to carry the two rear wheels. Thus it could easily be extended to accommodate different sizes of body.

Control was by handlebars which carried the gear lever as well as the usual items and the whole front end could be quickly detached for service or repair. The petrol tank alone travelled on the main frame with a flexible connection to the engine.

This strange design does not seem to have passed beyond the prototype stage and shortly afterwards the company ceased trading.

SGS

The initials stood for Sid Gleave Special and he was to make his mark on TT history by winning the 1933 Lightweight riding an Excelsior. Before then he was in business in a small way as a manufacturer and for 1930 was offering five models with JAP or Villiers engines.

The two-strokes were of 196 or 247 cc and went in loop frames with a three-speed Burman gearbox. The JAP engines were 245 cc sv and ohv units plus a 346 ohv, which was a super sports engine that went into a diamond frame (built for SGS by the Diamond works at Wolverhampton) with a three- or four-speed gearbox to create a TT model.

Like many others Sid found the 1930s hard going for making motorcycles and left this to others while he got on with racing.

Above **Strange front-wheel-drive New Progress Seal from 1932 in its prototype form**

Left **A 1924 Seal pictured at a rally in 1959. Very unusual front suspension and frame built up from four long tubes. Driver travelled in the sidecar**

Below **1930 SGS with Villiers engine and auto-lube. Nice but short-lived**

169

Sharratt

A 1920s firm that used proprietary engines but which by 1930 was only in limited production. For that year they listed just three models, all of which had 346 cc JAP engines.

The model F had a side-valve unit, but the FS was ohv, as was the FSS. All drove three-speed gearboxes and went into a conventional set of cycle parts.

For 1931 only the FS and FSS ohv models were listed and that was the last year for them. After that the firm turned to car dealing, which in time became a substantial business.

Below **The 1931 SOS model CY fitted with the 343 cc Villiers engine which was changed for the longer stroke 346 cc one the next year**
Far right **1934 Magnetic model C SOS with 249 cc water-cooled Villiers engine**

SOS

At first Super Onslow Special and later So Obviously Superior, but through the 1930s the SOS was considered exclusive and superior to the usual run of Villiers-powered machines. They were produced at first at Hallow, near Worcester, by Len Vale-Onslow and as there was no gas supply laid on he had, perforce, to adopt electric welding.

This led to a duplex frame with steel stampings for the fork ends in place of forged lugs. A platform was welded between the tubes under the mechanics to brace the frame and the result was a rigid structure. At the front went tubular girders and the wheels had good-sized brakes.

In 1930 SOS were still fitting JAP engines, and there were two models so equipped in 250 and 350 cc sizes, both with ohv. The rest of the range used Villiers power and came in 172, 196, 247 and 343 cc capacities. They were nicely constructed and continued for 1931 alone, for the JAP engines were dropped from the line-up.

For 1932 manufacture was transferred to Birmingham and the two-stroke range continued, with the largest model changing its engine to the long-stroke of 346 cc. There was also a suggestion that the four-strokes would return with 250 and 350 cc JAP and Python engines, but no more was heard of these.

What was seen early in the year was a water-cooled SOS. This was the prototype on test and later in the year came more details. There were to be two sizes of engine of 148 and 172 cc. The bottom half was pure Villiers, but the top was SOS with a separate head and barrel, both in iron and water-cooled. The water passages were generous in size and cooling was by a radiator mounted beneath the petrol tank with enclosing cowls.

The remainder of the machine was stock SOS with three-speed Burman gearbox, flywheel magneto ignition and an upswept option for the larger model which also had auto-lube and a separate oil tank. Coil ignition and dynamo lighting was an option for any model. The 148 cc machine had a Villiers carburettor, while the 172 cc one could have that or an Amal. To complete the range for 1933 there was a 172 cc air-cooled model which was fitted with the super sports engine with extensive head fins. Like the others it had twin exhaust systems.

In July a 249 cc water-cooled model was added to the range and was on the same lines as the others, and in October control of the firm passed to Tommy Meeten. Production remained in Birmingham, but at that time Meeten's shop was in Redhill, Surrey, where he sold Francis-Barnett and Villiers.

His range for 1934 was retyped, given names and included air- and water-cooled engines. All were fitted with Albion gearboxes, mainly handchange but some with the option of footchange and two with four speeds. The range began with the 172 cc Speed A, which was built for track use and had auto-lube and the option of hand or foot for changing its three gears. Next was the Club B, also of 172 cc but water-cooled, with auto-lube and handchange. The Club D was similar but had the 249 cc engine and footchange. There were two Magnetic models, the water-cooled 249 cc model C and the air-cooled 346 cc model F, both with three speeds and handchange, but the F was on petroil while the C had auto-lube.

Finally came the 249 cc water-cooled E and 346 cc air-cooled G Superb models, both with auto-lube and fully enclosed and with oil bath primary chaincases, then a rare feature for a small two-stroke. Both also had a four-speed gearbox with the option of hand or footchange and were fitted with legshields.

The range continued on these lines for 1935 with the option of three or four speeds for models A and B. For 1936 the designations were altered to indicate the type of engine cooling and the AA became the Brooklands model, available in track, road racing or trials trim to order. The water-cooled models became the BW, CW, DW and EW

Stanley

and were joined by three new machines. These had air-cooling and were the CA, DA and EA, all of 249 cc with Villiers engines. Tuned engines were also offered, and no doubt this was done by Meeten at the shop.

During 1936 Tommy Meeten opened new premises on the Kingston by-pass at Shannon Corner. He named them Meetens Motor Mecca and they became very well known until a fly-over was built at the junction in the mid-sixties. His range for 1937 was as before plus two more Club models with 249 cc engines and air- or water-cooling.

These had high-compression engines and other options were easy to arrange, for production was always in small numbers. If necessary modifications could always be done at the shop and for some models there was an option of frame wheelbase in one of two lengths.

The range was the same for 1938, but the AA name changed to Racing and in 1939 it was listed for grass or road racing with trials an option, and the 346 cc models became water-cooled as the FW and GW. All the names were the same and the range did represent the quality end of the utility market. Several models were offered with all-weather equipment—legshields, under-shields plus well-valanced mudguards—while there were cheaper versions with fewer fittings but as good a reputation.

When war came Meeten offered his facilities to the authorities but was turned down; he closed the Birmingham factory and turned to farming. His intention to restart production post-war was foiled by looting of his stock of engine units, so the Mecca became a shop specializing in Villiers-powered products.

This was a tricycle fitted with a 98 cc Villiers engine in the manner of an autocycle but with three wheels. It appeared in 1932 and was intended to offer stability and a little power assistance to the elderly.

The machine was based on a normal tricycle complete with pedalling gear and differential back axle. Into this was fitted a metal-to-metal cone clutch, while the engine hung just under the axle on the left side. Spur gears connected the engine to the alloy housing carrying the clutch and differential and there were dog clutches to connect the pedalling gear normally or to the engine for starting purposes.

The fitments were bicycle with a stirrup front brake and external contracting one on each rear wheel. The latter were interconnected to a single handlebar lever.

It was a nice idea, but was launched at a difficult time, and no more was heard of the little machine from Egham in Surrey.

Stevens HP6 model of 1936 with 495 cc engine. This was the competition version of the standard model and like it had a megaphone silencer

Stevens

When the old AJS firm was taken over by Matchless the Stevens brothers were left with the Wolverhampton factory and some old machine tools. There were also some engine jigs and at first they kept going by making a light van powered by a modified motorcycle engine. Then in March 1934 they re-entered the motorcycle market.

Their machine was a straightforward ohv single of 249 cc with vertical cylinder, twin pushrod tubes, exposed valve gear and rear-mounted mag-dyno. Lubrication was by pump supplied from a tank mounted in front of the crankcase with any surplus oil returned to it.

Transmission was by oil bath, pressed-steel chaincase to a four-speed, footchange Burman gearbox. The frame was a duplex cradle with single top tube and Druid forks were fitted with a central spring. Details and fittings were well executed and options included hand gearchange, Amal or Bowden carburettor and upswept or low-level exhaust system for the single-port head.

This machine was typed the DS1 and continued for 1935 with rubber insulation for the handlebars, an oil feed to the inlet valve and one to the rear chain among its detail changes. It was joined by the LL4, which was the same machine fitted with a 348 cc ohv engine. Both had the options as for 1934.

In April 1935 they were joined by a third model of 495 cc and listed as the LP5. This was much as the others, but had a different frame and the oil tank beneath the saddle, although the system remained total loss. The engine was a single-port type but with hairpin valve springs.

All three models continued for 1936 and their most obvious change was the adoption of mega-phone-shaped silencers for the 348 and 495 cc models. Inside the end was a reverse cone at the end of the spiral baffles, but from the side these were not to be seen. The smaller models had their oil tanks moved to beneath the saddle and there were new big-ends and petrol tanks for both.

For competition use the three models were available with suitable changes as the US2, HL3 and HP6 in the three capacities. They and the road trio all ran on into 1937 with a figure 7 added to their typing. There were few changes, but the 249 cc road machine changed to the megaphone silencer and this had extra spirals to reduce noise, as maybe the police had been showing an interest.

The same range was listed with the same type numbers for 1938, but during that year the brothers finally ceased making motorcycles and turned to other work.

Sun

Like many, this firm had its roots in the cycle industry and hailed from Birmingham. Motorcycles came prior to World War 1 and continued after it with JAP, Villiers and other engines, including a disc-valve two-stroke.

By 1930 the range of models numbered six and they were much as others of that time. Two models had Villiers engines of 147 and 196 cc and the other four were JAP powered. Two had side valves and were of 300 and 490 cc capacity and the ohv were of 346 and 490 cc. All had the engines set vertically, handchange and the 346 cc ohv the option of three or four speeds. In April the 490 cc ohv appeared in a revised form with four speeds.

The only models to continue as they were for 1931 were the 196 cc two-stroke and the two 500s with sv and ohv. New was a larger 343 cc two-stroke with Villiers engine and a model with an inclined 245 cc ohv JAP engine with rear magneto.

In May 1931 the range was joined by a miniature which used a 98 cc Villiers engine inclined in the simple diamond frame. A single exhaust system went on the left and the engine drove a two-speed Albion gearbox with direct-acting handchange. Lubrication was by petroil and ignition by flywheel magneto. Blade girders were used and the machine had direct lighting and with this was sold for 16 guineas.

In August 1931 the firm announced another model, which had a 147 cc Villiers engine, a two-speed Albion gearbox, flywheel magneto and a simple diamond frame with blade girders. The engine was mounted vertically and a saddle tank was fitted for the petroil mixture. An oil tin was clipped to the seat tube and the machine slotted well into the 150 cc tax class.

The 1932 range comprised four models plus the two newcomers of 98 and 147 cc, now called Tourist models. In addition the two 490 cc JAP-powered machines continued to be sold to use up stocks. The 196 cc machine ran on as the Utility and a Sports model was added with a 148 cc Villiers engine with three-speed Albion gearbox. The other two machines were again called Tourist models and both had 346 cc engines inclined in similar frames with tubular girders, but one had an ohv single-port JAP engine with dry sump lubrication and magneto ignition while the other used a Villiers engine with auto-lube and flywheel magneto.

In April 1932 a second version of the 148 cc model appeared and was fitted out to a fuller specification. It had coil ignition, a dynamo which clamped to the seat tube and was chain driven, electric horn, three-speed Moss gearbox, Webb

Sun four-stroke with 490 cc JAP engine in a 1931 model

blade girders and legshields with foot-trays and side valances.

This model ran on for 1933 along with the 98, 147 and 196 cc machines plus the two 346 cc ones. These six models ran on for that year, but then Sun gave up producing their own make for several years. They continued to make parts and even complete machines for other firms, but it was 1940 before another Sun was seen.

This was an autocycle powered by a 98 cc Villiers engine and produced in three forms. The standard one had the standard engine and the others the de luxe unit. These also had a Webb sprung front fork and the Super de luxe had louvred engine shields as well. With the war production stopped again but they did return to motorcycles in the post-war years.

Sunbeam

Sunbeam were one of several companies whose best years lay in their early history. They had built up a tremendous reputation for quality and finish, but to do this had to keep all the work in-house. They bought in castings and the usual proprietary items such as carburettor and magneto, but all

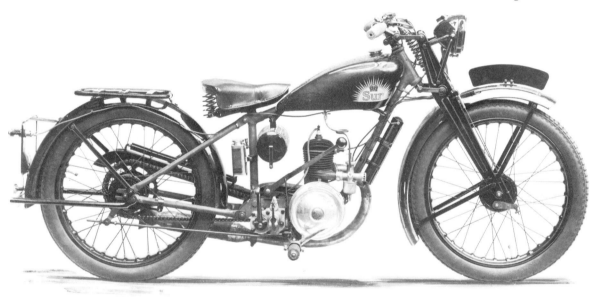

Above **Sun two-stroke Tourist with 147 cc Villiers engine**
Below **1931 Sunbeam Lion with 489 cc side-valve engine**

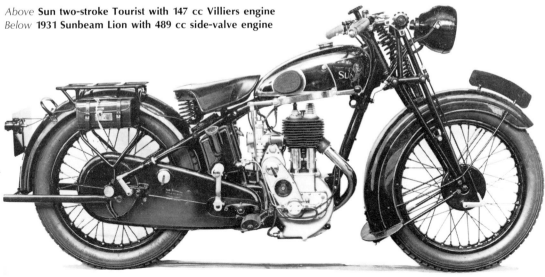

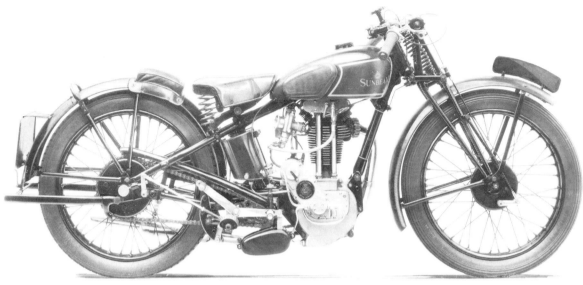

Above 1933 Sunbeam Little 90 racing machine of 246 cc
Below 1935 Model 16 with 248 cc high-camshaft engine

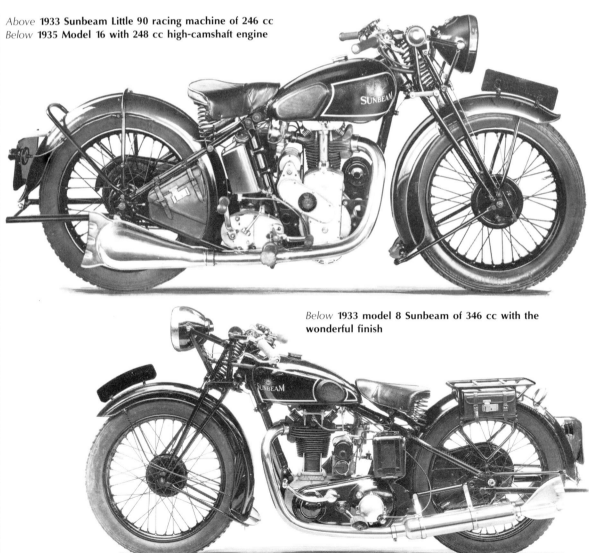

Below 1933 model 8 Sunbeam of 346 cc with the wonderful finish

machining, plating and painting was done on the premises to the very high standards first set by the founder, John Marston.

In 1928 Sunbeam became part of the large ICI concern, but despite the benefits of improved conditions the workforce were not over-enamoured with the notion. Instinctively and correctly they could see that the future could bring unwelcome directives from afar and preferred the discipline of management on the spot.

Sunbeam won four Senior TTs in the 1920s—in 1920, 1922, 1928 and 1929, along with many other races, but from then on success was to elude them. As the 1930s progressed the works began to feel the hand of the ICI accountants on them and much of the tradition began to go. More parts were bought in and slowly some of the quality went, although the standard of painting remained as high as ever.

The 1930 range reflected the 1920s Sunbeam line-up and although the company had changed to saddle tanks there was still the 599 cc side-valve model 7 with flat tank made to special order.

At the bottom of the list were the 346 cc side-valve Touring model 1 and Sporting model 2. With a 491 cc engine these became the models 5 and 6, which did have dry sump lubrication. With ohv there were the 346 cc model 8 and 493 cc model 9 and all these models had tall vintage-style engines with rear magneto. The gearbox was of the cross-over type, so while the primary chain remained as usual on the left, the final drive one was on the right and could be fully enclosed.

Of more interest to the enthusiast were the TT models 80 and 90, also of 346 and 493 cc, but with hairpin valve springs and replicas of the TT winning machines. They had much racier lines and were replicas in the same sense as the camshaft Norton and Rudge Ulster, although their lines were still vintage. There was one further competition model, which was the DTR for speedway use. It had a single-port 90 engine in cycle parts which at first were nearly impossible to use on the track, but in time these changed. Very few were made.

In June 1930 one more model was added to the list. This was the 6, also called the Lion, and had a 489 cc side-valve engine. It replaced the old model 6 and went on into the 1931 range. It heralded a new style of Sunbeam with Webb forks and chrome-plated tank, while the model list was shortened. The models 9 and 90 were still there with coil valve springs and the model 6 Lion was

trimmed down to cut the price. New was the 10 with 344 cc ohv engine with wet sump, three-speed gearbox and no rear chain enclosure option.

In July 1931 the old model 7 became a second version of the Lion with a 599 cc side-valve engine, and a tuned version of the 10 was listed. For 1932 there was only a single 344 cc ohv and the 9 and 90 continued in the list. To them was added the 599 cc ohv 9A and in the Lion range there was the 489 cc sv model from 1930 and a 599 cc version. The old flat-tank model 7 entered its final year to special order as before.

There was not much change for 1933, but the 346 cc ohv models 8 and 80 returned, much as they were in 1930 but with twin-port engines. The 9, 9A, 90 and two sizes of Lion continued and were joined by one newcomer. This was the 250 Long-stroke model 14, produced by reducing the bore of the 8 to give a 246 cc capacity. It did make for a heavy machine despite the fitting of some lighter parts. It was joined in January 1933 by the Little 90, a racing version built in small numbers which retained the long stroke of the stock engine.

In the same style came the 95, which was the 493 cc version of racing specification but for use on the road, and later the Little 95, which was the 1934 model of the 246 cc machine. Both had hairpin valve springs. The rest of the 1934 range was as for the year before less the 80 and 90. This left the two side-valve Lions, two touring ohv models, the 246 and 596 cc ohv machines and two 95 race replicas.

The company was, however, in trouble with the ICI accountants, for they built too good a product. Hard though this must have sounded it was true at the time, for price was all in the early 1930s and customers had to be found by skimping quality and cutting prices to the bone. This was not the Sunbeam way, of course, and they found it near impossible to change their habits. Sadly there were few about who could afford the price of good work and those who could tended to be snapped up by George Brough.

The 1935 range had the stalwart 8, 9, 9A and Lion models and three more, two revisions and one new. The revisions were the 95L for the sports rider and the 95R, which was without a kickstarter. Both models had four speeds, footchange and larger brakes. The new machine was the 248 cc ohv model 16 with a high camshaft, hairpin valve springs and a bulbous silencer on its single exhaust pipe. It had a Burman gearbox, so the final drive chain went on the left, but proved to be a poor design and was not at all successful.

The larger Lion and 596 cc ohv 9A remained as they were for 1936, but the other models went over to Burman gearboxes, so the final drive was moved to the left side of the machine. The 493 cc ohv model 9 had a new single-port head and a new cradle frame, while the 346 cc 8 and 246 cc 14 had diamond frames. Both had single-port engines and the smaller was much as it had been two years earlier.

The 489 cc Lion went in the cradle frame with a Burman box and the engine had an alloy head and fully enclosed valve gear. There was also a sports version of the 9 in the list and this had an upswept exhaust and a change of tyre sizes. Even this model was without the hairpin valve springs pioneered by the marque, but all models were still very well made and very quiet running thanks to anti-backlash gears in the timing chest and other measures.

The sports 493 cc model was joined in February 1936 by versions with 246 and 346 cc engines. These still retained the diamond frame of their base model but had the upswept sports exhaust system.

There was little change for 1937, although all models now had the Burman gearbox and the oil pump pipes disappeared within the timing cover. The valve gear of the 9 and 9A was fully enclosed and the range was nearly as before. The change was the appearance of a 493 cc ohv Light Solo in standard and sports forms and this was intended for solo use only. Both 246 and 346 cc ohv models

were listed in the two forms and the Lions in two sizes.

1937 saw the end of the road for Sunbeam as a part of ICI, for they were not producing the profit required of them. The result was a sale of the business to the AJS and Matchless combine in London, and late in 1937 the parts and data were moved south. The workforce in Wolverhampton was absorbed into other ICI activities on the same site and the London firm learnt a great deal about high-quality paint finishes, which went on to their machines from then on. The combination of the three firms became AMC.

For 1938 all ten models were listed with new designations but little other change. One item that had to go was the black painting of the gearbox end cover, as AMC production did not allow for this to happen to the Burman boxes.

The two old Lion models of 489 and 599 cc with side valves continued as the B29 and B30 in 1939, but the rest of the range had new engines. These were of an AMC design with ohv moved by a chain-driven high camshaft. The chain also drove the mag-dyno and had a Weller tensioner, the whole enclosed by a large triangular cover carrying the Sunbeam name in script.

Four sizes of engine were produced in 245, 348, 497 and 598 cc capacities. The three largest shared the same stroke, and dimensions were common with AMC engines. Hairpin valve springs were used and a duplex gear oil pump went in the base of the crankcase.

In addition to the four standard models the three smaller were listed in Sports and Com-

petition forms. The first of these had polished engine internals, upswept exhaust and a change of mudguard and tyres. The second was built for trials use with a smaller petrol tank, 4 in. rear tyre and alloy mudguards, but were still heavy machines, as were all the models in the series.

In June 1939 a rear suspension system was announced for the larger ohv singles. It looked like a plunger one but was not, although the springs were in plunger boxes at the rear of the frame. The wheel was, however, carried in a pivoted fork and this in turn linked to the plungers by a shackle—common practice in Italy and Germany at that time but not in England.

This went into the 1940 range, which comprised ten models in all including the three with rear suspension. The same three plus the 245 cc model were listed in rigid frames and the 348 and 497 cc ones in sports guise. Last but not least came the 599 cc sv Lion as the C30.

In practice very few spring-frame models were made and before long the AMC works was fully engaged in producing the Matchless G3 for the services. This brought the Sunbeams to a halt and in 1943 AMC sold the name to the BSA group. Post-war this resulted in the totally new in-line twin and there were no more Sunbeams in the John Marston style. AMC continued to benefit from the paint know-how for many years and gained a high reputation for their finish, although few realized where this had come from.

Left **The AMC-designed B28 Sunbeam of 598 cc from 1939 with chain drive for the high camshaft and plunger rear suspension**

Three Spires

This make appeared late in 1931 for the following year's season and was produced by Coventry Bicycles, who had, in the past, made the Coventry-B&D, and the Wee McGregor. Their new machine was a lightweight and powered by a 147 cc Villiers engine. It, and a two-speed Albion gearbox, were housed in a diamond frame with the cylinder vertical and tubular girder forks went at the front.

Lubrication was by petroil and ignition by flywheel magneto, which also powered the direct lighting. A Lycett saddle was provided along with a centre stand and a tank that contrived to look triangular, although it was of the saddle type. A pair of long legshields were provided on the model and a second machine was listed minus both these and the lighting.

The machine failed to survive past the end of the 1932 season and no more was heard of it.

Below **1932 Three Spires model with 147 cc Villiers engine and only listed for that one year**

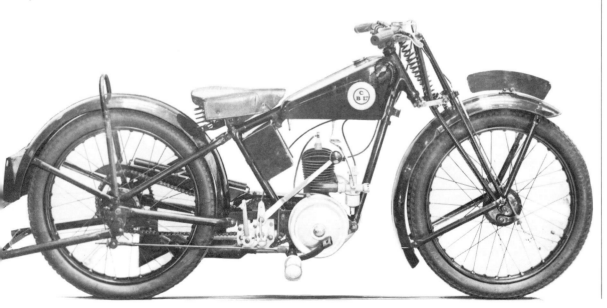

Triumph

In 1930 the range of Triumph motorcycles was made in Coventry and at that time the same parent firm built and sold bicycles and motor cars. The first of these was sold off early in the decade, but it was 1936 before the cars went their own way. They had run the company into financial difficulties and the initial decision was to stop all motorcycle production.

This situation became known to Jack Sangster, who already owned the Ariel firm, and he completed a deal to take over the two-wheeled side as the Triumph Engineering Company early in 1936. It was to become very successful and make a lot of money.

Back in 1930 the future was less clear and the heady days of the 1920s were giving way to the dark ones of the depressed early thirties. Like everyone else Triumph had to trim their range to suit people's pockets above all else.

To do this they kept to six models to begin the year, all with vertically mounted engines, three-speed gearboxes and conventional construction. From the 1920s came the odd-capacity model WS with its 278 cc side-valve engine and mechanical oil pump supplemented by a foot pump. It was aimed at the market for machines that qualified for the low tax due to their weight and gave as much capacity as was feasible within the limit.

Also from older days was the 549 cc side-valve model NSD, which had the same type of lubrication system. The remaining models were from 1929 and the smallest was the 348 cc ohv model CO. Next came the CN with a side-valve 498 cc engine and the CTT with a twin-port ohv unit of the same capacity. Finally came the model CSD with 549 cc side-valve power. All the C range had rear magnetos and the two larger sizes shared a common crankshaft stroke, with the capacity change coming from a larger bore.

Common to the range were very clean handlebars with integral controls. This was not done by the use of inverted levers but by curving the bars and placing the lever pivots at the bends. This was done with both air and ignition controls as well as the clutch and front brake.

Early in 1930 another model was added to the range and this was unusual in that it was a unit construction 174 cc two-stroke with a two-speed gearbox. The design was original in many respects and the first point was that the carburettor faced forward and was clipped directly to the inlet port. The exhaust went on the left, where it connected to a pipe and silencer on that side, while the transfer was on the right. The piston deflector therefore ran fore and aft and its two rings were formed to lock together, so piston pegs were not needed.

Each flywheel bob-weight was formed with a gear beside it and these meshed with two larger gears carried to the rear. Between them went an alloy packer to fill the space and keep the primary compression ratio up. Within it slid a selector dog which was moved by a rack-and-pinion device to lock one or other gear into mesh. All this was carried within the crankcase castings, and outboard of these on the gearbox shaft went a clutch with ball ramp lift mechanism. From the clutch a chain drove the rear wheel.

This unit went into a frame made from twin tubes which ran from the rear wheel spindle, curved easily at the headstock and ran back under the engine. There were no forgings in the frame construction, only pressings. Forks were girder and the petroil tank fitted within the frame with bolted and rubber mounting. Ignition and lighting were provided by a Lucas unit on the left end of the crankshaft and were included in the under £25 price. The machine was called the Junior.

For the spring of 1930 the very old-fashioned NSD was replaced by another model of the same typing but fully revised. The engine retained its dimensions while the cylinder was inclined forward and a dry sump lubrication system adopted and supplied from a tank cast as the front section of the crankcase. The magneto went behind the cylinder and a three-speed gearbox was fitted. The front wheel stand was unusual, for it was a pressed-steel item which pivoted from the underside of the crankcase. The front brake was a friction band, but the rear was the normal drum type.

The odd-sized WS went from the range for 1931 along with the CO and in their places came the 249 cc ohv WO and 343 cc ohv NM. Both had

Above **1931 Triumph model NSD with 549 cc side-valve inclined engine**

Above **Silent Scout model A Triumph of 1932 fitted with 549 cc engine**
Right **The 1933 model WA with partial enclosure of its 249 cc engine**

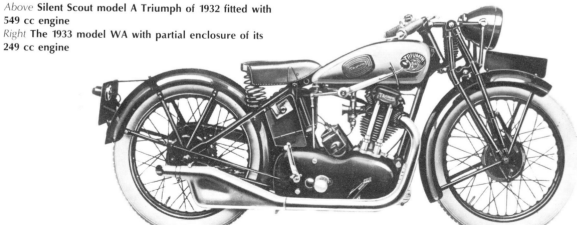

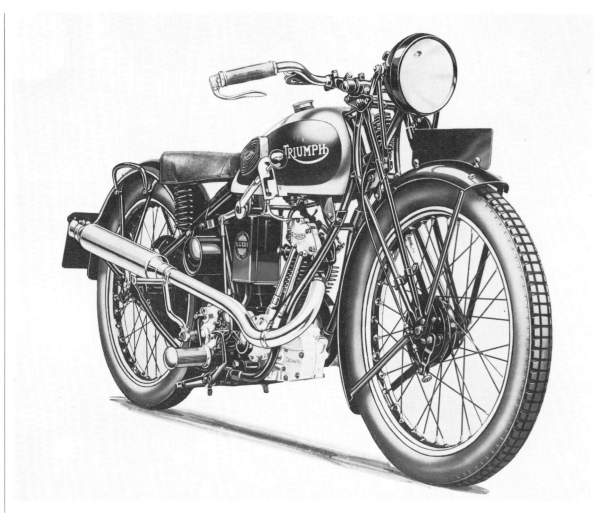

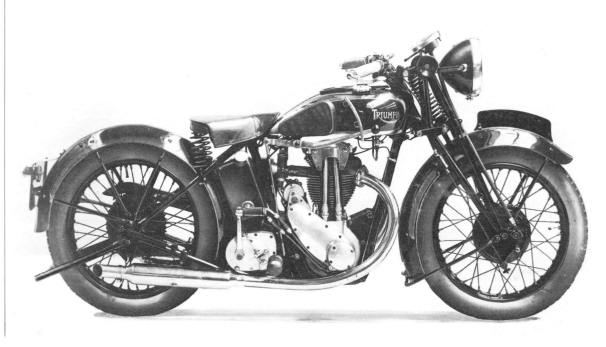

Above **The 647 cc twin-cylinder Triumph model 6/1 with matching sidecar on show late in 1934**
Left **Triumph 1934 model XO5/1 with three-speeds and 148 cc engine**
Bottom left **De luxe model 5/4 Triumph with 493 cc engine in 1934**

inclined engines and dry sump lubrication as on the NSD, which continued along with the CSD, CN and CTT with vertical cylinders, semi-dry sump oiling and cradle frames.

New was the 348 cc side-valve WL built on the lines of the WO, while the 174 cc two-stroke continued as the model X. Later additions to the programme were the de luxe ND with 549 cc side-valve engine and the NT with a 493 cc ohv unit. Both followed the theme of the NSD and had the right side of the crankcase and gearbox enclosed by a single pressing. This greatly cleaned up the appearance of that side of the machine and also meant that the castings did not need to be polished. The enclosure began to be available for other N or W series models.

1932 brought further changes to the range as the firm sought to offer something for every possible buyer. At the bottom end of the scale the two-stroke had its bore reduced to take the capacity down below the 150 cc tax barrier and in this size was sold as the Z, while the X was still available.

Only the CSD still had a vertical cylinder among the four-strokes, while the rest were inclined with the dry sump built into the front of the crankcase. The right side enclosing panel was improved to allow it to be detached more easily. The WO, WL, NM, NT and ND were all much as before and were joined by three newcomers. The WA was a single-port version of the twin-port 249 cc WO and the other two were competition models based on the standard road ones.

For a little off-road use the exhausts were high level, a sump plate was fitted and the enclosing side panel was dispensed with. Both machines had ohv and were the 343 cc CA and 493 cc CD.

At the end of March 1932 two further models were announced as the Silent Scouts. They were simply the A with a 549 cc sv engine and the B with a 493 cc ohv one. Both followed the Triumph format of the year with inclined cylinder, dry sump cast into the front of the crankcase and rear-mounted mag-dyno. As with some others of the range a Bowden carburettor was fitted. To reduce the noise level the pushrods were enclosed and harmonic cams fitted, while a concentration on quality in manufacture kept the noise down. A styling point was that the cylinder fins were parallel to the ground and thus not at right angles to the bore.

Aside from the aim to be quiet the machine also carried the notion of enclosure further. As an option either model could be fitted with combined leg and side shields which enclosed the area below the fuel tank and back to the rear wheel. Access was provided for essential services.

There were further changes for 1933, although the Silent Scouts A and B, competition 500 CD, road 500 NT, touring side-valve ND and one- or two-port 250s WO and WA all ran on. The two-strokes went, as did the 350s with either side or overhead valves and the old CSD. New was the BS, which was a sports version of the Silent Scout with a crankcase shield and without the option of the enclosure panels. A second new model was the WP, which was a sports model based on the stock 249 cc ohv machine with a four-speed gearbox, no side panel option and twin tubular silencers.

The third new model was the XO, a 148 cc ohv single with well-inclined cylinder and horizontal cooling fins. It was designed to come within the capacity tax class, and with a compression ratio of 7:1 and dual valve springs was a sporting unit. The machine had a three-speed gearbox and the frame was duplex, much as the two-stroke, with a pressed-steel seat post-member. Tension spring front forks were fitted. Coil ignition was used with the points in the timing cover, while the dynamo was clamped to the rear of the crankcase. An outside flywheel was fitted on the left under a pressed-steel cover. With a 47 mph top speed it made a sprightly ride-to-work machine.

In July 1933 an important step in Triumph history took place with the announcement of a model fitted with a 647 cc vertical twin engine.

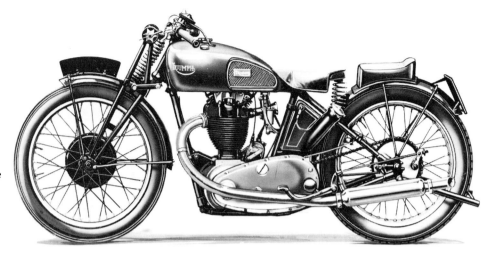

When Triumph made a road-racing model. This is the 1935 5/10 with tuned 493 cc engine and supplied with road silencer

This was not the firm's first engine in that style for they had built one as early as 1913, but it was the start of a modern trend. The twin was designed by Val Page and its form was to reappear post-war in the BSA twin.

For Triumph, Page laid down an engine based on 70 × 84 mm dimensions with overhead valves moved by a single gear-driven camshaft mounted to the rear of the crankcase. The mag-dyno was gear driven from the camshaft and lubrication was dry sump with the oil tank built into the crankcase. A flywheel was carried on the left of the crankshaft and outboard of it went the primary drive, which was by double helical gears, an expensive design at any time, let alone in 1933; this caused the engine to run backwards.

The gearbox was bolted to the back of the crankcase and contained four speeds with handchange. It and the engine were housed in a massive duplex frame supported by heavy-duty girder forks at the front. This was done because the machine was intended for sidecar use in the main, so it was solid and rather lacking in ground clearance for solo use.

Both brakes were 8 in. in diameter and were interconnected. In addition they could be locked on using a hand trigger on the primary chaincase. Depression of the brake pedal automatically released this device. Coupled brakes were also used on some of the other models.

To match the twin there was a special design of sidecar with a body that hid the chassis, and with this attached the firm ran the outfit round Brooklands for 500 miles at 60 mph, after it had been taken through the ISDT, that is, and for this they won the Maudes Trophy.

The twin was the largest model in the 1934

range, which was one of the most extensive in the industry. In addition most of it was new, although the B and BS Silent Scouts continued to be offered, as did the inclined-engine 150 with ohv. This became the XO5/1 in standard form and the XO5/5 when fitted with a four-speed gearbox. The /5 indicated a sports model with raised compression ratio, stronger valve springs, polished combustion chamber and a plum finish to the tank, mudguards and wheels. Also for all except the 150, footchange and a polished alloy chaincase were fitted.

The 150 was bored out a little to create the 175 cc XO7/1 and XO7/5, both of which used the light frame of the 150 along with all its other details. The same frame was also used by the XV/1, which was powered by a 148 cc Villiers engine coupled to a three-speed gearbox.

Three models used the medium-weight frame and all had new engines with vertical cylinders designed by Val Page. As was usual with his work they were straightforward in layout, dependable in use but a trifle solid in appearance. They sold well to those who could see their worth, but at that point lacked any touch of glamour.

The design could not have been more conventional and was much as the Ariel that Page had designed before. The magneto was gear driven rather than by chain as Triumph had the facilities for this, but for the rest it was a basic single with rear mag-dyno, dry sump lubrication and the expected cycle parts.

The three medium-weight models were the 2/1 and 2/5 which had 249 cc ohv engines and the 3/1 with a 343 cc side-valve unit. The rest of the range had a heavier frame and into this went touring and sports 343 cc ohv engines to give the 3/2 and 3/5. All these ohv models had twin-port heads, as did

Model 5/1 with 549 cc side-valve engine in 1936 to make a sidecar single for the Triumph range

the three of 493 cc. These were the 5/2, 5/4 de luxe and 5/5 sports, which were joined by a pair of 549 cc sv models labelled the 5/1 and 5/3 de luxe.

In April 1934 a further 493 cc single appeared as the road-racing 5/10. This was shown as a prototype and was based on the road model but with a lowered frame and modified engine. A longer rod and barrel were fitted and a choice of pistons made available for use with petrol-benzole or alcohol. Fixtures and fittings were for racing, but each of the two exhaust pipes terminated in a small, upturned silencer. Three of these machines were run in the TT by the factory, but all retired.

There was curtailment of the range for 1935 with the 148 cc ohv and two-stroke models being available to special order only and the 175, B and BS going from the range. This left the same line of singles with vertical cylinders as listed for 1934 plus the 647 cc twin and one new model.

The addition was a 249 cc single with ohv and one-port head with fully enclosed valve gear. It followed the lines of the other models in other respects and had a new lightweight four-speed gearbox. The frame had a single downtube, unlike the other models, and the machine was typed the L2/1.

To advertise the range the entire line-up of 13 models was taken to Brooklands in September 1934 and each given a one-hour run round the track under ACU observation. All managed to complete the run with only three minor stops.

The range announced for 1936 seemed to have been reduced, as the 2/5, 3/5, 5/3 and 5/4 were no longer listed. In effect they remained with their special fittings available as options. The rest of the range also received attention, with the 2/1 and 3/2 both becoming single-port engines with fully

enclosed valve gear. The frame remained a duplex but of light construction.

The side-valve 3/1 and 5/1 engines were fitted with light alloy cylinder heads and received detail improvements. The 5/2 gained an alloy chaincase, while the L2/1 was fitted with a fully enclosed primary chainguard with an adjustable oil feed to the chain.

The 5/5 continued with shorter forks and a reduction in height, while competition tyres were available for it as an option, as were high-level pipes. The 5/10 was still listed and could be had with TT or standard close-ratio gears. The twin continued with a price reduction.

Early in 1936 the company changed hands and a statement was issued that the range would continue in production and that Edward Turner would be the General Manager. He set to work with his special skills to give real style to selected models and the result came in April.

What Turner did was simple and effective. He took the 250, 350 and 500 models and fitted them with sports specification engines as a start. The alloy cases were polished and a high-level exhaust system fitted. He then added to the sparkle by fitting petrol tanks finished with chrome-plating and silver sheen panels lined in blue. The final and brilliant sales pitch was the names Turner gave the models, which were the Tiger 70, 80 and 90 in the three sizes.

There were further major changes for 1937 with new frames, forks and gearboxes with improved engines and revised model typing. Aside from the Tigers this used a number to indicate capacity and a letter to show valve position. The range was also reduced to remove the L2/1, which was nice but expensive to make, and the 6/1 twin, which was about to be replaced by the Turner design.

Each Tiger model was balanced by a de luxe version and these were listed as the 2H, 3H and 5H. For customers who preferred a side-valve engine the 343 cc 3S was available and for sidecar use a 598 cc one. This was the 6S and was a new and larger-size single built on the same lines as the others. It was a good compact range with plenty of appeal to buyers.

In January 1937 the range was extended by offering all three Tiger models in a competition form. These were intended for trials use, so the fittings were altered to suit, as were the gearbox ratios and the engine characteristics.

The Turner touch worked like magic on the public. Sports riders turned to the Tigers in droves, while the more sedate owners bought the standard models whose lines had been improved with new tanks and some polish where it mattered.

The Tigers were chosen for another attempt on the Maudes Trophy in March. One of each size was selected at random from dealers' stock and subjected to three hours at speed at Donington followed by flying laps at Brooklands. This brought them the trophy once again.

1938 saw the range of singles continue with minor changes in the form of a new rear number-plate shape, a Bakelite instrument panel and a twistgrip with spring plunger to hold it in any open position. There were two additions which had coil ignition in place of a magneto and were the 2HC and 3SC.

The very special event for Triumph was the advent of the Turner-designed model T, which became the Speed Twin or 5T. It had a simple ohv engine that was compact enough to fit the existing frame and in it were twin gear-driven camshafts, a built-up crankshaft and the twin-plunger oil pump. A mag-dyno was driven from the inlet cam gear and the iron block was held by six studs.

The cycle parts were as per the single and the finish amaranth red with the tank chromed before its panels were painted. The result was a very smart machine with tremendous appeal and a good turn of speed. It was immediately successful

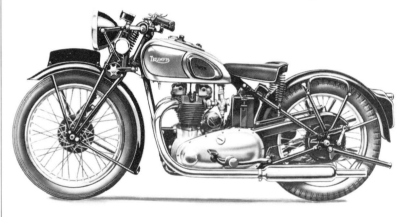

Left **The famous Speed Twin of 1938 with its 499 cc twin engine that was to run on for so many years**

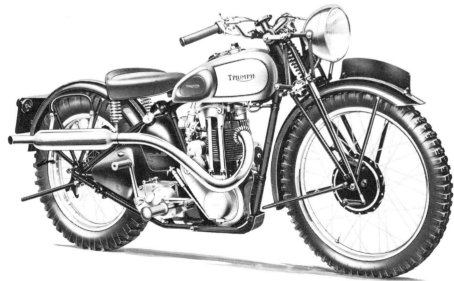

Right **Triumph Tiger 80 from 1937 with 343 cc engine and in competition form with tyres to suit**

and started a trend to twins that was to affect all the major firms in post-war days.

Logically it had to have a Tiger version, and in 1939 this arrived as the T100 and replaced the T90 in the process. With its arrival came an eight-stud block fixing, chromed front number plate surround and a change to a silver sheen finish for the mudguards with a black stripe in reverse to the earlier Tigers. The machine was set-off by megaphone-style exhausts with rounded ends and tailpipes which could readily be detached. An optional bronze cylinder head was available to take advantage of the special pistons fitted.

The rest of the range stayed much as it was, but the T70 and T80 both adopted the T100 mudguard finish, while the 5T took the eight-stud block. All were fitted with the new style front number-plate surround and a new tank motif, cast and then coloured to match the machine finish. The T90 went, but a further side-valve model appeared as the 493 cc 5S on the lines of its larger and smaller brothers.

Triumph decided to have another try for the Maudes Trophy in 1939 and for this used a Speed Twin and Tiger 100 selected by the ACU at random from dealers' stocks. They were taken to Coventry for a delivery check and then ridden to Brooklands but via John o'Groats and Land's End. The observer car was a Triumph Dolomite, which was a nice touch.

The 1806 miles were covered at a 42 mph average despite poor weather and a puncture for the T100. At Brooklands the machines were checked and then sent on a six-hour run round the track during which both averaged over 75 mph. In November the company learnt that they had won the trophy despite competition, but by then everyone had other problems to worry about.

No competition Tigers were in the 1940 model list and neither was the 5H, whose place had been taken by the 5T. Also out were the coil ignition 2HC and 3SC models, but the latter really remained as the economy 3SE. This was a low-price machine with a trimmed specification and it was joined by the larger 5SE, which retained the mag-dyno.

The other models remained, so that although supply was limited there was a choice for civilians. Not seen at all was the new 350 cc twin in its touring 3T guise or its Sports Tiger 85 one. That lay six long years away and was to be from another factory at Meriden.

Velocette

A family of motorcyclists built the Velocette and this showed through in the design and quality of manufacture. They were the Goodmans and three generations were to control the Hall Green firm over the years. Correct engineering solutions and nice machines resulted from this to enhance their reputation as builders of fine motorcycles.

By 1930 they had made their name in the TT with Junior wins in 1926, 1928 and 1929 using their ohc engine. They had also reached the end of development for their first two-stroke engine and so had a new one to offer.

This was the 249 cc GTP and it moved away from the overhung crankshaft of its predecessors to the more normal type. A large flywheel went on the left end with the engine sprocket and the right drove the oil pump and the ignition cam for the coil ignition. The rest of the machine was conventional, although the three-speed gearbox did have the outboard final drive sprocket and the usual slim Velocette clutch.

The other machines all had the 348 cc ohc engine with its slim, light lines and bevel-and-shaft drive on the right. The magneto went to the rear, where it was chain driven, lubrication was dry sump and the dynamo, when fitted, went in front of the crankcase and was driven by a flat belt.

There were three models, with the KSS the one for sporting road work. For the racer there was the Mk I KTT, the first production racing machine to be sold to the public and based firmly on the 1928 works model. It was light, rigid and had an open exhaust and big brakes. The third machine was the KTP, which had coil ignition, the points cam on the end of the camshaft, a dynamo in the magneto position and twin exhaust ports. These last did nothing but harm to the performance and the cut-price electrics did not match the ohc specification at all.

The same range was there for 1931 but with the KTT in a modified form which became known as

Top **The well-known ohc Velocette KTS from 1932**
Centre **Drive side of 1934 KTS shows outboard gearbox sprocket**
Right Velocette KTT Mk IV of **1934 on show and powered by the famous 348 cc ohc engine**

188

the Mk II. The practice of allocating mark numbers was introduced for stores identification purposes, but in time went into general rider use. The II was much as the I but had some engine changes. With it ran the KSS and the much less successful KTP, while the GTP ran on well and proved a popular lightweight.

For 1932 the KTP was replaced by the much nicer KTS, which was simply a KSS with touring mudguards and tyres. Both had an oil bath chaincase and detail improvements, as did the KTT, which became the Mk III. The GTP had a link fitted between the throttle and the oil pump to give the latter a variable output depending on the opening of the former. Novel at the time.

1933 brought four-speed gearboxes to the KSS and KTS models, while the KTT became the Mk IV with a new cylinder head and hairpin valve springs. The GTP continued as it was. This was all very well, but left a big gap between the small two-stroke and the sports camshaft models.

To fill this Velocette experimented in 1931 with a side-valve 350 which lacked power and then came up with another classic, the 248 cc MOV.This had ohv, a high gear-driven camshaft, enclosed valves and nearly square dimensions. It was obviously going to be able to rev and have a lively performance and no one was disappointed, for early road models were good for 60 mph and later tuned racers for 100 mph.

The basically simple engine with rear magneto, front dynamo and dry sump lubrication went into a cradle frame with a four-speed, handchange gearbox. None of the cycle parts came from the other models, but the result looked every inch a Velocette.

The MOV was announced in June 1933 and it and the other models made up the initial range for 1934. Footchange went on to the MOV as it did the KSS and KTS. The KTT remained the Mk IV but acquired an aluminium-bronze head, while the GTP was fitted with a new barrel with revised ports. These models were then joined by a second ohv machine, the 349 cc MAC, which came from extending the stroke of the MOV to 96 mm to copy the dimensions of an experimental long-stroke KTT. In other respects it was a copy of the smaller model and was to have an even longer history.

In April 1934 the GTP was given a face-lift with a four-speed, footchange gearbox and an oil bath primary chaincase. The dynamo continued to be mounted aft of the crankcase and its belt drive was outboard of the case under a small shield. The outside flywheel was fixed to it by six studs so access was easy enough. Some were built with magneto ignition, but most kept to the coil.

The six models were all listed for 1935 without any real change, but in April a new version of the KTT was announced as the Mk V. While it followed the same lines as before it was extensively altered, although the engine dimensions did stay as they were, so the capacity remained 348 cc.

The engine retained its ohc and drive, but the barrel was shorter and sunk more deeply into the larger crankcase. Long studs secured both the aluminium-bronze head and the barrel, while the valves continued with hairpin springs. Lubrication was still dry sump but modified to ensure that oil drag was kept to a minimum.

The gearbox still had four speeds and footchange, but all the mechanics went into a new full cradle frame. The equipment was pure racing with a suitable carburettor and magneto, open exhaust and, as before, a left-side filler for the oil tank to suit the TT pits. A tyre pump was mounted beneath the large petrol tank and a prop-stand was fitted to the left chainstay.

To complete a good year for Velocette enthusiasts a 495 cc edition of the high-camshaft ohv design was launched in June 1935. Its capacity came from boring the MAC out and the new model was typed the MSS, but it was developed as much from the works 495 cc ohc racing engine, as it followed the MOV engine configuration. The engine design was on the same lines as the others, but the frame was based on the new KTT one. It was to run on in various forms for a long time.

There was little change to the ohv machines or the two-stroke for 1936, but the KSS and KTS were redesigned. The differences between them remained simply tyres and mudguards, but the engines now had an alloy, one-piece head and cam box casting. The valve gear was fully enclosed, eccentric rocker spindles enabled the gaps to be set and coil valve springs were fitted. The magneto remained behind the barrel and the dynamo ahead of the crankcase with its belt drive. The gearbox was the usual Velocette one with four speeds and a full cradle frame was employed. Both machines were fully equipped, and in effect the KTS was an MSS with a KSS engine.

The main change to the ohv engines for 1937 was the adoption of automatic ignition advance using a weight system in the magneto driving gear, very forward for a time when enthusiasts generally

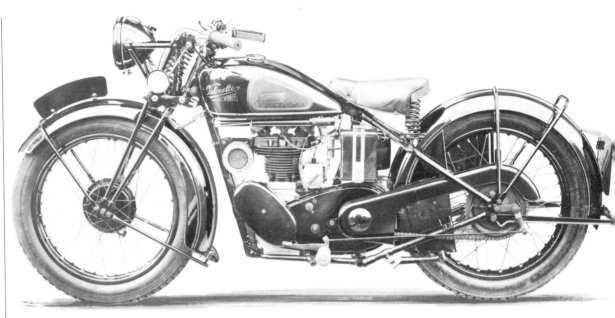

Above **Engine of a 1934 Velocette 249 cc model GTP with throttle-controlled oil pump. Later in the year it was fitted with a four-speed footchange gearbox**
Top **The 248 cc ohv model MOV Velocette in 1934**

preferred to have a lever to play with. Otherwise it was detail changes to the range which was without the KTT pending major alterations.

For 1938 the company decided to price the range on an all-in basis and not list essentials such as the speedometer as an extra. This was prompted in part by the legal need for the fitment from October 1937, but the industry at large still quoted it as an extra years later.

In May 1938 the KTT returned to the list as the Mk VII. The capacity was, as always, 348 cc, but it now had an alloy head and barrel, both massively finned, and the head casting included the rocker box and large wells for the hairpin valve springs.

The camshaft was still driven by shaft and bevels and the magneto occupied its usual position and was turned by chain. Lubrication was dry sump and valve adjustment by eccentric rocker spindles.

The engine and four-speed gearbox went into a full cradle frame with new girder forks. The hubs contained 7 in. brakes and were laced to rims carrying racing tyres. Equipment included a rev-counter, megaphone exhaust, saddle, rear pad and large petrol tank. A prop-stand was still included and went in the same place.

There were no changes to the road models for 1939, but the KTT became the Mk VIII with pivoted fork rear suspension. This was unusual in that it was controlled by units using air as the suspension medium and oil for damping. There were no

springs at all, but the air was pumped up to a level based on the rider's weight and the circuit he was competing on.

The road range was listed for 1940, but before production could really get under way war broke out and the firm was switched to general service contracts.

These then were the production Velocettes, but there were others built by the works as experiments, one-offs and for their own racing. With the easy interchange of many parts or assemblies this was often no trouble to arrange and the practice spread to private owners as well.

One such exercise which came at the end of the 1920s was the KDT. This was built for speedway use and had a bored out 407 cc KTT engine in suitable frame and forks. Very few were made, just 25 being shown in the factory records.

In 1930 there was the long-stroke KTT which was a works one-off that showed no advantage over the normal engine, so was converted to a larger size, and later the motor went into a road model. Its dimensions, however, became those of the MAC.

The next year brought the supercharged KTT known as Whiffing Clara and the name came from Harold Willis, as did so many of the Velocette names and sayings of the period. His wit and humour were as remarkable as his engineering abilities and he pushed the marque forward for a decade.

1931 also brought the 350 side-valve, whose poor power and high noise level led to the MOV. Two years later the works raced KTT models with enclosed rockers which became known as the Dog Kennel engines due to the head casting shape, and these were built in 350 and 500 cc sizes. 1936 brought the Mk VI KTT, which had a KSS head on a Mk V engine. One was labelled by Willis as 'the little rough 'un' but did win the Manx that year, while, in all, eight were built using what was to become the frame for the Mk VII.

The works had three twin ohc machines for that year's TT, but the vertical shaft coupling on one failed early on and the design was put away for over a decade. There were also 500 cc KTT machines for the works and these first appeared in Dog Kennel form in 1934. From 1937 they were in the style of the KTT with the engine dimensions of the MSS.

One of these engines was enlarged to 596 cc for use in the 1937 ISDT in a sidecar outfit and proved very good in this role. The following year it was used again and during this period Velocette were working on a road MSS with pivoted fork rear suspension. This machine was made more novel by the use of a stressed-skin construction for the rear frame section and slots which allowed the spring unit angle to be varied to alter their effect.

This method of construction and suspension system also went onto the model O twin-cylinder prototype built in 1939. Its engine differed greatly from other firms' twins, for the two crankshafts lay along the frame and were geared to contra-rotate. Capacity of the engine was 587 cc and it had ohv, twin carburettors and low-level exhausts. The right crankshaft drove the transmission and the left the dynamo. Final drive was by shaft.

The road model was matched by a racing one known as the Roarer and built on the same lines using MOV dimensions and KTT-style heads. The right crankshaft drove a supercharger and the left the transmission to the shaft final drive. It ran in practice in the 1939 TT, but was never raced.

Post-war most of the road models survived for a varying number of years, as did many of the special racing ones in one form or another.

Vincent-HRD

Philip Vincent was a determined man who had some firm ideas on how a motorcycle should perform and how it should be built. He read Mechanical Science at Cambridge and had a poor opinion of many of the features of contemporary machines, so in the 1920s built his first motorcycle. Like all the others it had rear suspension with a triangulated pivoted fork and the springs mounted beneath the saddle to work against the upper frame. The engine was a Swiss MAG, the gearbox Moss, forks Webb and hubs Enfield.

At the age of 19 in 1927 he decided to go into the business of making motorcycles and after taking advice from Arthur Bourne, editor of *The Motor Cycle*, bought the established HRD name from the OK Supreme company. It might have only been three years old, but the name of Howard R. Davies was very well known for he had tied for second in the 1914 Senior TT, been reported killed in action in 1917 and had won the 1921 Senior with his 350 AJS. Having formed his firm he then was second in the Junior and won the Senior in 1925.

With this background the marque was in demand but was under-financed and was bought out before the name went on to Vincent. Davies was rather surprised at the motorcycle that resulted, for the very fine rigid frame had gone, so the resulting machine was totally changed other than in the use of a proprietary engine.

By 1930 Vincent-HRD were known as makers of high-class, hand-built machines and were building these in very small numbers. Thanks to the Depression they could hardly have chosen a more inauspicious time and if that was not enough the use of rear suspension was a major point against the marque. There was a great prejudice against such things at that time and any engineering reasoning was simply countered by the statement that TT winners used rigid frames.

So Vincent sales were minimal and a little in the

manner of Broughs as a club for the dedicated. For all that they gradually improved and for 1930 went to Olympia with a range powered by JAP engines. For touring there were 490 and 600 cc side-valve engines and for sporting use the same sizes of ohv units. The competition rider was cultivated by a pair of racing JAP engines and finally there was a 350 cc Grass Track Racer. The last named was successful in racing but not commercially as only two were sold. However, this was significant to Vincent, as his sales for 1930 were 36, although this was 50 per cent up on 1929.

They progressed to 48 in 1931 and in that year began to indicate Rudge Python engines as an option after experiencing a run of trouble with the JAP units. However, the odd appearance of the machines plus the sprung frame was a considerable handicap to sales, so it was decided to design a new diamond frame which would have a conventional appearance while retaining the rear suspension. It was late in 1931 that Phil Irving joined the firm and was immediately involved with the new frame. His practical knowledge was to complement the innovations that came from Vincent to produce good, working motorcycles.

The new frame really set the format for the pre-war Vincent and had single tank, seat and down-tubes. The engine was part of the structure with small front plates and massive rear ones. The latter surrounded the gearbox and also provided the mounting for the rear fork pivot and its taper roller bearings. The rear suspension springs and dampers went beneath the saddle and were loaded by the triangulated rear fork. Damping was provided by friction material between the inner

and outer spring box covers and could be adjusted by external clamps.

In this frame the purchaser could have a 490 cc JAP engine or a 499 cc Python in standard or sports form. For those who preferred the older style there were five further models listed, but hardly any were sold.

For 1933 a lightweight model was added to the list as the L and was powered by either a 247 cc Villiers engine or a 245 cc side-valve JAP, but it never actually went into production. The one prototype had the two-stroke power unit and was interesting as it was partially enclosed with panels round the crankcase and transmission. It retained the diamond sprung frame, as did the other models, which were all of 500 cc with ohv. There was one with a JAP engine and two with Pythons in two states of tune. With both Vincent and Irving keen riders the models had many points that met with the approval of enthusiasts.

The two-stroke was extensively modified for 1934 and became the model W with a water-cooled 249 cc Villiers engine. Its enclosure was extended to completely hide the engine, which had the radiator in front of the cylinder and a cast-alloy expansion box ahead of the crankcase. This feature was as it had been on the L. The panelling included legshields.

The frame of the W was new and unlike the others except in its retention of a triangulated rear fork and spring unit under the seat. The main frame member was a malleable iron backbone to which were bolted two downtubes. These were attached to a channel section which ran under the engine and gearbox to another acting as a seat

1933 Vincent-HRD with 499 cc Python engine

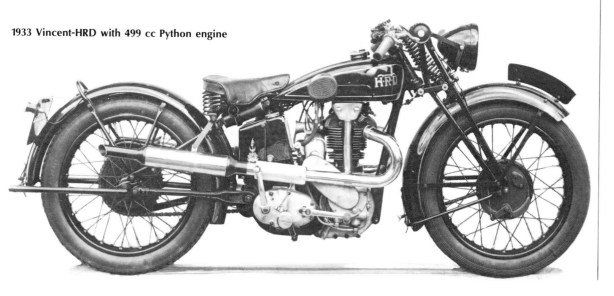

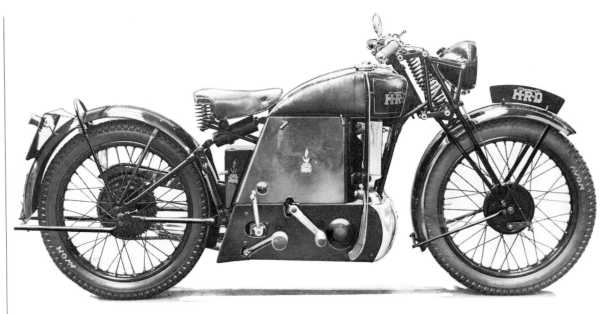

stay and rear fork pivot support. Strip stays braced the construction.

In addition to the W there was the JW, which used a 600 cc side-valve, water-cooled JAP engine and was built as a combination. It had the same form of enclosure but only the show model was ever made.

The three 500s continued to be offered, but could now stop well, for they had Super-power Duo-brakes with two drums on each hub. The spoke flanges were separate to ensure that the drums were not distorted during wheel building and the rear assembly carried two sprockets for easy gearing changes. Each brake was a single leading shoe type with separate pin mounting for

Above **1935 Vincent-HRD 499 cc single with Vincent engine**
Top **Enclosed 1934 Vincent-HRD model W with 249 cc Villiers engine and usual Vincent rear suspension**

each shoe and a system of levers and cables gave compensation from one side to the other. While the compensation system was to continue on the front brake to the end, that at the rear proved to be too complicated and spongy. It was therefore soon replaced by a pair of adjustable brake rods.

Phil Vincent was badly let down by JAP engines in the 1934 TT and with Rudge units becoming hard to get he decided the only answer was to make his own. He had four months to do it in if he was to exhibit at the next show.

He succeeded with the usual show rush and the design set the style for all his future engines. The valve gear was what set the Vincent apart from others and began with a camshaft placed very high up with short pushrods splayed out to run parallel to the valve line. This allowed the rockers to run straight across the head to the valves.

The next unusual feature was that each valve had two guides and the rocker located on it between them. The hairpin valve springs went above the rocker, and thus well away from the heat, and were fully exposed. The top of the valve stem was threaded and the upper spring holder screwed to it. Two external pipes supplied oil to the rocker chambers and were the subject of Press criticism, but, as Vincent pointed out, others just relied on grease guns.

The timing gear was simple with a large idler meshing with gears on the crankshaft, camshaft and magneto, which went behind the cylinder. Both head and barrel were iron and a dry sump lubrication system was used. The crankcase was tall and very well ribbed to provide a compact and rigid engine.

It was built in three stages of tune as the standard Meteor, sports Comet and racing TT model and all had the sprung frame and twin brakes on each wheel. Also in the list was the J with a 490 cc ohv JAP engine and the W water-cooled two-stroke which was to special order.

For 1936 all models had the Vincent engine and this was modified so that the sump went to the rear of the crankcase and the pushrod tubes had gland joints. A Miller mag-dyno was adopted for the road machines and there were five models in all.

The Meteor, Comet and racing TT were as before and were joined by the Comet Special and the TT road model. Both these had the TT engine but in a revised state of tune to make them suited to fast road work.

Four of the singles went forward for 1937 as Meteor, Comet, Comet Special and racing TT Replica with little change. The news that made the headlines was the appearance of the Rapide with its V-twin 998 cc engine and tremendous performance. This came from the combination of two Meteor cylinders and heads on a common crankcase which slotted into a lengthened version of the existing frame. It was little heavier than a 500 and it all tucked in well in a remarkably compact form. The result was a very fast machine, too fast, it was soon found, for the transmission, which could easily wilt under all that torque.

The Comet Special was dropped for 1938, but the other three models of 499 cc continued along with the Rapide. There was a larger oil tank and toolbox for the road machines while the TT Replica was given a new camshaft, stiffer crankcase and aluminium-bronze cylinder head. This last item seems to have only actually appeared on works machines and not on customers' ones.

For 1939 only three models were listed, the Meteor, Comet and Rapide, and while the first was

1935 Vincent-HRD with 490 cc JAP engine listed as the model J

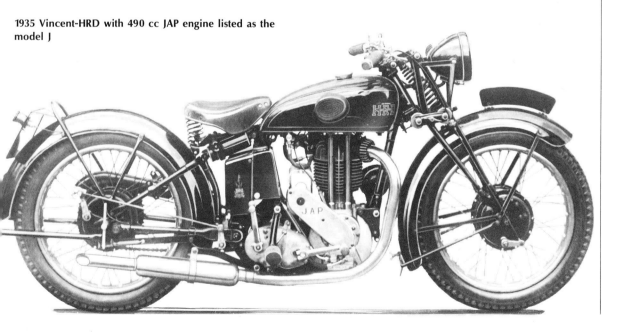

Whitwood

the touring machine, to enthusiasts they were fast, faster and fastest; apart from the clutch slip, which had been commented on in road tests. The works had a racing 1000 by this time and its power proved an embarrassment with petrol starvation, wheelspin and lifting front wheels all making life hard for the rider.

On the road the Vincents continued to offer discerning riders performance with useful features they wanted. The wheels were really quickly detachable, the pillion pad was linked to the frame to benefit from the rear suspension and details such as the prop-stand worked well.

Production of motorcycles ceased late in 1939 and the company turned to war work, some special designs for the services and thoughts of a high-speed tourer for the years to come.

Below **Vincent-HRD Rapide in 1939 with too much power from its 998 cc for the clutch**

This was a machine built by the OEC concern but listed separately once it was past the prototype stage. It represented another attempt to produce a car on two wheels and like the rest sold to a very limited market.

The model was announced in July 1934 and from the side did resemble a small saloon car with a short bonnet. Or it could have been a vast double adult sidecar hitched to and obscuring its towing machine. In fact it was a true body on two wheels with two doors, two seats in tandem form, a windscreen, side screens and a folding hood.

The mechanics were fully enclosed and there was a stabilizing wheel on each side to hold the machine up when at a standstill. Steering was by a wheel which was geared to the OEC duplex steering system used. A range of engines was to be

Right **Bird's eye view of the Whitwood showing its tandem seating, steering wheel and car type body**

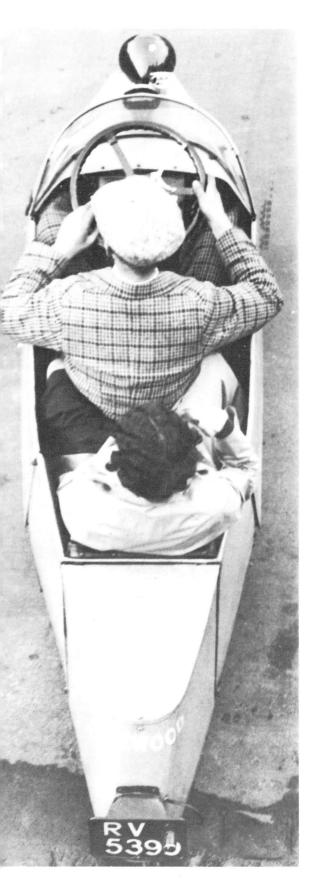

offered and the equipment included twin headlamps.

In October 1934 a fuller description was published along with the range of engine sizes to be offered. The power unit went under the front seat and was laid horizontally. The gearbox went under seat number two and the frame was similar to that of the OEC Atlanta with four tubes running fore and aft to carry the works. At the front they supported the duplex steering system, but there was no rear suspension.

The body was attached to the main frame and had the petrol and oil tanks located behind the passenger's backrest under a hinged lid. Steering was still by wheel and there was now only one headlamp mounted on the nose with the horn just behind it. The two retractable wheels were controlled by a lever on the left, the gearchange by one on the right and clutch and brake by pedals. A long hand lever enabled the engine to be started without the rider leaving his seat.

Four models were listed as the 150 cc Dart and 250 cc Sterling with two-stroke engines and the 500 cc Century and 1000 cc Regent, both with side valves and the latter a V-twin. If nothing else it was an enterprising design.

For 1936 there were quite a few changes and the most significant mechanical one was to move the engine to a position to the left of the rear wheel. It was still mounted horizontally but with the cylinder pointing to the rear and it drove forward to a cross-shaft which connected to the gearbox mounted on the right. This then drove back to the rear wheel.

A dynamo was tucked in above the cross-shaft and the engine had coil ignition. A self-starter was listed as an extra and in this case a dynamotor was fitted. Oil, petrol and battery all went on the left over the gearbox and the rear wheel was now sprung. At the front the duplex steering continued, but the steering wheel angle was altered from bus style to car style. This aided comfort but complicated the coupling gears.

Both seats now had backrests and the doors had permanent side screens which could be folded down. The windscreen had safety glass, so was no longer curved and could be folded forward. The folding hood was still provided and could be stowed behind the passenger seat. The hand starter remained, but the hand throttle was supplemented by a foot one. The side wheel mechanism was improved.

The revised machine was lower than before

with cleaner body lines and once again twin headlamps were fitted. Engine sizes were 250 cc ohv for the Devon model, 500 cc sv for the York and 750 cc sv V-twin for the Rutland.

Early in 1936 the firm established with the Ministry of Transport that it was classed as a motorcycle despite its total of four wheels. As the outrigger ones did not normally revolve they did not count, so there was no question of car taxation applying.

Not that this made much difference, for the make was no longer listed at the end of the year and sales were minuscule while it was available.

The Whitwood as seen from the side with its roof in place. The stabilizing wheel can be seen under the body on the left

Wolf

This company really was on the fringe of the industry but managed to stay there for a long time. It always used proprietary parts and had fluctuating fortunes, being made by Wearwell Cycles in Wolverhampton. The machines were first built in 1901, but there was an occasional lapse and the marque was not listed for 1930.

It returned in 1931 with two models using a simple loop frame. The smaller was called the Minor and was fitted with a 147 cc Villiers engine and the other had a 196 cc unit and was named the Utility. They were joined in May by the 98 cc Cub model, which had a two-speed gearbox and was of simple construction.

The range for 1932 included these three models as the 98 cc W1 Cub, 147 cc W3 Minor and 196 cc W7 Utility. The first two had two-speed gearboxes, but the W3 had the option of three speeds, which was standard for the W7, and this model had legshields and a rear carrier as standard. New

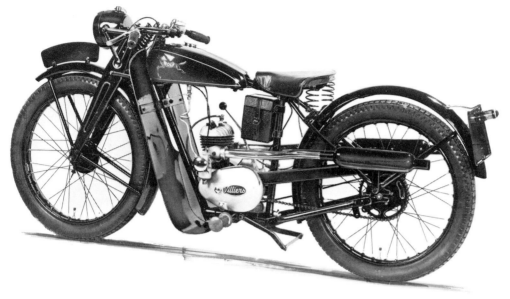

Above **Wolf 122 cc WA10 of 1937 with twin exhausts**
Below **Much earlier 1931 Wolf with 147 cc Villiers engine and listed as the Minor**

models were the W5 Vixen with a 148 cc long-stroke Villiers engine and also built as the W6 with a chrome-plated tank with blue panels in place of the standard black finish. Larger was the 196 cc W8 Silver Wolf, which had the super sports engine inclined in the frame, and this was also sold as the W9 with direct lighting.

There was little change for 1933 except that the W9 was not listed and only names were used. The Cub had a new frame with shorter wheelbase and was one of only three models continued for 1934, as the WA2. The other two were 148 cc Vixens as the standard model WA5 and brighter-finished WA6.

This range continued as it was for 1935, but for 1936 the 147 cc Minor with two-speed gearbox returned to the range and there were two new models. One was the Super-Sports with a 249 cc engine and the other had the new 122 cc unit with

twin exhausts feeding into an expansion box in front of the crankcase.

For 1937 this model, given the name Unit, was fitted with twin exhausts that ran straight back and a number of items to smarten its appearance. It was given the typing of WA10, while the Super-Sports became the WA9. The remaining models just kept their names and were the 147 cc Minor and 148 cc Vixen, so the Cub was no longer listed.

It was all back to type numbers for 1938 when the Minor became the WA4, the Super-Sports stayed as the WA9, the two Vixen models were the WA5 and WA6 and the Unit the WA10. A second 249 cc model appeared listed as the WA11, which had petroil lubrication and blade forks.

The range stayed the same for 1939, but was reduced for 1940 to the 122 cc machine and the two versions of the 148 cc before production came to a halt.

Zenith

This firm's best days were prior to World War 1 and in the twenties. In the first period they became very successful in the competitions of the day, which were mainly hillclimbs and sprints, thanks to their variable-ratio belt drive known as the Gradua; so successful, in fact, that they were barred from some classes in 1911 and adopted a trademark which reflected this by showing their machine behind bars and the legend 'barred'. In the 1920s they had many successes at Brooklands, including the first 100 mph lap, by Bert Le Vack in 1922, and they also built record breakers. With these they raised the absolute world record to over 124 mph in 1928 and to over 150 mph in 1930. The latter achievement was clouded by the OEC scandal, when the wrong machine was shown at Olympia, thus losing Zenith valuable publicity.

All this activity and success was heady stuff, but did not sell too many machines. For 1930 the range offered was all powered by JAP engines and comprised singles and twins. The side-valve single engines were installed upright while the ohv ones

were inclined. On offer were 300 and 490 cc sv plus 346 and 490 cc ohv singles and sv twins of 677 and 747 cc. Also available to special order were racing models of 350, 500 and 1000 cc, all with ohv and labelled 20TT, 22TT and 8.55 respectively. Finally came the 980 cc sv Super Eight model N.

Not enough machines were sold in 1930 and production ceased, but in 1931 the firm of Writer's, a large dealer in South London, took them over and in July announced a smaller range. In essence this comprised the 346 and 490 cc ohv singles, the 490 cc sv and the 677 and 747 cc sv twins much as before. The singles had Burman gearboxes and the twins Sturmey-Archer, but both had three speeds. Construction followed conventional lines and the finish remained black and purple.

These five models all continued for 1932 with redesigned frames and improved rear stands. All were available in standard or de luxe form and for the latter a four-speed Burman gearbox, full electrical equipment and a speedometer were fitted as part of the specification. They also had a chrome-plated tank with black top, purple sides and a heart-shaped instrument panel.

In May 1932 the range was expanded by adding models with two-port, ohv Blackburne engines. There were standard and de luxe versions with 350 and 500 cc engines plus two with a 600 cc dry sump unit. One of these was to the de luxe specification and the other in competition form with raised pipes, special tyres and other suitable fittings.

1936 Zenith CP with 1100 cc side-valve V-twin JAP engine

For 1933 Zenith listed no less than 20 models from a combination of JAP or Blackburne engines and standard or de luxe specifications. All had interconnected brakes and the model list was as before. There were thus five machines with JAP engines and three with Blackburne all built in two ways. In addition there were three more V-twins with one, the model N, a revival from the 1930 list with the 980 cc sv JAP engine. The others were the NP with an 1100 cc sv engine and the 680 ohv de luxe with engine of that type, both units being JAPs and both machines having four-speed gearboxes. The final model was the new B5 Special Sports, which had a specially tuned 490 cc JAP engine, four-speed Burman gearbox, upswept pipes and a mag-dyno.

1934 saw the range shrink to 14 models and only two still had Blackburne engines. The type designations also changed, so the 490 cc models became the CS5 in standard or de luxe forms with side valves, C5 with ohv in the two styles, which were also the two with the Blackburne option, and C5 Special Sports for the tuned model.

The 677 and 747 cc V-twins ran on in a rather vintage format, both still available in the two styles, and the largest one continued as the CP1100. The remaining pair of models were new and listed as the 245 cc LC1 and 346 cc LC2. Both had ohv JAP engines inclined in a duplex cradle frame that was of mainly bolted construction. Ignition was by coil with a dynamo mounted

Single cylinder Zenith model LC1 with 245 cc JAP power in 1934 and typical of the many machines in the range

behind the cylinder and an upswept exhaust was fitted. The gearbox was a four-speed Burman with footchange and the petrol tank chrome-plated with the nose in black and purple. Both the name transfer and lining were now in white instead of the gold used before.

The Blackburne engines were no longer listed in 1935, but otherwise the range was the same and the models were fitted with new petrol tanks. There were 11 machines for 1936 and among them were new versions of the LC1 and LC2 with magneto ignition. Also new was the C5 Super with a 498 cc TT Replica JAP engine with dry sump lubrication and Miller Dyno-mag. This sat upright in a duplex cradle frame with Druid tubular girder forks.

Of the other models the side-valve CS5 expanded to 600 cc and the de luxe ohv C5 became the C5 sports. The C5 continued, as did the 750 and CP V-twins, the last being the 1100 cc side-valve model. The 750 was listed in two forms, one with detachable cylinder heads, and both retained pump lubrication. The rest of the range was now on dry sump.

For 1937 the C5 Sports became the Special and only one 747 cc V-twin was listed as the de luxe. The other models remained as they were and were joined by one new one, the HC5. This had a new 500 cc JAP engine with a high-mounted camshaft which was chain driven from the crankshaft. Ignition was by magneto and lubrication dry sump. It went in a cradle frame with Druid forks and drove a four-speed Burman gearbox with footchange as fitted to the whole range.

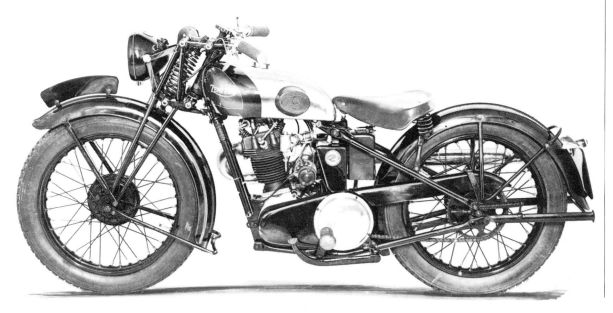

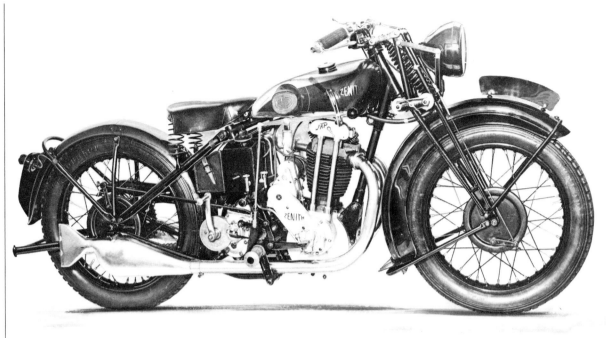

1938 saw two further models with high-camshaft JAP engines, these being the 250 cc HC1 and 350 cc HC2 on the lines of the HC5, which continued. The C5, C5 Super, CS5, LC1, 750 and CP also ran on with detail changes, but not the LC2 or the C5 Special.

The high-camshaft models failed to stay in the list for 1939, which was down to six models. Those left were the LC1 in two forms with coil or magneto ignition, the 490 cc ohv C5, 600 cc sv

Zenith B5 in 1932 with 490 cc JAP engine and chrome-plated tank

CS5 and the 750 and CP V-twin models, both with side valves. They were all listed for 1940, but with the war, production ceased at the Hampton Court works. Post-war a 750 was listed and it is supposed that about 250 were built before production ceased in 1950.

Right **Typical lightweight used in town during the 1930s when you just jumped on to the machine and rode to your meeting. Machine is a Montgomery Terrier with 122 cc Villiers engine**

A 1940 picture taken at a small show to promote the use
of the autocycle for basic transport in wartime

Model charts

These have been included to supplement the text and show how models and capacities varied through the decade. By using them the changes, or otherwise, over the years can be seen along with their place in the general pattern for each marque.

The lists also show the full range of machines for each year, including those introduced during the season. In most cases the model year ran from about September of the previous calendar year, so a 1935 model would have been on sale from late in 1934. Note that in those times firms and dealers went to great lengths to obtain sales, so an obsolete model could be built from spares or sold from old stock.

The charts show each basic model as given by the maker, which could include standard, de luxe and sports versions of the same machine. These are included, but further variations in terms of electrical equipment and options are not. The reason is space as, for example, nearly all of the 18 models listed by BSA for 1930 could have three standards of lighting equipment.

Each chart shows the bore and stroke of most or all models plus the calculated capacity and the position of the valves. Under each year the model number is given to indicate existence and these are official numbers, names or abbreviations in most cases. Where none exist the basic capacity has been used to show when the model was built. In a few cases the firm themselves did this, but reference to the text will indicate when this occurred.

In most cases the charts are arranged to run from smallest to largest model with each size in the valve order of sv, ohv, ohc. Singles are followed by twins. Where it worked better this arrangement was altered to a date basis, as this suited some firms, Vincent-HRD for example.

Firms varied a good deal in their use of type letters and numbers. From the charts it can be seen that some changed their system more than once in the decade and adopted new principles. Some never really changed at all and Norton is perhaps the best example. Others varied a great deal and Royal Enfield were one of the best at confusing dealers and public alike. They used the same letter for machines of different capacity and at other times changed the designation without really altering the machine. In their case major changes have been shown by using a new line even when the letter, bore and stroke remained common.

Where a maker kept to a common power unit but revamped the model and its typing the charts use the minimum number of lines. Montgomery is a good example with a stream of JAP engines used to power a great variety of models whose existence is noted without indication of continuance of line.

Use of the text with the charts will help to avoid confusion, it is hoped.

Many charts carry abbreviations and those relating to the marque are listed beneath its data. However, some are common and are given here to avoid repetition.

Bl — Blackburne

JAP — J. A. Prestwich

Py — Python (Rudge)

SA — Sturmey-Archer

ts — two-stroke

Vil — Villiers

The shape of things to come. The first of Phil Vincent's
own engines appeared for the 1935 season. This is the
499 cc Meteor

AER

	b × s	30	31	32	33	34	35	36	37	38	39	40
249 ts Vil	63 × 80										250	250
340 ts twin	57 × 66.7								350	350	350	350

Note: from 1933 all models used a year prefix to their type number; e.g. 33/12

AJS

	b × s	30	31	32	33	34	35	36	37	38	39	40
249 ohv	65 × 75	R12	S12		12	12						
245 ohv	62.5 × 80						12	12	12	12	12	12
245 ohv	62.5 × 80						22	22	22	22	22	22
245 ohv	62.5 × 80								22T	22T	22T	
245 ohv	62.5 × 80									22SS	22SS	
245 ohv	62.5 × 80										12M	
348 sv	74 × 81	R5	S5	T5	5	5	5	5				
348 sv	74 × 81	R4										
400 sv	74 × 93		S4									
348 ohv	74 × 81	R6	S6	T6	6	6	6					
348 ohv	74 × 81		SB6	TB6	B6	B6						
348 ohv	69 × 93						16	16	16	16	16	
348 ohv	69 × 93						26	26	26	26	26	26
348 ohv	69 × 93								26T	26T	26T	
348 ohv	69 × 93									26SS	26SS	26SS
348 ohv	69 × 93										16M	16M
346 ohc	70 × 90	R7	S7		7	7	7	7	7	7R	7R	
499 sv	84 × 90	R9	S9	T9	9	9	9	9				
497 sv	82.5 × 93						4	4	9	9	9	9
497 sv	82.5 × 93						14	14				
499 ohv	84 × 90	R8	S8	T8	8	8	8					
499 ohv	84 × 90		SB8	TB8	B8	B8	18					
497 ohv	82.5 × 93							8	8	8	8	8
497 ohv	82.5 × 93							18	18	18	18	
497 ohv	82.5 × 93								18T	18T	18T	
497 ohv	82.5 × 93									18SS	18SS	8SS
495 ohc	79 × 101	R10	S10		10	10	10	10				
498 sv twin	65 × 75		S3									
495 ohc four	50 × 63							20				
998 sv twin	84 × 90	R2	S2									
982 sv twin	85.5 × 85.5				2	2	2	2	2	2	2	2

AJW

	b × s	30	31	32	33	34	35	36	37	38	39	40
172 ts Vil	57.15 × 67	BF	BF	BF								
196 ts Vil	61 × 67	Ut										
196 ts Vil	61 × 67	BF	BF	BF								
247 ts Vil	67 × 70	SF	SF	SF								
249 ts Vil	63 × 80										L	L
249 ts Vil	63 × 80										Ldl	Ldl
343 ts Vil	79 × 70	SF	SF									
346 ts Vil	70 × 90		SF	SF								
348 ohv Py	70 × 90.5		Py	FF	FF							
348 ohv Py	70 × 90.5				Vt							
498 ohv JAP	80 × 99	500										
499 ohv Py	85 × 88		Py	FF	FF	FF						
499 ohv Py	85 × 88			V	V	RF						
499 ohv Ul	85 × 88				FV	FV						
499 ohv Ul	85 × 88				FF							
488 ohv JAP	85.5 × 85						RF	RF	RF			
488 ohv JAP	85.5 × 85						FF	FF	FF	FF	FF	FF
498 ohv JAP							FV					
495 ohv St	79 × 101							SV				
500 ohv Bl		500										
677 ohv JAP	70 × 88	680	680	680								
982 sv JAP	85.5 × 85.5	980	8HP									
982 sv JAP			8.30									
995 ohv JAP	80 × 99	8/55	8/55									
994 ohv An	78 × 104	Spec	Race									

An – Anzani   Ldl – Lynx de luxe   Ul – Ulster
BF – Black Fox   RF – Red Fox   Ut – Utility
FF – Flying Fox   SF – Silver Fox   V – Vixen
FV – Flying Vixen   St – Stevens   Vt – Vixenette
L – Lynx   SV – Silver Vixen

AKD

	b × s	30	31	32	33	34	35	36	37	38	39	40
148 ohv	56 × 60		Co	Co								
172 ohv	60 × 61	10	Or	Or								
172 ohv	60 × 61	70	Me	Me								
172 ohv	60 × 61	80	Or	Or								
196 ohv	63 × 63	20	Ju	Ju								
196 ohv	63 × 63	60										
248 ohv	64 × 77	90										
248 ohv	64 × 77	100	Ne	Ne								
296 sv	70 × 77	40										
349 sv	76 × 77		Po	Po								

Co – Comet   Ne – Neptune
Ju – Jupiter   Or – Orion
Me – Mercury   Po – Polar

ARIEL

	b × s	30	31	32	33	34	35	36	37	38	39	40
249 sv	65 × 75	LB	LB31	LB32								
249 ohv	65 × 75	LF	LF31	LF32								
249 ohv	65 × 75	LG										
248 ohv	61 × 85					LF	LF	LG	LG	LG	OG	OG
248 ohv	61 × 85				LH	LH	LH	LH	LH	LH	OH	OH
346 sv	72 × 85			MB32								
346 ohv	72 × 85		MF31	MF32	NF	NF	NF	NG	NG	NG	NG	NG
346 ohv	72 × 85			MH32	NH	NH	NH	NH	NH	NH	NH	NH
499 sv	81.8 × 95										VA	VA
499 ohv	81.8 × 95	E						VG	VG	VG	VG	VG
499 ohv	81.8 × 95	F	VF31				VH	VH	VH	VH	VH	VH
499 ohv (4V)	81.8 × 95	G										
499 ohv (4V)	81.8 × 95		VG31									
498 ohv	86.4 × 85		SF31		VF	VF	VF					
498 ohv	86.4 × 85				VG	VG	VG					
498 ohv	86.4 × 85				VH	VH						
498 ohv (4V)	86.4 × 85		SG31	SG32								
498 ohv (4V)	86.4 × 85			VG32								
498 ohv (4V)	86.4 × 85			VH32								
557 sv	86.4 × 95	A	SB31	SB32	VA	VA	VA					
557 sv	86.4 × 95	B	VB31	VB32	VB	VB	VB					
598 sv	86.4 × 102							VB	VB	VB	VB	VB
498 ohc -4	51 × 61		4F31	4F/5.32								
601 ohc -4	56 × 61			4F/6.32	4F/6	4F/6	4F/6	4F/6				
599 ohv -4	50.4 × 75										4F	4F
995 ohv -4	65 × 75								4G	4G	4G	4G
995 ohv -4	65 × 75										4H	4H

ASCOT PULLIN

	b × s	30	31	32	33	34	35	36	37	38	39	40
496 ohv	82 × 94	500										

BAKER

	b × s	30	31	32	33	34	35	36	37	38	39	40
172 ts Vil	57.15 × 67	55										
172 ts Vil	57.15 × 67	65										
196 ts Vil	61 × 67	50										
196 ts Vil	61 × 67	58										
247 ts Vil	67 × 70	60										
343 ts Vil	79 × 70	62										
249 sv James	64 × 77.5	250										

BAUGHAN

	b × s	30	31	32	33	34	35	36	37	38	39	40
250 sv Bl			250	AH	AH	AH	AH	250				
250 ohv Bl				MH	AM	MH	MH	250				
298 sv Bl		300										
300 sv SA				AH3								
348 sv Bl		350					SL	350				
348 sv SA		350		SL	SL	SL						
346 sv JAP			350									
348 ohv Bl		350	350	350	350		0	350				
348 ohv SA		350	SA	0	0	0						
346 ohv JAP			350									
496 sv SA			500	SC		SC						
498 sv Bl							SC	500				
496 ohv Bl		500		500	SW		WH	500				
496 ohv SA		500	500	WH	SW	WH						
500 ohv s/c				SW		SW						
498 ohv Bl						SD	SWD	SWD				

s/c – sidecar

BERWICK

	b × s	30	31	32	33	34	35	36	37	38	39	40
247 ts Vil	67 × 70	250										
343 ts Vil	79 × 70	350										

BROUGH SUPERIOR

	b × s	30	31	32	33	34	35	36	37	38	39	40
491 ohv twin	62.5 × 80		500									
677 ohv twin	70 × 88	680	680	680	680 ohv	680	680	680				
680 sv twin					680 sv							
800 sv four	57.9 × 76			Str. 4	Str. 4	Str. 4						
981 sv twin	85.7 × 85	SS80	SS80	SS80	SS80							
982 sv twin	85.5 × 85.5						SS80	SS80	SS80	SS80	SS80	SS80
982 sv twin	85.5 × 85.5									TT		
995 ohv twin	80 × 99	SS100	SS100	SS100	SS100	SS100	SS100					
982 ohv twin	85.5 × 85.5							SS100	SS100	SS100	SS100	SS100
998 ohv four	71 × 63										GD	
1096 sv twin	85.7 × 95				11.50	11.50	11.50	11.50	11.50	11.50	11.50	11.50

GD – Golden Dream
Str – Straight
TT – Transverse Twin

BSA

	b × s	30	31	32	33	34	35	36	37	38	39	40
149 ohv	52 × 70					X34-0	X35-0	X0				
174 ts	60 × 61.5	A30-2										
249 sv	63 × 80	B30-3	B31-1		B33-1	B34-1	B35-1	B1	B20	B20		
249 sv	63 × 80									C10	C10	C10
249 ohv	63 × 80	B30-4	B31-2	B32-1	B33-2	B34-2	B35-2	B2	B21	B21	B21	
249 ohv	63 × 80		B31-3		B33-3	B34-3	B35-3	B3	B22	B22	C11	C11
249 ohv	63 × 80					B34-17		B18				
348 sv	72 × 85.5	L30-5	L31-4	L32-2								
348 sv	72 × 85.5	L30-6	L31-5	L32-4								
348 sv	71 × 88								B23	B23	B23	C12
348 ohv	72 × 85.5	L30-11	L31-6	L32-3								
348 ohv	72 × 85.5			L32-5								
348 ohv	71 × 88				R33-4	R34-4	R35-4	R4	B24	B24	B24	B29
348 ohv	71 × 88				R33-5	R34-5	R35-5	R5	B25	B25	B25	
348 ohv	71 × 88					R34-6		R17	B26	B26	B26	
348 ohv	71 × 88							R19				
348 ohv	71 × 88							R20				
349 ohv	68.8 × 94								M19	M19		
493 sv	80 × 98	S30-7	S31-7									
493 sv	80 × 98	S30-9										
493 sv	80 × 98	S30-18										
499 sv	85 × 88			W32-6	W33-6	W34-7	W35-6	W6				
496 sv	82 × 94								M20	M20	M20	M20
493 ohv	80 × 98	S30-12	S31-9	S32-8								
493 ohv	80 × 98	S30-13	S31-10									
493 ohv	80 × 98	S30-18										
493 ohv	80 × 98	S30-19										
499 ohv	85 × 88			W32-7	W33-7	W34-8	W35-7					
499 ohv	85 × 88				W33-8	W34-9	W35-8					
499 ohv	85 × 88				W33-9	W34-10	W35-9					
499 ohv	85 × 88					FF						
496 ohv	82 × 94							Q7	M22	M22	M22	
496 ohv	82 × 94							Q8	M23	M23	M23	M23
496 ohv	82 × 94							Q21		M24	M24	
556 sv	85 × 98	H30-8	H31-8	H32-9								
556 sv	85 × 98	H30-10										
596 sv	85 × 105				M33-10	M34-12	M35-10	M10	M21			
591 sv	82 × 112									M21	M21	M21
596 ohv	85 × 105				M33-11	M34-13	M35-11					
499 ohv twin	63 × 80					J34-11	J35-12	J12				
748 ohv twin	71 × 94.5							Y13	Y13	Y13		
771 sv twin	76 × 85	E30-14	E31-11									
985 sv twin	80 × 98	G30-15	G31-12	G32-10	G33-12	G34-14	G35-14	G14	G14	G14	G14	G14
985 sv twin	80 × 98	G30-16			G33-13							

CALTHORPE

	b×s	30	31	32	33	34	35	36	37	38	39	40
245 ohv	62.5 × 80										250	
247 ts	67 × 70			Minor								
247 ohv	67 × 70					Minor	Minor	R2/36	R2/37	R2/38		
348 ohv	74 × 81	II	III	III			Junior	K4/36				
348 ohv	74 × 81			Comp				Comp				
350 ohv	72 × 86								K5/37	K5/38		
350 ohv	72 × 86								Comp	Comp		
348 ohv	69 × 93										350	
494 ohv	85.5 × 86			IV	Major	Major	Major	M4/36	M5/37	M5/38		
494 ohv	85.5 × 86			Comp				Comp	Comp	Comp		
497 ohv	82.5 × 93										500	

Note: 1932 Minor also known as P1, the III as K2
and IV as M1. 1933 Major also known as M2

CARLTON

	b×s	30	31	32	33	34	35	36	37	38	39	40
122 ts Vil	50 × 62								125	125	125	125

CHATER-LEA

	b×s	30	31	32	33	34	35	36	37	38	39	40
247 ts Vil	67 × 70	Su Spt										
348 ohc	71 × 88	Ca	Su Sp	Ca	Ca	Ca	Ca					
545 sv	85 × 96	Sp	Sp	Sv	Sv	Sv	Sv	Sv				

Ca – Camshaft
Sp – Sports
Su Sp – Super Sports

Su Spt – Super Sportette
Sv – Side-Valve

CHELL

	b×s	30	31	32	33	34	35	36	37	38	39	40
98 ts Vil	50 × 50										100	
122 ts Vil	50 × 62										125	

COTTON

	Engine	30	31	32	33	34	35	36	37	38	39	40
122 ts	Vil										125/39	125/40
147 ts	Vil			1V	1V	1V	1V	1V	1V	1V	1V	1V
148 sv	JAP			1J	1J	1J						
150 ohv	Bl					1B	1B	1B		1B		
150 ohv	JAP						1J	1J	1J			
247 ts	Vil	1			2V	2V						
250 sv	JAP				2J	2J	2J	2J	2J	2J	2J	2J
250 sv	JAP						2JC	2JC	2JC	2JC	2JC	2JC
242 ohv	JAP	11	11J									
245 ohv	JAP				30J	30J	30J	30J	250/37	250/38	250/39	250/40
248 ohv	Py				30RP	30RP						
250 ohv	JAP					6J	6J	6J				
250 ohv	Bl					6B	6B	6B				
250 ohv	JAP/Bl								GB	GB		
250 ohv	JAP hc								30 Spec	30 Spec	30 Spec	30 Spec
295 sv	Bl	3										
300 sv	JAP	3J		3J	3J	3J						
348 sv	Bl	7										
350 sv	JAP	7J		7J	7J	7J						
348 ohv	Bl	9										
348 ohv	Bl	90SF	90SF									
350 ohv	Bl	29	29B	29B	29B	29B	29B	29B				
348 ohv	Py		29RP	29RP	29RP							
350 ohv	JAP	29J	29J	29J	29J	29J	29J	29J	350/37	350/38	350/39	350/40
350 ohv	JAP	9J		9J	9J	9J	9J	9J	9/37	9/38		
350 ohv	JAP hc								9 Spec	9 Spec	9 Spec	9 Spec
495 sv	Bl	8										
500 sv	JAP	8J		8J	8J	8J						
495 ohv	Bl	5										
495 ohv	Bl	25	25B	25B	25B	25B	25B	25B				
495 ohv	SA	25SA	25SA									
500 ohv	JAP	25J	25J	25J	25J	25J	25J	25J	500/37	500/38	500/39	500/40
499 ohv	Py		25RP	25RP	25RP	25RP						
500 ohv	JAP	5J						5J	5 Spec	5 Spec		
500 ohv	JAP hc								25 Spec	25 Spec	25 Spec	25 Spec
596 ohv	Bl			26B	26B		26B	26B				
596 ohv	JAP					26J	26J	26J	600/37	600/38	600/39	600/40

JAP hc – JAP high camshaft
Spec – Special

COVENTRY EAGLE

	b × s	30	31	32	33	34	35	36	37	38	39	40
98 ts Vil	50 × 50			H16								
98 ts Vil	50 × 50									P7	Q7	
98 ts Vil	50 × 50										Q9	
98 ts Vil	50 × 50										Q12	R12
98 ts Vil	50 × 50											R14
98 ts Vil	50 × 50											R0
122 ts Vil	50 × 62									P8	Q8	
122 ts Vil	50 × 62										Q10	
147 ts Vil	55 × 62	F21			J19							
147 ts CE	55 × 62			H18								
147 ts CE	55 × 62			H19								
148 ts Vil	53 × 67				J18	K1	L2	M2	N2	P2	Q2	
148 ts Vil	53 × 67						L1	M1	N1	P1	Q1	R1
172 ts Vil	57.15 × 67	F23	D25									
196 ts Vil	61 × 67	F24	G24									
196 ts Vil	61 × 67	F25	G25									
196 ts Vil	61 × 67		G22	H22								
245 ohv JAP	62.5 × 80					K3						
245 ohv JAP	62.5 × 80					K6	L7					
245 ohv M	62.5 × 80								N25	P25	Q25	
246 ohv Bl	63 × 79							M12				
247 ts Vil	67 × 70				J20							
247 ts Vil	67 × 70						L3	M3	N3	P3	Q3	
247 ts Vil	67 × 70						L4	M4	N4	P4	Q4	R4
247 ts Vil	67 × 70					K2	L5	M5	N5	P5	Q5	
247 ts Vil	67 × 70					K2A	L6	M6	N6	P6	Q6	
247 ts Vil	67 × 70					K4						
247 ts Vil	67 × 70							M10				
249 ts Vil	63 × 80							M9				
249 ts Vil	63 × 80							M11	N11	P11		
300 sv JAP	70 × 78	F35										
346 sv JAP	70 × 90	F45										
346 sv SA	70 × 90		G45	H45								
346 ohv JAP	70 × 90	F46	G46	H40								
348 ohv SA	71 × 88	F44	G44	H44								
348 ohv M	69 × 93								N35	P35	Q35	R35
482 sv JAP	85 × 85	F50										
495 sv SA	79 × 101	F52	G52									
490 ohv JAP	85.7 × 85	F55	G55	H55								
495 ohv SA	79 × 101	F54	G54									
497 ohv M	82.5 × 93								N50	P50	Q50	R50
976 sv JAP	85.5 × 85	F130	G130									
988 sv JAP	85.5 × 86	F150	G150									
995 ohv JAP	80 × 99	F160										

CE – Coventry Eagle (by Levis)
M – Matchless

COVENTRY-VICTOR

	Engine	30	31	32	33	34	35	36	37	38	39	40
499 ohv	FT	RS	RS	RGS	RGS	RGS						
499 ohv	FT	Sp	Sp	DT1	DT1							
600 ohv	FT			DT2	DT2							
600 ohv	FT				SS							
688 sv	FT	SS	SS	SS	SS	SS	SS					

DT – Dirt Track No.   RS – Royal Sports
FT – Flat Twin engine   Sp – Speedway
RGS – Royal Grand Sports   SS – Super Six

CYC-AUTO

	b × s	30	31	32	33	34	35	36	37	38	39	40
98 ts C-A	50 × 50					A	A	A	C	C		
98 ts C-A	50 × 50						B	B	D	D		
98 ts Vil	50 × 50								CV	CV		
98 ts Vil	50 × 50								DV	DV		
98 ts Sc	50 × 50										G	G
98 ts Sc	50 × 50										Gdl	Gdl
98 ts Sc	50 × 50										L	L
98 ts Sc	50 × 50										Ldl	Ldl
98 ts Sc	50 × 50										Tr	Tr

C-A – Cyc-Auto   L – Ladies
dl – de luxe   Sc – Scott
G – Gents   Tr – Tradesman

DAYTON

	b × s	30	31	32	33	34	35	36	37	38	39	40
98 ts Vil	50 × 50										Auto	

DIAMOND

	b × s	30	31	32	33	34	35	36	37	38	39	40
148 ts Vil	53 × 67				150 TS							
245 ohv JAP	62.5 × 80		250 OHV									
247 ts Vil	67 × 70	250 TS	250 TS	250 TS								
346 ts Vil	70 × 90		350 TS	350 TS								
346 ohv JAP	70 × 90		350 OHV	350 OHV								
490 ohv JAP				500 SV								

DOT

	b × s	30	31	32	33	34	35	36	37	38	39	40
98 ts Vil	50 × 50		Midget	Midget								
147 ts Vil	55 × 62		Minor	Minor								
148 ts Vil	53 × 67			Major								
196 ts Vil	61 × 67	V5										
196 ts Vil	61 × 67	V6										
247 ts Vil	67 × 70	V	V31									
343 ts Vil	79 × 70		VL31									
346 ts Vil	70 × 90		V31									
346 ohv JAP	70 × 90	V7										
349 ohv Br			B31									

Br – Bradshaw

DOUGLAS

	b × s	30	31	32	33	34	35	36	37	38	39	40
148 ts	53 × 67				Bantam	X	5X			CL38		
245 sv	51 × 60					Y	5Y	Aero				
348 sv	60.8 × 60	H3	A31	A32		Y1	5Y1	Aero	Aero			
348 sv	60.8 × 60	L3	B31	B32								
350 ohv				K32								
499 sv	62.25 × 82	S5	C31	C32								
489 sv	72 × 60					Y2						
494 sv	68 × 68						End	End				
494 sv	68 × 68						5Y2	Aero	Aero			
499 ohv	62.25 × 82	DT5	DT5	DT5		OW	50W					
499 ohv	62.25 × 82	SW5	SW5	SW5								
500 ohv			F31	F32								
500 ohv				M32								
596 sv	68 × 82	T6	D31	D32		Z	5Z	Aero	Aero			
596 sv	68 × 82	S6	E31	E32								
585 sv	74 × 68									DC38	DC39	
596 ohv	68 × 82	DT6	DT6	DT6		OW1	5OW1					
596 ohv	68 × 82	SW6	SW6	SW6								
600 ohv			G31	G32								
750 sv				H32								
744 sv	76 × 82					Z1	5Z1					

DUNELT

	b × s	30	31	32	33	34	35	36	37	38	39	40
148 ts Vil	53 × 67			V1	V1	V1	V1					
148 ts Vil	53 × 67				V1S	V1S	V1S					
249 ohc SA	60 × 88	T										
249 ts		K										
249 ts Vil	63 × 80				V2	V2	V2					
249 ts Vil	63 × 80					V2S	V2S					
248 ohv Py	62.5 × 81				TS	TS						
245 ohv JAP	62.5 × 80						TS					
297 sv SA	65.5 × 88		Cy									
346 ts Vil	70 × 90		Mo	V2								
348 ohv SA	71 × 88	Mon	Vu	V3	V3							

	b × s	30	31	32	33	34	35	36	37	38	39	40
348 ohv SA	71 × 88			V3S	V3S							
495 ohv SA	79 × 101	Ma										
495 ohv SA	79 × 101	SD	Dr	V4	V4							
495 ohv SA	79 × 101				V4S							
499 ohv Py	85 × 88					V4S						
490 ohv JAP	85.7 × 85						V4S					
598 sv SA	86.8 × 101		He	V5	V5							

Cy – Cygnet
Dr – Drake
He – Heron
Ma – Majestic

Mo – Monarch
Mon – Montlhéry
S – Special
Vu – Vulture

EXCELSIOR

	b × s	30	31	32	33	34	35	36	37	38	39	40
98 ts Vil	50 × 50		A0	B0	C0	D0	E0				J0	
98 ts Vil	50 × 50									Auto	Auto	Auto
122 ts Vil	50 × 62							F0	G0	H0	J0	K0
147 ts Vil	55 × 62	0										
147 ts Vil	55 × 62	1		BE2								
147 ts Vil	55 × 62	2	A2	B2								
148 ts Vil	53 × 67			B4	CV1	DV1	E1	F1	G1	H1	J1	K1
148 ts Vil	53 × 67			BE4	CE1	DE1	ED1	FD1	GD1	HD1	JD1	KD1
148 ts Vil	53 × 67			150	C1	D1	E2	FX1				
149 ohv	49 × 79				C4	D4	E3					
149 ohv	49 × 79					Wasp						
196 ts Vil	61 × 67	3	A3	B3	C3	D3						
196 ts Vil	61 × 67	4	A4		CV3							
196 ts Vil	61 × 67		AE4		CE3							
245 ohv JAP	62.5 × 80	9	A9									
245 ohv JAP	62.5 × 80	10	250									
245 ohv JAP	62.5 × 80	13	A14									
246 ohv	63 × 79				C7	D7	E7	F7				
246 ohv	63 × 79					DE7	E8	F8	G8	H8		
246 ohv	63 × 79					D14	E6					
246 ohc	63 × 79						E11	F11				
246 ohc	63 × 79						ER11	FR11				
247 ts Vil	67 × 70	5	A5	B5			E4	F4	G4	H4	J4	K4
247 ts Vil	67 × 70	7	A7				ED4	FD4	GD4	HD4	JD4	KD4
247 ts Vil	67 × 70		AE5	BE5								
249 ohv	67 × 70.69										J8	
249 ts Vil	63 × 80				C5	D5	E5	F5	G5			
249 ts Vil	63 × 80				C6	D6						
249 ts Vil	63 × 80					D9	E9					
249 ohc	67 × 70.65								G11	H11	J11	K11
249 ohc	67 × 70.65								GR11	HR11	JR11	
249 ohc	67 × 70.65										J11/S	
249 ohc	67 × 70.65										JRS11	
300 sv JAP	70 × 78	6	A6									
300 sv JAP	70 × 78	8										
344 ohv	69 × 92							F9	G9	H9	J9	
344 ohv	69 × 92							F10				
346 sv JAP	70 × 90		A8	B8	C8	D8						
346 ohv JAP	70 × 90		A10	B9								

	b × s	30	31	32	33	34	35	36	37	38	39	40
346 ohv JAP	70 × 90		A11	B10	C10	D10						
346 ohv	70 × 90		350									
349 ohc	75 × 79						E12	F12	G12	H12	J12	K12
349 ohc	75 × 79						ER12	FR12	GR12	HR12	JR12	
349 ohc	75 × 79										J12/S	
349 ohc	75 × 79										JRS12	
490 sv JAP	85.7 × 85	11										
490 ohv JAP	85.7 × 85	12	A12	B12	C12							
490 ohv JAP	85.7 × 85			B11	C11	D11	E10					
496 ohc	82 × 94							F14	G14	H14	J14	K14
496 ohc	82 × 94								G15	H15	J15	
498 ohv JAP				B14	C14							
600 sv JAP	85.7 × 104		A13	B13	C13							

Auto – Autobyk

FAGAN

	b × s	30	31	32	33	34	35	36	37	38	39	40
148 ts Vil	53 × 67						150	150				

FEDERATION

	b × s	30	31	32	33	34	35	36	37	38	39	40
147 ts Vil	55 × 62			2	2	2						
148 ts Vil	53 × 67				2A	2A	148	148	148			
245 ohv JAP	62.5 × 80				3	3	250	250	250			
300 sv JAP	70 × 78	2										
346 sv JAP	70 × 90	3	3	3								
346 ohv JAP	70 × 90	4	4	4								
498 sv JAP	80 × 99	5										
490 sv JAP	85.7 × 85		5	5								
490 ohv JAP	85.7 × 85		6	6	4	4	500	500				
677 sv JAP	70 × 88		7	7								

FRANCIS-BARNETT

	b × s	30	31	32	33	34	35	36	37	38	39	40
98 ts Vil	50 × 50				SNIPE					H49	J49	K49
98 ts Vil	50 × 50				POWERBIKE						J50	K50
122 ts Vil	50 × 62				SNIPE					H48	J48	K48
147 ts Vil	55 × 62	4	19	23				MERLIN				
147 ts Vil	55 × 62		20	24				KESTRAL				
148 ts Vil	53 × 67			25	27	33		LAPWING				
148 ts Vil	53 × 67				28	34		LAPWING				
148 ts Vil	53 × 67					35		LAPWING				
148 ts Vil	53 × 67				PLOVER	40		F/40	G/40	H40	J40	K40
148 ts Vil	53 × 67				PLOVER	41		F/41	G/41	H41	J41	K41
172 ts Vil	57.15 × 67	9		26				CONDOR				
196 ts Vil	61 × 67	14	BH	21	29	36	36	BLACK HAWK				
196 ts Vil	61 × 67				30	37		BLACK HAWK				
196 ts Vil	61 × 67	15	F	22	31	38		FALCON				

	b × s	30	31	32	33	34	35	36	37	38	39	40
247 ts Vil	67 × 70	12						EMPIRE				
247 ohv Bl	68 × 68		STAG				44	F/44	G/44			
247 ohv Bl	68 × 68		RED STAG						G/46			
249 ts Vil	63 × 80		CRUISER		32	39	E39	F/39	G/39	H39	J39	K39
249 ts Vil	63 × 80		SEAGULL				42					
249 ts Vil	63 × 80		SEAGULL				43	F/43	G/43	H43	J43	K43
249 ts Vil	63 × 80		CRUISER					F/45	G/45	H45	J45	K45
249 ts Vil	63 × 80		SEAGULL						G/47	H47	J47	K47
343 ts Vil	79 × 70	16	DOMINION									

GLORIA

	b × s	30	31	32	33	34	35	36	37	38	39	40
98 ts Vil	50 × 50			100	100							
147 ts Vil	55 × 62				150							

GRINDLAY-PEERLESS

	Engine	30	31	32	33	34	35	36	37	38	39	40
172 ts	Vil	175										
196 ts	Vil	200										
247 ts	Vil	250										
245 ohv	JAP	250 JAP										
248 ohv	Py			T. Cub	T. Cub	T. Cub						
248 ohv	Py				S. Cub							
346 ohv	JAP		350 JAP	350 JAP								
346 ohv	JAP		350 SS	350 SS								
348 ohv	Py			350 Py								
490 sv	JAP	500 SV										
490 ohv	JAP		500 JAP	500 JAP								
490 ohv	JAP		500 SS	500 SS								
490 ohv	JAP		500 TT									
499 ohv	Py			P4	T.	T.	T.					
499 ohv	Py			500Py								
499 ohv	PyUl			500Ul	T.C.	T.C.	T.C.					
499 ohv	PyUl				S.C.	S.C.						
499 ohv	PyTT				R.500	R.500						
680 sv twin	JAP	680 SV										
680 ohv twin	JAP	680 JAP										
750 sv twin	JAP	750 SV										

R – Racing
S – Speed
S.C. – Speed Chief

T. – Tiger
T.C. – Tiger Chief
Ul – Ulster

GROSESPUR

	b × s	30	31	32	33	34	35	36	37	38	39	40
122 ts Vil	50 × 62									Su	Su	Su

Su – Superb

HEC

	b × s	30	31	32	33	34	35	36	37	38	39	40
80 ts HEC											HEC	HEC

HUMBER

	b × s	30	31	32	33	34	35	36	37	38	39	40
349 sv	75 × 79	SV										
349 ohv	75 × 79	OHV										
349 ohc	75 × 79	OCS										

IXION

	b × s	30	31	32	33	34	35	36	37	38	39	40
249 sv NH	63 × 80	250										

NH – New Hudson

JAMES

	b × s	30	31	32	33	34	35	36	37	38	39	40
98 ts Vil	50 × 50										K17	L17
98 ts Vil	50 × 50									J18	K18	L18
98 ts Vil	50 × 50											L20
122 ts Vil	50 × 62							H17	I17	J17	K17	L17
148 ts J	55 × 62.5		D15	E15	F15	G15	H15					
148 ts J	55 × 62.5		D14	E16	F16	G16	H16					
148 ts Vil	53 × 67							I15	J15	K15	L15	
148 ts Vil	53 × 67							I16	J16	K16	L16	
172 ts Vil	57.15 × 67	B11	C10									
196 ts Vil	61 × 67	B9	C9									
196 ts Vil	61 × 67	B10	C11	D11								
196 ts Vil	61 × 67		C12	D12				I12	J12			
196 ts J	61 × 67			E12	F12	G12	H12					
197 ts Vil	59 × 72									K12	L12	
247 ts Vil	67 × 70	B8	C8	D8						K8	L8	
249 ts Vil	63 × 80			E8	F8	G8	H8	I8	J8			
249 ts Vil	63 × 80						H9	I9	J9	K9	L9	
249 sv J	64 × 77.5	B7	C7	D7	E7	F7	G7					
249 ohv J	64 × 77.5		C5	D5	E5	F5	G5					
347 sv J	73 × 83			D4								
349 sv J	73 × 83.5	B5										
349 ohv J	73 × 83.5	B4	C4									
499 ohv Py	85 × 88		C3									
499 sv Jt	64 × 77.5	B2	C2	D2	E2	F2	G2					
499 sv Jt	64 × 77.5	B3										
499 ohv Jt	64 × 77.5	B1	C1	D1								
499 ohv Jt	64 × 77.5	B6										

J – James
Jt – James twin

LEVIS

	b × s	30	31	32	33	34	35	36	37	38	39	40
247 ts	67 × 70	Z	Z		TS	TS	TS	TS	TS		MTS	TS
247 ts	67 × 70	6 port							Baby		MTS	TS
247 sv	67 × 70	C	C									
247 ohv	67 × 70	B	Bs	Bs	B33	B34	Bs	Bs	Bs	Bs	Bs	Bs
247 ohv	67 × 70							L250				
247 ohc	67 × 70					CB	CB	CB				
346 sv	70 × 90										SV	SV
346 ohv	70 × 90	A1		Pop A2				L350	LA37	SP3	CAs	CAs
346 ohv	70 × 90	A2	A2	A2	A33	A34	As	As	As	As	As	As
346 ohv	70 × 90										SF350	SF350
498 ohv	80 × 99				D33	D34	Ds	Ds	Ds	Ds	Ds	Ds
498 ohv	80 × 99							L500	LD37	SP5	CDs	CDs
498 ohv	80 × 99										SF500	SF500
591 ohv	82 × 112								600	600	600	600

CAs – competition A Special
CDs – competition D Special
L – Light
MTS – Master Two-Stroke

Pop – Popular
s – Special
SV – Side Valve
TS – Two-stroke

LGC

	b × s	30	31	32	33	34	35	36	37	38	39	40
247 ts Vil	67 × 70	TS/1	TS/1									
300 sv JAP	70 × 78	S/1	S/1									
346 ohv JAP	70 × 90	O/1	O/1									
346 ohv JAP	70 × 90	O/2										

MAJESTIC

	b × s	30	31	32	33	34	35	36	37	38	39	40
249 ohv St	65 × 75				250							
348 ohv St	74 × 81				350							
499 ohv St	84 × 90				500							

St – Stevens

Note: from 1933 all models used a year prefix to their type number; e.g. 33/D7

MATCHLESS

	b × s	30	31	32	33	34	35	36	37	38	39	40
245 sv	62.5 × 80	R/4	R/7	R/7	D7	F7	F7	F7	G7	G7	G7	G7
245 ohv	62.5 × 80	R/6	D/S	D/S	D2	D2		G2	G2	G2	G2	
245 ohv	62.5 × 80					F	F4	G2M	G2M	G2M	G2M	G2M
245 ohv	62.5 × 80								G2MC	G2MC	G2MC	
348 sv	69 × 93		D	D	D							
348 ohv	69 × 93	T/S2		D/6	D/6		G3	G3	G3	G3	G3	G3
348 ohv	69 × 93				D6		G3C	G3C	G3C	G3C	G3C	
348 ohv	69 × 93			D/3	D3	D3	D3			G4	G4	G4
497 sv	82.5 × 93	T/5	D/5	D/5	D/5							

b×s	30	31	32	33	34	35	36	37	38	39	40
497 sv	82.5 × 93				D5	D5	D5	D5	G5	G5	G5	G5
491 ohv	85.5 × 85.5	V/3	C/S	C/S	CS	CS	CS					
497 ohv	82.5 × 93				D80	D80	D80	G80	G80	G80	G80	G80
497 ohv	82.5 × 93						D90	G90	G90	G90	G90	G90
497 ohv	82.5 × 93							G80C	G80C	G80C		
497 ohv	82.5 × 93							G90C	G90C		G90C	
583 sv	85.5 × 101.6V/6		C	C	C	C	C					
394 sv twin	54 × 86	A	A2	A2	A2							
592 ohc four	50.8 × 73		B	B	B	B	B					
982 sv twin	85.5 × 85.5	X/2	X/3	X/3	X3	X4	X4	X4	X	X	X	X
982 sv twin	85.5 × 85.5	X/R2	X/R3	X/R3	XR3	XR4						

MONTGOMERY

b×s	30	31	32	33	34	35	36	37	38	39	40
98 ts Vil	50 × 50										T	T
122 ts Vil	50 × 62							T	T	Std	T	T Std
122 ts Vil	50 × 62							Tdl	Tdl	Std. dl		TMDL
148 ts Vil	53 × 67				148							
197 ts Vil	59 × 72											T
247 ts Vil	67 × 70	250TS	250TS		250	250						
245 sv JAP	62.5 × 80									T		
245 ohv JAP	62.5 × 80	250 OHV	250 OHV		250 Std		32T	T	T	T	T Std	T Std
245 ohv JAP	62.5 × 80		G250		250G	250G	36T	Tdl	G	Tdl	TMDL	TMDL
245 ohv JAP	62.5 × 80									R		
300 sv JAP	70 × 78	300 SV	300 SV									
346 sv JAP	70 × 90	350 SV	350 SV									
346 ohv JAP	70 × 90	350 OHV	350 OHV	350 OHV			36-350T	T	T	T Std	T Std	T Std
346 ohv JAP	70 × 90		G350	G350	350G	350G	39T	Tdl	G	Tdl	TMDL	TMDL
346 ohv JAP	70 × 90									R		
490 sv JAP	85.7 × 85	500 SV	500 SV							T Sp		
490 ohv JAP	85.7 × 85	500 OHV	500 OHV	500 OHV	500 B	500 B						
490 ohv JAP	85.7 × 85		G500	G500	500G							
499 ohv JAP	85 × 88						41G	G	T	G	G Std	G Std
499 ohv JAP	85 × 88					Su G	46 G	Gdl	G	G	GMDL	GMDL
499 ohv JAP	85 × 88						50 SpG	Sp		R		
550 sv JAP						550						
600 sv JAP			600 SV	600 SV						T Std		
600 ohv JAP						600 B						
680 ohv JAP	vee		G680		680 Tw	680 Tw						
750 sv JAP	vee	750 SV	750 SV		750 Tw	750 Tw						
994 sv JAP	vee		1000 SV									

B – Bulldog   R – Retriever   Su – Super
dl – de luxe   Sp – Sports   T – Terrier
G – Greyhound   Std – Standard   Tw – Twin

NEW COMET

	b × s	30	31	32	33	34	35	36	37	38	39	40
172 ts Vil	57.15 × 67	175										
196 ts Vil	61 × 67		SS									

SS – Super Sports

NEW GERRARD

	b × s	30	31	32	33	34	35	36	37	38	39	40
346 ohv JAP	70 × 90	350	350	350	350	350	350	350	350	350	350	350

NEW HENLEY

	b × s	30	31	32	33	34	35	36	37	38	39	40
172 ts Vil	57.15 × 67	V1										
196 ts Vil	61 × 67		V1									
196 ts Vil	61 × 67	V2	V2									
247 ts Vil	67 × 70	Bryn	Bryn									
346 ohv JAP	70 × 90	3	3									
346 ohv JAP	70 × 90		4									
490 sv JAP	85.7 × 85	6	6									
490 sv JAP	85.7 × 85		7									
490 ohv JAP	85.7 × 85	5	5									
490 ohv JAP	85.7 × 85		4A									
750 ohv JAP		8	8									

NEW HUDSON

	b × s	30	31	32	33	34	35	36	37	38	39	40
98 ts Vil	50 × 50											Auto
249 sv	63 × 80	80										
249 ohv	63 × 80	91										
346 sv	70 × 90	83	std									
346 sv	70 × 90		dl	32	32							
346 ohv	70 × 90	85	std									
346 ohv	70 × 90	87	dl	34	34							
346 ohv	70 × 90		spec									
496 sv	79.5 × 100	84										
496 ohv	79.5 × 100	86	std									
496 ohv	79.5 × 100	88	dl									
496 ohv	79.5 × 100	89	spec									
493 sv	83.5 × 90			01	01							
493 ohv	83.5 × 90			3	3							
493 ohv	83.5 × 90			4	4							
493 ohv	83.5 × 90			BW	BW							
548 sv	83.5 × 100		std	1	1							
548 sv	83.5 × 100		dl	2	2							

BW – Bronze Wing
dl – de luxe
spec – special
std – standard

NEW IMPERIAL

	b × s	30	31	32	33	34	35	36	37	38	39	40
148 ohv UC	55 × 62.5			23	23	23	23	23	23	23	23	
148 ohv UC	55 × 62.5					23DL	23DL					
148 ohv UC	55 × 62.5						25					
148 ohv UC	55 × 62.5						27					
245 ohv	62.5 × 80	9	9	8		50	50	50			50	
245 ohv	62.5 × 80			20				90	90	90		
245 ohv	62.5 × 80			22								
247 ohv UC	67 × 70				30	30	30	30		36L	36L	
247 ohv UC	67 × 70					30DL	30DL	36	36	36	36	
247 ohv UC	67 × 70						35		36DL	36DL	36DL	36DL
247 ohv UC	67 × 70						37					
344 sv	74 × 80	2	2	2	2							
344 sv	74 × 80	DL2	DL2									
346 ohv	70 × 90	10	10			60	60	60			60	
346 ohv	70 × 90							100	100	100		
344 ohv	74 × 80		B10	15								
344 ohv BP	74 × 80		F10	F10	F10	F10	F10					
344 ohv	74 × 80			19								
344 ohv	74 × 80			21								
344 ohv BP	74 × 80			Comp								
344 ohv UC	74 × 80			16	16	16	47	46	46	46	46	46
344 ohv UC	74 × 80				16A	16A	49	49	46DL	46DL	46DL	46DL
344 ohv UC	74 × 80					40	40	40				
344 ohv UC	74 × 80						45					
499 sv	84 × 90	7	7	18	18	18	18					
496 sv UC	82 × 94						80					
499 ohv	84 × 90	7B	7B	Comp								
499 ohv	86 × 86		11A									
499 ohv BP	86 × 86		11	F11	F11	F11	F11					
499 ohv UC	86 × 86			17	17	17						
499 ohv UC	86 × 86				17A	17A						
496 ohv UC	82 × 94						70	70	110	110	110	110
496 ohv UC	82 × 94							76	76	76	76	76
496 ohv UC	82 × 94								76DL	76DL	76DL	76DL
554 sv UC	84 × 100							80				
491 ohv UC	62.5 × 80						90					
491 ohv UC	62.5 × 80						100					

BP – Blue Prince
DL – De Luxe
UC – Unit Construction

NEWMOUNT

	b × s	30	31	32	33	34	35	36	37	38	39	40
198 ts Zun	60 × 70	198	200 s	200 s	200 s							
198 ts Zun	60 × 70		Lw	Lw	Lw							
300 ts Zun	68 × 82.5		300	300	300							
348 ohv Py	70 × 90.5		350	350	350							
499 ohv Py	85 × 88		500 s	500 s	500 s							
499 ohv Py	85 × 88		500 sp	500 sp	500 sp							

Lw – Lightweight
s – standard

sp – special
Zun – Zundapp

NORMAN

	b × s	30	31	32	33	34	35	36	37	38	39	40
98 ts Vil	50 × 50										Mo	St Mo
98 ts Vil	50 × 50											Dl Mo
98 ts Vil	50 × 50											Ca Mo
98 ts Vil	50 × 50											Lw
122 ts Vil	50 × 62										Lw	Lw

Ca Mo – Carrier Motobyke
Dl Mo – De Luxe Motobyke
Lw – Lightweight

Mo – Motobyke
St Mo – Standard Motobyke

NORTON

	b × s	30	31	32	33	34	35	36	37	38	39	40
348 ohv	71 × 88	JE	JE		50	50	50	50	50	50	50	
348 ohv	71 × 88			55	55	55	55	55	55	55	55	
348 ohc	71 × 88	CJ	CJ	CJ	CJ	CJ	CJ	CJ	CJ	CJ	CJ	
348 ohc	71 × 88			40	40	40	40	40	40	40	40	
490 sv	79 × 100	16H	16H	16H	16H	16H	16H	16H	16H	16H	16H	16H
490 sv	79 × 100	2	2	2								
490 ohv	79 × 100	18	18	18	18	18	18	18	18	18	18	
490 ohv	79 × 100	20	20	20	20	20	20	20	20	20	20	
490 ohv	79 × 100	21										
490 ohv	79 × 100	22	22									
490 ohv	79 × 100	ES2	ES2	ES2	ES2	ES2	ES2	ES2	ES2	ES2	ES2	
490 ohc	79 × 100	CS1	CS1	CS1	CS1	CS1	CS1	CS1	CS1	CS1	CS1	
490 ohc	79 × 100			30	30	30	30	30	30	30	30	
588 ohv	79 × 120	19	19	19								
588 ohv	79 × 120	24										
597 ohv	82 × 113				19	19	19	19	19	19	19	
634 sv	82 × 120	1	1	1	1	1	1	1	1	1	1	1
634 sv	82 × 120	14										
Trials spec.							Opt	Opt	Opt	Opt	Opt	

Opt – Option

NUT

	b × s	30	31	32	33	34	35	36	37	38	39	40
250 ohv					250							
350 sv		350 SV	350 SV	350 SV								
350 ohv		350	350	350								
500 ohv twin		500 T	500 T	500 T	500 T							
500 ohc twin					500 C							
700 ohv twin		700 T	700 T	700 T	700 T							
700 ohc twin					700 C							
750 sv twin		750 SV	750 SV	750 SV	750 SV							

OEC

	Engine	30	31	32	33	34	35	36	37	38	39	40
98 ts	Vil										100	
122 ts	Vil										125	
148 ts	Vil					34/1						
245 ohv	JAP				250 OHV			36/P1				
245 ohv	M					34/3	35/1	36/1				
245 ohv	M						35/2dl		37/1			
245 ohv	AJS								En	En		
249 ts	Vil					34/2						
249 ts	Vil					250 WC						
346 ts	Vil					350						
350 sv	Bl	350 SV										
350 sv	SA	350 SV										
346 sv	JAP		350 SV	350 SV	350 SV							
350 ohv	Bl	350 OHV										
346 ohv	JAP	350 OHV	350 OHV	350 OHV	350 OHV							
348 ohv	M					34/4	35/3					
348 ohv	M						35/4dl		37/2			
348 ohv	AJS								Ca	Ca	Ca	Ca
500 sv	Bl	500 SV										
490 sv	JAP	500 SV	500 SV	500 SV	500 SV							
497 sv	M					34/5						
500 ohv	Bl	500 OHV										
490 ohv	JAP	500 OHV	500 OHV	500 OHV	500 OHV							
497 ohv	M					34/6	35/5dl	36/2	37/3			
497 ohv	AJS								C'der	C'der	C'der	C'der
497 ohv	AJS										C'ore	C'ore
500 ohv	JAP							36/P2				
600 sv	JAP				600 SV	600 SV						
600 ohv	JAP				600 OHV	600 OHV						
592 ohc-4	M					34/8						
498 ohv-2	JAP		500 OHV	500 OHV								
680 ohv-2	JAP		680 OHV	680 OHV								
750 sv -2	JAP		750 SV	750 SV	750 SV			36/P3	37/4			

	Engine	30	31	32	33	34	35	36	37	38	39	40
980 ohv -2	JAP		1000 OHV	1000 OHV	1000 OHV							
1000 sv-2	JAP		1000 SV	1000 SV	1000 SV							
982 sv-2	M					34/7	35/6	36/3	37/5			
982 sv-2	AJS								Twin			
1100 sv-2	JAP								37/6			

Ca – Cadet
C'der – Commander
C'ore – Commodore
dl – de luxe

En – Ensign
M – Matchless
WC – Water-cooled

OK SUPREME

	b × s	30	31	32	33	34	35	36	37	38	39	40
148 sv JAP	51.5 × 71			P								
245 sv JAP	62.5 × 80								SV	SV	SV	SV
245 ohv JAP	62.5 × 80	TT				G2		GT70	AC			
245 ohv JAP	62.5 × 80		G	G	G	G	G	G	G	G	G	G
245 ohv JAP	62.5 × 80				GDL	GDL	GDL	GDL	GDL	GDL	GDL	GDL
245 ohv JAP	62.5 × 80						V	GT				
245 ohv JAP	62.5 × 80							G70	G70	G70	G70	G70
248 ohc	70 × 64.5		A	A	A							
248 ohc	66 × 72.5						HS	CG	CG	CG	CG	
248 ohc	66 × 72.5						RC	RC	RC	RC		
248 ohc	66 × 72.5						HT	HT				
300 sv JAP	70 × 78	B	B	B								
344 ohv JAP	74 × 80	J							GTS	GTS	GTS	
346 ohv JAP	70 × 90	TT/LS							BC			
346 ohv JAP	70 × 90	GH				GS2	GS2	GH	GH			
346 ohv JAP	70 × 90	H	H	GS	GS	GS	GS					
348 ohv AMC	69 × 93									BA	BA	
348 ohv AMC	69 × 93									CA	CA	
348 ohv AMC	69 × 93									GA	GA	
348 ohv AMC	69 × 93									JA	JA	
344 ohv JAP	74 × 80									RRS		
346 ohc	70 × 90						WS	WS	WS	WS	WS	
346 ohc	70 × 90						RCB	RCB	RCB	RCB		
346 ohc	70 × 90						WT	WT				
490 sv JAP	85.7 × 85	K										
490 sv JAP	85.7 × 85	K/31	N	N	N	N	N	N		N		
490 ohv JAP	85.7 × 85	K/32	L	L	L	L	L		L	L		
490 ohv JAP	85.7 × 85			R	LB	LB						
498 ohv	83 × 92							R				
498 ohv	83 × 92							S				
498 ohv JAP	80 × 99									HC		
497 ohv AMC	82.5 × 93										DA	DA
497 ohv AMC	82.5 × 93										HA	HA
600 sv JAP	85.7 × 104						OS	OS				
747 sv JAP	70 × 97	M	M									
750 sv JAP												750

Note: from 1931 all models have a year suffix number to read A/31, B/32, etc to G/40
AMC – Matchless

OMC

172 ts Vil	b × s	30	31	32	33	34	35	36	37	38	39	40
172 ts Vil	57.15 × 67	OMC										

P&P

	b × s	30	31	32	33	34	35	36	37	38	39	40
199 ts		60											
245 ohv JAP	62.5 × 80	80											
500 ohv		90											
500 ohc		S 500											

S – Silent

PANTHER

	b × s	30	31	32	33	34	35	36	37	38	39	40
147 ts Vil	55 × 62	15	15	10								
196 ts Vil	61 × 67	20	20									
247 ts Vil	67 × 70	25	25	20								
249 ohv	60 × 88			30								
249 ohv	60 × 88			40	40							
249 ohv RP	60 × 88				RP	20	20	20	20	20	20	
249 ohv RP	60 × 88					10	10				40	
249 ohv RP	60 × 88							70	71			
249 ohv Rw	60 × 88					70						60
249 ohv St	60 × 88					St	St	St	St	St		
348 ohv	71 × 88				45							
348 ohv RP	71 × 88					30	30	30	30	30	30	
348 ohv Rw	71 × 88					80	80	80				70
348 ohv Rw	71 × 88							85	85	85	85	
348 ohv St	71 × 88					St	St	St	St	St		
499 ohv	84 × 90	50	50	50	50	50	50					
499 ohv	84 × 90		55	Ex								
490 ohv Rw	79 × 100		90	90	90	90	90	90	90	90		
490 ohv Rw	79 × 100		95									
498 ohv Rw	79.6 × 100									95	95	90
594 sv Rw	87 × 100											80
594 ohv	87 × 100	60	60	60	60	60	60					
594 ohv	87 × 100		65									
594 ohv Rw	87 × 100	85										
594 ohv Rw	87 × 100			100	100	100	100	100	100	100	100	100

Ex – Express   Rw – Redwing
RP – Red Panther   St – Stroud

POUNCY

	b × s	30	31	32	33	34	35	36	37	38	39	40
148 ts Vil	53 × 67			Kid	Pup							
249 ts Vil	63 × 80				Pal	Pal	Pal	Pal				
346 ts Vil	70 × 90		Cob	Cob								
346 ts Vil	70 × 90			T.S	Mate	Mate						

T.S – Triple S

PRIDE & CLARKE

	b × s	30	31	32	33	34	35	36	37	38	39	40
122 ts Vil	50 × 62										Cub	

RADCO

	b × s	30	31	32	33	34	35	36	37	38	39	40
147 ts Vil	55 × 62	L	L	L	L							
147 ts Vil	55 × 62	M	M	M	M							
196 ts Vil	61 × 67	O	O	O	O							
196 ts Vil	61 × 67	N	N	N	N							
196 ts Vil	61 × 67			T	T							
196 ts Vil	61 × 67		S	U	U							
247 ts Ra	67 × 70	P	P	P	P							
247 ts Ra	67 × 70	R	R	R	R							
245 ohv JAP	62.5 × 80	E	E									
490 sv JAP	85.7 × 85	H	H									
490 ohv JAP	85.7 × 85	K	K									

Ra – Radco

RALEIGH

	b × s	30	31	32	33	34	35	36	37	38	39	40
225 sv	60 × 79.5	MG30										
248 sv		MJ30										
297 sv	65.6 × 88	MO30	MO31	MO32	MO33							
348 ohv	71 × 88	MT30	MT31									
348 ohv	71 × 88		MG31	MG32	MG33							
495 sv	79 × 101	MA30	MA31	MA32	MA33							
495 ohv	79 × 101	MH30	MH31	MH32	MH33							
598 sv	86.8 × 101			MB32	MB33							

RAYNAL

	b × s	30	31	32	33	34	35	36	37	38	39	40
98 ts Vil	50 × 50								Auto	Auto	DL	DL
98 ts Vil	50 × 50										Pop	Pop

DL – De Luxe
Pop – Popular

REX-ACME

	b × s	30	31	32	33	34	35	36	37	38	39	40
147 ts Vil	55 × 62	V10C	V11C									
172 ts Vil	57.15 × 67	V10S										
247 ts Vil	67 × 70	V10A										
249 ts Vil	63 × 80				13							
250 ohv JAP					13							
295 sv Bl	69 × 79	B10										
300 sv JAP	70 × 78		J11									
348 sv Bl	69 × 93	K10										
346 sv JAP	70 × 90	U10										
343 ts Vil	79 × 70	V10B										
348 ohv Bl	71 × 88	M101	M111									
348 ohv Bl	71 × 88	M102	M112									
346 ohv JAP	70 × 90	O10	O11	O12	O13							
490 sv JAP	85.7 × 85	C10	C11									
495 ohv SA	79 × 101	SA10	SA11									
499 ohv Py	85 × 88		P11									
499 ohv Py	85 × 88		Sp									
500 ohv JAP		Sp	Sp									
500 ohv Bl		Sp	Sp									
500 ohv JAP				R12	R13							
596 sv Bl	85 × 105	D10										
747 sv JAP	70 × 97	E10										

Sp – Speedway

REYNOLDS

	Engine	30	31	32	33	34	35	36	37	38	39	40
497/598 ts	Scott		Aero	Sp								
598 ts	Scott				Sp	Sp						

Sp – Special

ROYAL ENFIELD

	b × s	30	31	32	33	34	35	36	37	38	39	40
126 ts	54 × 55											RE
148 ts	56 × 60			Z	Z	Z	Z	Z				
148 ts	56 × 60				X	X						
148 ohv	56 × 60					T	T	T	T	T		
148 ohv	56 × 60								TM	TM		
225 ts	64 × 70	A										
225 ts	64 × 70		A31	A	A							
225 ts	64 × 70					A	A	A	A	A		
225 ts	64 × 70										A	
225 sv	64 × 70	B										
248 sv	64 × 77				B	B	B	B				
248 sv	64 × 77								B	B		
248 sv	64 × 77									BM	D	D
248 ohv	64 × 77				BO Bul	BO Bul	S2 Bul	S2 Bul				
248 ohv	64 × 77					S	S	S				
248 ohv	64 × 77								Bul	Bul		
248 ohv	64 × 77								S2	S2	S2	
248 ohv	64 × 77								S	S		
248 ohv	64 × 77								SM	S		
248 ohv	64 × 77										SF	SF
346 sv	70 × 90	C	C31	C		C	C	C				
346 sv	70 × 90								C	C	C	
346 sv	70 × 90	F	F31									
346 ohv	70 × 90	G	G31	G	G Bul	G Bul	G					
346 ohv	70 × 90							G	G	G	G Bul	G Bul
346 ohv	70 × 90							G comp	G comp			
346 ohv	70 × 90								G2			
346 ohv	70 × 90								Bul	Bul	Bul comp	
346 ohv	70 × 90	CO	CO31	CO								
346 ohv	70 × 90		CS31	CS								
346 ohv	70 × 90									CO	CO	CO
346 ohv	70 × 90										CM	
488 sv	85.5 × 85	D										
488 sv	85.5 × 85	H										
488 sv	85.5 × 85	HA	HA31									
499 sv	80 × 99.25			L	L							
499 sv	80 × 99.25			LC	LC				H	H		
488 ohv	85.5 × 85	E										
488 ohv	85.5 × 85	J										
488 ohv	85.5 × 85	JA	JA31									
488 ohv (4V)	85.5 × 85		JF31	LF	LF	LF						
488 ohv (3V)	85.5 × 85						LO					
499 ohv	80 × 99.25		J31	J								
499 ohv	84 × 90							J	J	J	J	J
499 ohv	84 × 90								J2	Bul	J2 Bul	J2 Bul
499 ohv (4V)	84 × 90							JF	JF Bul	Bul	J2 Bul	
499 ohv	84 × 90							J comp	500 comp	500 comp	comp	
499 ohv (4V)	84 × 90									500 comp	comp	
499 ohv	84 × 90								JM			
570 sv	85.5 × 99.25		H31	H		L	L	L				

231

	b×s	30	31	32	33	34	35	36	37	38	39	40
570 sv	85.5 × 99.25								L	L	L	L
570 sv s/c	85.5 × 99.25										H	
976 sv twin	85.5 × 85	K	K31	K	K	K	K	K				
1140 sv twin	85.5 × 99.25				K (ex)	K (ex)	K (ex)	K (ex)	K	K	K	
1140 sv twin	85.5 × 99.25								KX	KX	KX	

Bul – Bullet
comp – competition
(ex) – export model

s/c – sidecar outfit
3V – three-valve head
4V – four-valve head

ROYAL RUBY

	b×s	30	31	32	33	34	35	36	37	38	39	40
247 ts Vil	67 × 70	250										
249 ts Vil	63 × 80				Sp							
249 ts Vil	63 × 80				SS							
249 ts Vil	63 × 80				SS wc							
343 ts Vil	79 × 70	350										
346 ts Vil	70 × 90		RS	Club	SS							
346 ts Vil	70 × 90			Std.	Sp							

RS – Red Shadow
Sp – Sports
SS – Super-Sports

Std – Standard
wc – water-cooled

RUDGE

	b×s	30	31	32	33	34	35	36	37	38	39	40
248 sv JAP	64.5 × 76	250										
245 ohv JAP	62.5 × 80	250										
300 sv JAP	70 × 78	300										
248 ohv R	62.5 × 81		250	250	250	STD						
248 ohv R	62.5 × 81			TT	TT							
248 ohv R	62.5 × 81					Sp	Sp	Sp				
248 ohv 2V	62.5 × 81						To					
245 ohv 2V	62 × 81							Ra	Ra	Ra	Ra	
245 ohv 2V	62 × 81									Sp	Sp	
339 ohv P	70 × 88	340										
348 ohv R	70 × 90.5		350	350	350							
348 ohv R	70 × 90.5		TT	TT	TT							
499 ohv P	85 × 88	Spec	Spec	Spec	Spec	Spec	Spec					
493 ohv P	84.5 × 88							Spec	Spec	Spec	Spec	
493 ohv P	84.5 × 88								Sp Sp	Sp Sp	Sp Sp	
499 ohv P	85 × 88	Ul	Ul									
499 ohv R	85 × 88			Ul								
499 ohv SR	85 × 88				Ul	Ul	Ul	Ul	Ul	Ul	Ul	
499 ohv P	85 × 88	DT	DT									
499 ohv P	85 × 88		TT									
499 ohv R	85 × 88			TT								
499 ohv SR	85 × 88				TT							

DT – Dirt Track
P – Pent-roof 4-valve
R – Radial 4-valve
Ra – Rapid
Sp – Sports
Spec – Special
Sp Sp – Sports Special

SR – Semi-radial 4-valve
STD – Standard
To – Tourist
TT – TT Replica
Ul – Ulster
2V – Two-valve

SCOTT

	b × s	30	31	32	33	34	35	36	37	38	39	40
299	73 × 71.4	Sq	Sq									
499 or	68.25 × 68.25	F Sq T	F Sq T	F Sq T								
	or	dl	dl	dl								
597	74.6 × 68.25	Sp Sq	Sp Sq									
		Su Sq	Su Sq									
497		DT										
497 to 1938	66.6 × 71.4	TTR	TTR	TTR	Rep	Rep						
598 to 1939	73 × 71.4	Sp Sp	Sp Sp		F Sq T	F Sq T	F Sq	F Sq	F Sq	F Sq	F Sq	
					dl	dl					CS	
				F Sq Sp	F Sq Sp							
650			650									
986							3S	3S	3S			

CS – Clubman's Special
dl – de luxe (F Sq T)
DT – Dirt Track
F Sq – Flying Squirrel
F Sq Sp – Flying Squirrel Sports
F Sq T – Flying Squirrel Tourer

Rep – Replica
Sp Sp – Sprint Special
Sp Sq – Sports Squirrel
Sq – Squirrel
Su Sq – Super Squirrel
TTR – TT Replica

SGS

	b × s	30	31	32	33	34	35	36	37	38	39	40
196 ts Vil	61 × 67	200										
245 sv JAP	62.5 × 80	250										
245 ohv JAP	62.5 × 80	250										
247 ts Vil	67 × 70	250										
346 ohv JAP	70 × 90	350										

SHARRATT

	b × s	30	31	32	33	34	35	36	37	38	39	40
346 sv JAP	70 × 90	F										
346 ohv JAP	70 × 90	FS	FS									
346 ohv JAP	70 × 90	FSS	FSS									

SOS

	b × s	30	31	32	33	34	35	36	37	38	39	40
250 ohv JAP		GS1										
350 ohv JAP		GS2										
148 SOS	53 × 67				KUW							
172 Vil	57.15 × 67	K	K	K	K							
172 SOS	57.15 × 67				KW							
196 Vil	61 × 67	K	KZ	KS								
247 Vil	67 × 70	C	C	C								
343 Vil	79 × 70	C	CY									
346 Vil	70 × 90			CY								
172 Vil	57.15 × 67					A	A	AA	AA	AA	AA	
172 Vil	57.15 × 67					B	B	BW	BW	BW	BW	
249 Vil	63 × 80					C	C	CW	CW	CW	CW	
249 Vil	63 × 80							CA	CA	CA	CA	
249 Vil	63 × 80					D	D	DW	DW	DW	DW	
249 Vil	63 × 80							DA	DA	DA	DA	
249 Vil	63 × 80					E	E	EW	EW	EW	EW	
249 Vil	63 × 80							EA	EA	EA	EA	
249 Vil	63 × 80								DWHC	DWHC	DWHC	
249 Vil	63 × 80								DAHC	DAHC	DAHC	
346 Vil	70 × 90					F	F	FA	FA	FA		
346 Vil	70 × 90										FW	
346 Vil	70 × 90					G	G	GA	GA	GA		
346 Vil	70 × 90										GW	

STANLEY

	b × s	30	31	32	33	34	35	36	37	38	39	40
98 ts Vil	50 × 50			S								

STEVENS

	b × s	30	31	32	33	34	35	36	37	38	39	40
249 ohv	63 × 80					DS1	DS1	DS1	DS17	DS17		
249 ohv	63 × 80							US2	US27	US27		
348 ohv	74 × 81						LL4	LL4	LL47	LL47		
348 ohv	74 × 81							HL3	HL37	HL37		
495 ohv	79 × 101						LP5	LP5	LP57	LP57		
495 ohv	79 × 101							HP6	HP67	HP67		

SUN

	b × s	30	31	32	33	34	35	36	37	38	39	40
98 ts Vil	50 × 50		T	T	98							Auto
147 ts Vil	55 × 62	150 TS		T	147							
148 ts Vil	53 × 67			S								
148 ts Vil	53 × 67			150	150							
196 ts Vil	61 × 67	200 TS	200 TS	Ut	196							
245 ohv JAP	62.5 × 80		250 OHV									
300 sv JAP	70 × 78	300 SV										
343 ts Vil	79 × 70		350 TS									

	b × s	30	31	32	33	34	35	36	37	38	39	40
346 ts Vil	70 × 90			T	T							
346 ohv JAP	70 × 90	350 OHV		T	T							
490 sv JAP	85.7 × 85	500 SV	500 SV	500 SV								
490 ohv JAP		500 OHV	500 OHV	500 OHV								

S – Sports
T – Tourist
Ut – Utility

SUNBEAM

	b × s	30	31	32	33	34	35	36	37	38	39	40
246 ohv	59 × 90				14	14		14	14	A23		
246 ohv	59 × 90				Li 90	Li 95						
246 ohv	59 × 90							14 Sp	14 Sp	A23S		
248 ohv	64 × 70						16					
245 ohv	62.5 × 80										B23	C23
245 ohv	62.5 × 80										B23S	
245 ohv	62.5 × 80										B23T	
346 sv	70 × 90	1										
346 sv	70 × 90	2										
346 ohv	70 × 90	8			8	8	8	8	8	A24		
346 ohv	70 × 90	80			80							
344 ohv	74 × 80		10	10								
346 ohv	70 × 90							8 Sp	8 Sp	A24S		
348 ohv	69 × 93										B24	C24
348 ohv	69 × 93										B24S	C24S
348 ohv	69 × 93										B24T	
348 ohv	69 × 93											CH24
491 sv	77 × 105.5	5										
491 sv	77 × 105.5	6										
489 sv	77 × 105	Lion	Lion	Lion	Lion	Lion	Lion	Lion	Lion	A29	B29	
493 ohv	80 × 98	9	9	9	9	9	9	9	9	A27		
493 ohv	80 × 98	90	90	90	90		95L	9 Sp	Li S	A25		
493 ohv	80 × 98	DTR			95	95	95R		Li SSp	A26		
497 ohv	82.5 × 93										B25	C25
497 ohv	82.5 × 93										B25S	C25S
497 ohv	82.5 × 93										B25T	
497 ohv	82.5 × 93											CH25
599 sv	85 × 105.5	7		Lion	Lion	Lion	Lion	Lion	Lion	A30	B30	C30
596 ohv	88 × 98			9A	9A	9A	9A	9A	9A	A28		
598 ohv	90.48 × 93										B28	C28
598 ohv	90.48 × 93											CH28

THREE SPIRES

	b × s	30	31	32	33	34	35	36	37	38	39	40
147 ts Vil	55 × 62			150								

TRIUMPH

	b × s	30	31	32	33	34	35	36	37	38	39	40
148 ts	55 × 62.5			Z								
148 ts Vil	53 × 67					XV/1						
148 ohv	56.6 × 59				XO	XO5						
174 ts	59.5 × 62.5	X	X	X								
175 ohv	61.5 × 59					XO7						
249 ohv	63 × 80		WO	WO	WO	2/1	2/1	2/1	2H	2H	2H	2H
249 ohv	63 × 80			WA	WA	2/5	2/5	T70	T70	T70	T70	T70
249 ohv	63 × 80				WP		L2/1	L2/1		2HC	2HC	
278 sv	66.5 × 80	WS										
343 sv	70 × 89					3/1	3/1	3/1	3S	3S	3S	3S
343 sv	70 × 89									3SC	3SC	3SE
343 ohv	70 × 89		NM	NM		3/2	3/2	3/2	3H	3H	3H	3H
343 ohv	70 × 89			CA		3/5	3/5	T80	T80	T80	T80	T80
348 sv	72 × 85.5		WL	WL								
348 ohv	72 × 85.5	CO										
483 sv	84 × 89										5S	5S
493 sv	84 × 89											5SE
493 ohv	84 × 89		NT	NT	NT	5/2	5/2	5/2	5H	5H	5H	
493 ohv	84 × 89			CD	CD	5/4	5/4	T90	T90	T90		
493 ohv	84 × 89			B	B	B						
493 ohv	84 × 89				BS	BS						
493 ohv	84 × 89					5/5	5/5	5/5				
493 ohv	84 × 89					5/10	5/10	5/10				
498 sv	80 × 99	CN	CN									
498 ohv	80 × 99	CTT	CTT									
549 sv	84 × 99	NSD	NSD	A	A	5/1	5/1	5/1				
549 sv	84 × 99	CSD	CSD	CSD		5/3	5/3					
549 sv	84 × 99	ND	ND	ND								
598 sv	84 × 108								6S	6S	6S	6S
499 ohv twin	63 × 80									5T	5T	5T
499 ohv twin	63 × 80										T100	T100
647 ohv twin	70 × 84					6/1	6/1	6/1				

VELOCETTE

	b × s	30	31	32	33	34	35	36	37	38	39	40
249 ts	63 × 80	GTP	GTP	GTP	GTP	GTP	GTP	GTP	GTP	GTP	GTP	GTP
248 ohv	68 × 68.25				MOV	MOV	MOV	MOV	MOV	MOV	MOV	MOV
348 ohc	74 × 81	KTP	KTP									
348 ohc	74 × 81	KSS	KSS	KSS	KSS	KSS	KSS	KSS	KSS	KSS	KSS	KSS
348 ohc	74 × 81			KTS	KTS	KTS	KTS	KTS	KTS	KTS	KTS	KTS
348 ohc	74 × 81	KTT	KTT	KTT	KTT	KTT	KTT	KTT		KTT	KTT	
KTT Mk		I	II	III	IV	IV	V	V/VI		VII	VIII	
349 ohv	68 × 96					MAC	MAC	MAC	MAC	MAC	MAC	MAC
495 ohv	81 × 96						MSS	MSS	MSS	MSS	MSS	MSS

VINCENT-HRD

	b × s	30	31	32	33	34	35	36	37	38	39	40
247 ts Vil	67 × 70				L							
249 ts Vil	63 × 80					W	W					
350 ohv JAP			Sp									
350 ohv JAP		GTR	GTR	GTR								
350 ohv Py			Sp									
490 sv JAP	85.7 × 85	To	To									
490 ohv JAP	85.7 × 85	Sp	Sp	TJ								
490 ohv JAP	85.7 × 85			DJ	J	J	J					
498 ohv JAP	80 × 99	Ra	Ra	TJR								
499 ohv Py	85 × 88			DP	P	P						
499 ohv Py	85 × 88			DPS	PS	PS						
499 ohv Py	85 × 88			TP								
499 ohv Py	85 × 88			TPS								
600 sv JAP		To	To			JW						
600 ohv JAP		Sp										
600 ohv JAP		Ra										
499 ohv	84 × 90						M	M	M	M	M	
499 ohv	84 × 90						C	C	C	C	C	
499 ohv	84 × 90							CS	CS			
499 ohv	84 × 90						TTm	TTm	TTR	TTR		
499 ohv	84 × 90							TTrm				
998 ohv	84 × 90								Rap	Rap	Rap	

C – Comet
CS – Comet Special
GTR – grass-track racer
M – Meteor
Ra – race
Rap – Rapide

Sp – Sports
TGR – triangulated grass-track
To – touring
TTm – TT model
TTR – TT Replica
TTrm – TT road model

WHITWOOD

	b × s	30	31	32	33	34	35	36	37	38	39	40
150 ts Vil							Dart					
250 ts Vil							St					
250 ohv JAP								Devon				
500 sv JAP							Ce	York				
750 sv JAP							Re	Ru				

Ce – Century
Re – Regent

Ru – Rutland
St – Sterling

WOLF

	b × s	30	31	32	33	34	35	36	37	38	39	40
98 ts Vil	50 × 50		Cub	W1	Cub	WA2	Cub	Cub				
122 ts Vil	50 × 62							Unit	WA10	WA10	WA10	WA10
147 ts Vil	55 × 62		M	W3	M			M	M	WA4	WA4	
148 ts Vil	53 × 67			W5	V	WA5	V	V	V	WA5	WA5	WA5
148 ts Vil	53 × 67			W6	V	WA6	V	V		WA6	WA6	WA6
196 ts Vil	61 × 67		U	W7	U							
196 ts Vil	61 × 67			W8	SW							
196 ts Vil	61 × 67			W9								
249 ts Vil	63 × 80							SS	WA9	WA9	WA9	
249 ts Vil	63 × 80									WA11	WA11	

M – Minor
SS – Super-Sports
SW – Silver Wolf

U – Utility
V – Vixen

ZENITH

	b × s	30	31	32	33	34	35	36	37	38	39	40
245 ohv JAP	62.5 × 80					LC1	LC1	LC1	LC1	LC1	LC1	LC1
245 ohv JAP	62.5 × 80							LC1(M)	LC1(M)	LC1(M)	LC1(M)	LC1 (M)
250 ohv JAP										HC1		
300 sv JAP	70 × 78	300 SV										
346 ohv JAP	70 × 90	B2	B2	B2	B2							
346 ohv JAP	70 × 90			B2dl	B2dl	LC2	LC2	LC2	LC2			
346 ohv JAP	70 × 90							LC2(M)	LC2(M)			
346 ohv JAP	70 × 90	20TT								HC2		
350 ohv Bl				std	B2							
350 ohv Bl				dl	B2dl							
490 sv JAP	85.7 × 85	BS5	BS5	BS5	BS5	CS5	CS5					
490 sv JAP	85.7 × 85			BS5dl	BS5dl	CS5dl	CS5dl					
490 ohv JAP	85.7 × 85	B5	B5	B5	B5	C5	C5	C5	C5	C5	C5	C5
490 ohv JAP	85.7 × 85			B5dl	B5dl	C5dl	C5dl	C5Spo	C5Spe			
490 ohv JAP	85.7 × 85				B5SS	C5SS	C5SS					
498 ohv JAP								C5Su	C5Su	C5Su		
500 ohv JAP			22TT						HC5	HC5		
500 ohv Bl				std	B5	C5						
500 ohv Bl				dl	B5dl	C5dl						
600 sv JAP								CS5	CS5	CS5	CS5	CS5
600 ohv Bl				dl	B6dl							
600 ohv Bl				Co	B6Co							
677 sv JAP	70 × 88	680	680	680	680	680	680					
677 sv JAP	70 × 88			680 dl	680 dl	680 dl	680 dl					
680 ohv JAP					680 OHV							
747 sv JAP	70 × 97	750	750	750	750	750	750	750				
747 sv JAP	70 × 97			750dl	750dl	750dl	750dl	750dl	750dl	750	750	750
980 sv JAP		N			N							
1000 ohv JAP		8.55										
1100 sv JAP					NP	CP1100	CP1100	CP	CP	CP	CP	CP

Co – Competition
dl – de luxe

(M) – magneto
Spe – Special

Spo – Sports
SS – Special Sports

std – standard
Su – Super

Acknowledgements

This one was for myself as it covers the machines my friends and I rode in the early post-war days when a tired pre-war model was all we could afford. So this is nostalgia first and reference second, although the engineer in me has insisted on checking capacities from bore and stroke which has corrected a few ancient figures.

Help came from many quarters to check the text as much of it went to the relevant marque specialists of the Vintage Motorcycle Club for their tender care. Their kind notes, corrections and suggestions were incorporated as were others from similar knowledgeable sources.

The long list of helpers includes Ray Carter (AJS), Peter Gasson (AJW), Don Bassett (AKD), Jim Lee (Ariel), Pete Staughton, Mike Leatherdale, John Wallis and Barry Robinson (all Brough Superior), Dick Lewis (BSA), Dick Weeks (Calthorpe), Jeff Davies (Chater-Lea), Eddie Collin (Cotton and Rex-Acme), E. G. Butler (Excelsior), John Cottrell (Humber), Dennis Prydie (Ivy), Don Mitchell (James), Dick Platt (Levis), Harold Butterfield (Matchless), Eric Londesbrough (New Hudson), Fred Pateman (New Imperial), Wally Flew (Norton), Martin Shelley (OEC and Whitwood), John Minns (OK Supreme), Dave Earnshaw (Panther), Eddie Keightley (Quadrant), John Deane (Radco), Dave Comber (Raleigh), John Cliffe (Royal Enfield), Bryan Reynolds (Rudge), John Underhill (Scott, AER and Reynolds), Jack Sizer (Sun), Ivan Rhodes (Velocette), Pete Green (Vincent HRD) and Tony Donnithorne (Zenith).

Thank you, gentlemen, one and all, for your help and good wishes. Also my thanks to Bob Currie who not only checked the whole text but also wrote me a kind foreword in very quick time – as always.

Nearly all the pictures came from the EMAP archives which hold the old *Motor Cycle Weekly* files for which I am most grateful. A few came from the National Motor Museum at Beaulieu and all bar two (I think) are contemporary. Some were none too easy to use due to their age but the Osprey staff persevered with them as many show an interesting background to that pre-war era.

Roy Bacon
Niton, Isle of Wight
July 1986